A Perspective of Human Resource Management

Dr.B. Jayanthi

Dr.P. Kavitha

Dr. Suja Sundram

Published by

A Perspective of Human Resource Management

ISBN 978-93-86638-63-2

Authors

Dr.B. Jayanthi

Dr.P. Kavitha

Dr. Suja Sundram

Bonfring

309, 2nd Floor, 5th Street Extension, Gandhipuram,

Coimbatore-641 012.

Tamilnadu, India.

E-mail: info@bonfring.org

Website: www.bonfring.org

Phone: 0422 4213231

Preface

During the course of Teaching and Research career of more than fifteen years, we have seen the emergence of handling workforce, employers, managers, supervisors and students need to update with current trends as well as possess a strong theoretical foundation of human resource practices.

We strongly felt that these HRM practices are in the fact the 'technologies' which help in realizing the potentials of people. Human resources management (HRM) is a growing discipline. With the culmination of innovative and refined approach to managing people, it is an extended behavioural science. For creating a performing organization and to sustain the performance HR orientation needs to be top down and also to involve the line managers to ensure sustainable peak performance. Human resource practice helps the organization in increasing organizational productivity and in turn the profitability. The latest developments, ideas, research and best practice, this book intends to examine the technological implications of the last changes taking place and how they affect the management and motivation of HR belonging to these organizations.

Therefore these practices enable releasing the potentials of people when implemented with the right kind of knowledge, methods, tools etc. With rising competitive environment the organization would like to leverage their human resources as strategic advantage which fits to the firm.

However, the success rate is very low because of the cultural mismatch and the failure to manage Human resources properly. It is basically the people and their way of managing the organization that is differentiating factor between successful organizations.

This new edition covers is underpinned by a strategic approach to HRM, focusing on the three-way linkage between strategy, people and performance. Based on the roles and responsibilities of HR managers, units are divided into five parts As the authors explain, the HRM function can be developed to help the organisation create value and sustain competitive advantage in business. The HR function also plays a major role in initiatives that promote employee well-being. Each chapter highlights the strategic achievements that have occurred within each HR topic and addresses the key challenges central to the effective management of people, managing for innovation; attracting and retaining talent; and managing for sustainability.

This straight forward and accessible text takes the reader through both practical and theoretical aspects of the subject and is ideal for those studying HRM for the first time. This textbook combines the main theoretical underpinning for the subject area with large number of practical examples and situational cases to assist the learning process.

The view behind the book is to emphasis more on HRM issues and policies or general managers who apply HRM policy but also who have a profound effect on the success or failure of HRM. We continue to point out the discrepancies between HRM findings from research and practice of HRM.

Perhaps the most important improvement in the book is in writing. An extra effort has been made to simplify and improve the writing and the transition from topic to topic. This text book remains the only HR book that attempts to directly link student learning experiences.

This text continues to appeal to a wide audience. The analysis of current academic knowledge and major areas of HRM practice provides an informed handbook for students, academics and practitioners. The text could easily be used in an undergraduate or graduate HR unit or as a comprehensive HR handbook for managers. For instructors, the text includes numerous pedagogical features such as extensively updated case study material that provides a sound basis for teaching; and for students, it successfully reinforces the link between theory, practice and critical thinking.

This book covers five units consists of Unit 1-A Perspective of Human Resource Management discusses Nature of HRM, objectives, Functions challenges and roles of HR manager, policies of HRM, Human resource accounting and HRA (Human resource audit). Unit 2 explains the concepts of Best fit employees which covers on Human resource Planning, Process, factors affecting HRP, Recruitment & its sources, selection process, Job analysis and Socialization & its methods. Unit 3 explains on Training & Executive Development which covers Importance of training, Need Assessments, Methods of training, Evaluation of training, Executive Development, Methods, Knowledge Management, Approaches and Self-development. Unit 4 explains on sustaining employees' interest which covers compensation plans & its modes, Factors affecting compensation plans, Job evaluation and its methods, Motivation & its theories, career management, stages, steps in career management. Mentoring, Rewards & its types. Unit 5 explains performance evaluation and control process which covers performance appraisal, process, methods, Job changes, Employee separation, Employee empowerment, employee grievances, participative management and collective bargaining.

Each part in this book received equal weightage in terms of treatment and coverage. Thus, the readers will find an elaborate discussion even on newer areas of Human resource management.

Acknowledgement

We wish to express ourdeep gratitude to everyone who helped us in their own way in writing this book. We gratefully acknowledge all organizations and institutions, Ministry of labour of the Government of India. Political and economical risk consultancy for their permission to utilize the information pertaining to them in this book.

We would like to thank **Bonfring Publications** for enabling us to publish this book. Above all we want to thank our family, who supported and encouraged us in spite of all the time it took us away from them. It was a long and difficult journey for them.

We also thank our parents, family members' students, colleagues for their valuable support to complete this book successfully. I am extremely thankful to all participants for helping us in the process of selection and editing this book. It gives us immense pleasure to record our thanks to our research scholars for value addition to collective bargaining and labour relations topics.

Finally we acknowledge the **Bonfring Publications** for publishing this book. We welcome any critical reviews and feedback from readers, and would consider those as the real reward for writing this book.

Dr.B. Jayanthi

Dr.P. Kavitha

Dr. Suja Sundram

Units	Contents	Page No

UNIT 1

A PERCEPTIVE OF HUMAN RESOURCE MANAGEMENT

Objective of the Unit 1

- Understand nature of Human Resource Management.
- Know the differences Between Personnel Management and Human Resource Management.
- Understand Objectives of Human Resource Management.
- Know the Functions of Human Resource Management.
- Understand Importance of Human Resource Management.
- Highlight the future Challenges of HR Managers.
- Roles and Qualities of HR Managers.
- HR Policies and its types.
- Human resource Audit & its approaches.
- Human resource accounting & its benefits.

1.1. INTRODUCTION TO HRM

Human Resource Management (HRM) is a relatively new approach to managing people in any organisation. People are considered the key resource in this approach. It is concerned with the people dimension in management of an organisation. Since an organisation is a body of people, their acquisition, development of skills, motivation for higher levels of attainments, as well as ensuring maintenance of their level of commitment are all significant activities. These activities fall in the domain of HRM. Human Resource Management is a process, which consists of four main activities, namely, acquisition, development, motivation, as well as maintenance of human resources."Our people are our greatest asset" "Nothing is more important than our employees". Effective human resource management has become more important in recent times. Here are some reasons:

- Most businesses now provide services rather than produce goods – people are the critical resource in the quality and customer service level of any service business
- Competitiveness requires a business to be efficient and productive – this is difficult unless the workforce is well motivated, has the right skills and is effectively organised
- The move towards fewer layers of management hierarchy (flatter organizational structures) has placed greater emphasis on delegation and communication.

As a result, if a business is to be successful and achieve its objectives, then it needs to manage its human resources effectively. The key is to remember that **HRM is a strategic approach**. HRM uses a variety of **tools** to help meet the strategic needs of the business, each of which needs together in an integrated way. The key tools are:

- Workforce planning.
- Recruitment & selection.
- Training & development.
- Rewarding and motivating staff.
- Communication.
- Roles and responsibilities (organisational structures).

INTRODUCTION TO HUMAN RESOURCES MANAGEMENT

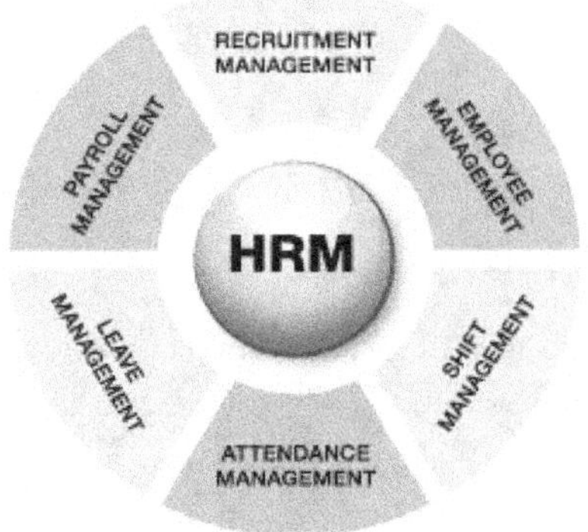

Human Resource Management (HRM)

Scott, Clothier and Spriegel have defined Human Resource Management as that branch of management which is responsible on a staff basis for concentrating on those aspects of operations which are primarily concerned with the relationship of management to employees and employees to employees and with the development of the individual and the group.

Human Resource Management is responsible for maintaining good human relations in the organisation. It is also concerned with development of individuals and achieving integration of goals of the organisation and those of the individuals.

Northcott considers human resource management as an extension of general management, that of prompting and stimulating every employee to make his fullest contribution to the purpose of a business. Human resource management is not something that could be separated from the basic managerial function. It is a major component of the broader managerial function. French Wendell defines-Human resource management as the recruitment, selection, development, utilization, compensation and motivation of human resources by the organisation.

According to Edwin B. Flippo, Human resource management is the planning, organising, directing and controlling of the procurement, development, resources to the end that individual and societal objectives are accomplished. This definition reveals that human resource (HR) management is that aspect of management, which deals with the planning, organising, directing and controlling the personnel functions of the enterprise.

1.2.   NATURE OF HUMAN RESOURCE MANAGEMENT

The emergence of human resource management can be attributed to the writings of the human relations who attached great significance to the human factor. Lawrence Appley remarked, Management is personnel administration. This view is partially true as management is concerned with the efficient and effective use of both human as well as non-human resources. Thus human resource management is only a part of the management process. At the same time, it must be recognized that human resource management is inherent in the process of management. This function is performed by all the managers. A manager to get the best of his people must undertake the basic responsibility of selecting people who will work under him and to help develop, motivate and guide them.

However, he can take the help of the specialised services of the personnel department in discharging this responsibility. The nature of the human resource management has been highlighted in its following features:

1. **Inherent Part of Management:** Human resource management is inherent in the process of management. This function is performed by all the managers throughout the organisation rather that by the personnel department only. If a manager is to get the best of his people, he must undertake the basic responsibility of selecting people who will work under him.

2. **Pervasive Function:** Human Resource Management is a pervasive function of management. It is performed by all managers at various levels in the organisation. It is not a responsibility that a manager can leave completely to someone else. However, he may secure advice and help in managing people from experts who have special competence in personnel management and industrial relations.

3. **Basic to all Functional Areas:** Human Resource Management permeates all the functional area of management such as production management, financial

management, and marketing management. That is every manager from top to bottom, working in any department has to perform the personnel functions.

4. **People Centered:** Human Resource Management is people centered and is relevant in all types of organisations. It is concerned with all categories of personnel from top to the bottom of the organisation.

    The broad classification of personnel in an industrial enterprise may be as follows: (i) Blue-collar workers (i.e. those working on machines and engaged in loading, unloading etc.) and white-collar workers (i.e. clerical employees), (ii) Managerial and non-managerial personnel, (iii) Professionals (such as Chartered Accountant, Company Secretary, Lawyer, etc.) and non-professional personnel.

5. **Personnel Activities or Functions:** Human Resource Management involves several functions concerned with the management of people at work. It includes manpower planning, employment, placement, training, appraisal and compensation of employees. For the performance of these activities efficiently, a separate department known as Personnel Department is created in most of the organisations.

6. **Continuous Process:** Human Resource Management is not a ‗one shot' function. It must be performed continuously if the organisational objectives are to be achieved smoothly.

7. **Based on Human Relations:** Human Resource Management is concerned with the motivation of human resources in the organisation. The human beings can't be dealt with like physical factors of production. Every person has different needs, perceptions and expectations. The managers should give due attention to these factors. They require human relations skills to deal with the people at work. Human relations skills are also required in training performance appraisal, transfer and promotion of subordinates.

Personnel Management VS Human Resource Management

Contemporary Human Resource Management, as a part and parcel of management function, underscores strategic approach to management in areas of acquisition, motivation, and management of people at work. Human Resource Management derives its origin from the practices of the earlier personnel management, which assisted in the management of people in an organisation setup. Human Resource Management leverages setting up the systems and procedures for ensuring efficiency, controlling and providing equality of opportunities for all working for the organisation. Human Resource Management (HRM) differs from Personnel Management (PM) both in scope and orientation. HRM views people as an important source or asset to be used for the benefit of organisations, employees and society. It is emerging as a distinct philosophy of management aiming at policies that promote mutuality-mutual goals, mutual respect, mutual rewards and mutual responsibilities. The belief is that policies of mutuality will elicit commitment, which in turn, will yield both better economic performance and greater Human Resource Development (HRD). Though a distinct philosophy, HRM cannot be treated in isolation. It is being integrated into the overall strategic management of businesses. Further, HRM represents the latest term in the evolution of the subject. There are several similarities between Human Resource Management (HRM) and Personnel Management (PM) (a) Both models emphasize the importance of integrating personnel/HRM practices with organisational goals. (b) Both models vest Personnel/HRM firmly in line management. (c) Human Resource Management (HRM) and Personnel Management (PM) both models emphasizes the importance of individuals fully developing their abilities for their own personal satisfaction to make their best contribution to organisational success. (d) Both models identify placing the right people into the right jobs as an important means of integrating personnel/HRM practice with organisational goals.

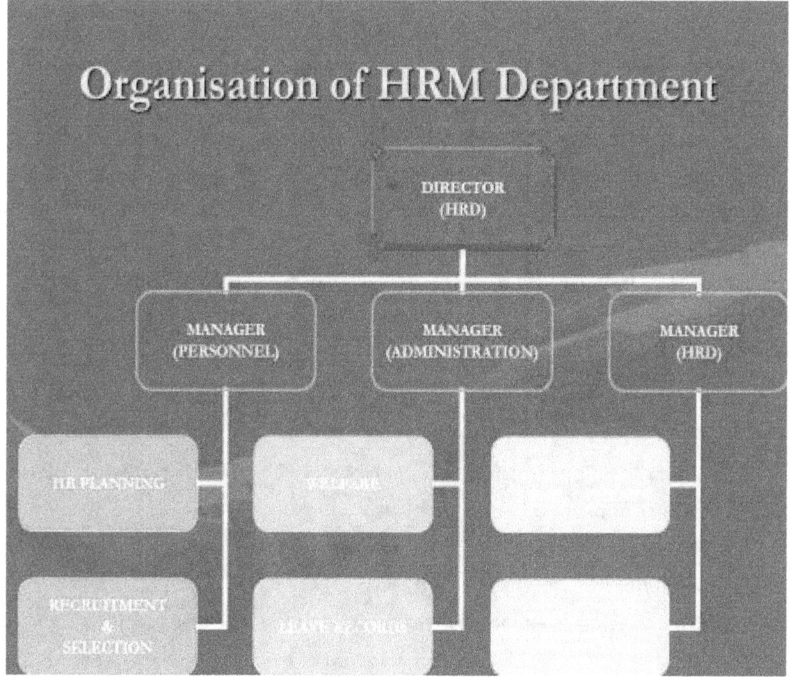

1.3.   OBJECTIVES OF HUMAN RESOURCE MANAGEMENT

According to Scott, Clothier and Spriegal, The objectives of Human Resource Management, in an organisation, is to obtain maximum individual development, desirable working relationships between employers and employees, and to affect the moulding of human resources as contrasted with physical resources. The basic objective of human resource management is to contribute to the realisation of the organisational goals. However, the specific objectives of human resource management are as follows:

1. To ensure effective utilization of human resources, all other organisational resources will be efficiently utilized by the human resources.

2. To establish and maintain an adequate organisational structure of relationship among all the members of an organization by dividing of organisation tasks into functions, positions and jobs, and by defining clearly the responsibility, accountability, authority for each job and its relation with other jobs in the organisation.

3. To generate maximum development of human resources within the organisation by offering opportunities for advancement to employees through training and education.

4. To ensure respect for human beings by providing various services and welfare facilities to the personnel.

5. To ensure reconciliation of individual/group goals with those of the organisation in such a manner that the personnel feel a sense of commitment and loyalty towards it.

6. To identify and satisfy the needs of individuals by offering various monetary and non-monetary rewards. In order to achieve the above objectives, human resource management undertakes the following activities:

   1) Human Resource Planning, i.e. determining the number and kinds of personnel required to fill various positions in the organisation.

   2) Recruitment, selection and placement of personnel, i.e., employment function.

   3) Training and development of employees for their efficient performance and growth.

   4) Appraisal of performance of employees and taking corrective steps such as transfer from one job to another.

   5) Motivation of workforce by providing financial incentives and avenues of promotion.

   6) Remuneration of employees. The employees must be given sufficient wages and fringe benefits to achieve higher standard of living and to motivate them to show higher productivity.

7)   Social security and welfare of employees.

1.4.   FUNCTIONS OF HUMAN RESOURCE MANAGEMENT

The Main functions of human resource management are classified into two categories:

a)   Managerial Functions.

b)   Operative Functions.

A.   **Managerial Functions:** Following are the managerial functions of Human Resources Management.

1.   **Planning:** The planning function of human resource department pertains to the steps taken in determining in advance personnel requirements, personnel programmes, policies etc. After determining how many and what type of people are required, a personnel manager has to devise ways and means to motivate them.

2.   **Organisation:** Under organisation, the human resource manager has to organise the operative functions by designing structure of relationship among jobs, personnel and physical factors in such a way so as to have maximum contribution towards organisational objectives. In this way a personnel manager performs following functions:

   a)   Preparation of task force.

   b)   Allocation of work to individuals.

   c)   Integration of the efforts of the task force.

   d)   Coordination of work of individual with that of the department.

3.   **Directing:** Directing is concerned with initiation of organised action and stimulating the people to work. The personnel manager directs the activities of people of the organisation to get its function performed properly. A personnel manager guides and motivates the staff of the organisation to follow the path laid down in advance.

4.   **Controlling:** It provides basic data for establishing standards, makes job analysis and performance appraisal, etc. All these techniques assist in effective control of the qualities, time and efforts of workers.

B.   **Operative Functions:** The following are the Operative Functions of Human Resource Management

1.   **Procurement of Personnel:** It is concerned with the obtaining of the proper kind and number of personnel necessary to accomplish organisation goals. It deals specifically with such subjects as the determination of manpower requirements, their recruitment, selecting, placement and orientation, etc.

2. **Development of Personnel:** Development has to do with the increase through training, skill that is necessary for proper job performance. In this process various techniques of training are used to develop the employees. Framing a sound promotion policy, determination of the basis of promotion and making performance appraisal are the elements of personnel development function.

3. **Compensation to Personnel:** Compensation means determination of adequate and equitable remuneration of personnel for their contribution to organisation objectives. To determine the monetary compensation for various jobs is one of the most difficult and important function of the personnel management. A number of decisions are taken into the function, viz., job-evaluation, remuneration, policy, inventive and premium plans, bonus policy and co-partnership, etc. It also assists the organisation for adopting the suitable wages and salaries, policy and payment of wages and salaries in right time.

4. **Maintaining Good Industrial Relation:** Human Resource Management covers a wide field. It is intended to reduce strife's, promote industrial peace, provide fair deal to workers and establish industrial democracy. It the personnel manager is unable to make harmonious relations between management and labour industrial unrest will take place and millions of man-days will be lost. If labour management relations are not good the moral and physical condition of the employee will suffer, and it will be a loss to an organisation vis-a-visa nation. Hence, the personnel manager must create harmonious relations with the help of sufficient communication system and co-partnership.

5. **Record Keeping:** In record-keeping the personnel manager collects and maintains information concerned with the staff of the organisation. It is essential for every organisation because it assists the management in decision making such as in promotions.

6. **Personnel Planning and Evaluation :** Under this system different type of activities are evaluated such as evaluation of performance, personnel policy of an organisation and its practices, personnel audit, morale, survey and performance appraisal, etc.

1.5. IMPORTANCE OF HUMAN RESOURCE MANAGEMENT

Human Resource Management has a place of great importance. According to **Peter F. Drucker,** The proper or improper use of the different factors of production depends on the wishes of the human resources. Hence, besides other resources human resources need more development. Human resources can increase cooperation but it needs proper and efficient management to guide it. Importance of personnel management is in reality the importance of labour functions of personnel department which are indispensable to the management activity itself. Because of the following reasons human resource management holds a place of importance.

1. It helps management in the preparation adoption and continuing evolution of Personnel programmes and policies.
2. It supplies skilled workers through scientific selection process.
3. It ensures maximum benefit out of the expenditure on training and development and appreciates the human assets.
4. It prepares workers according to the changing needs of industry and environment
5. It motivates workers and upgrades them so as to enable them to accomplish the Organisation goals.
6. Through innovation and experimentation in the fields of personnel, it helps in reducing casts and helps in increasing productivity.
7. It contributes a lot in restoring the industrial harmony and healthy employer-employee relations.
8. It establishes mechanism for the administration of personnel services that are delegated to the personnel department.

Thus, the role of human resource management is very important in an organisation and it should not be undermined especially in large scale enterprises. It is the key to the whole organisation and related to all other activities of the management i.e., marketing, production, finance etc.

Human Resource Management is concerned with the managing people as organizational resources rather than as factors of production. It involves a system to be followed in business firm to recruit, select, hire, train and develop human assets. It is concerned with the people dimension of an organization.

The attainment of organizational objectives depends, to a great extent, on the way in which people are recruited, developed and utilized by the management. Therefore, proper co-ordination of human efforts and effective utilization of human and others material resources is necessary.

1.6. SCOPE OF HRM

The scope of HRM is indeed vast. All major activities in the working life of a worker- from this time of his or her entry into an organization until he or she leaves- come under the preview of HRM.

Specifically, the activities included are – HR planning, job analysis and design, recruitment & selection, orientation and placement, Training & Development, performance appraisal and job Evaluation, employee and executive remuneration, motivation and communication, welfare, safety and Health, industrial relations (IR) and the like. For the sake of convenience, we can categories all this functions into seven sections- (i) Introduction to HRM, (ii) Employee Hiring (iii) employee and executive remuneration (iv) Employee Motivation (v) Employee maintenance (vi) IR and, (vii) prospects of HRM. HRM differs from Personnel management both in scope and orientation. HRM views people as an important source or asset to be used for the benefit of the organization, employees and the society. It is emerging as a distinct philosophy of management aiming at politics that promotes mutuality – mutual goals, mutual respect, mutual rewards   and mutual responsibilities.

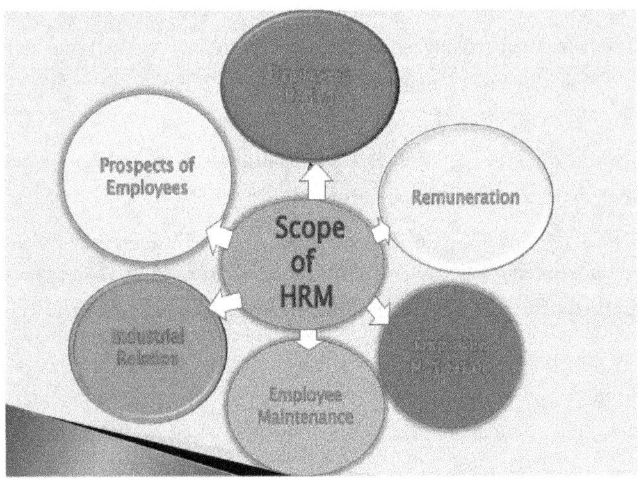

1.7.   CHALLENGES TO HRM

The role of the Human Resource Manager is evolving with the change in competitive market environment and the realization that Human Resource Management must play a more strategic role in the success of an organization. Organizations that do not put their emphasis on attracting and retaining talents may find themselves in dire consequences, as their competitors may be outplaying them in the strategic employment of their human resources. With the increase in competition, locally or globally, organizations must become more adaptable, resilient, agile, and customer-focused to succeed. And within this change in environment, the HR professional has to evolve to become a strategic partner, an employee sponsor or advocate, and a change mentor within the organization.

In order to succeed, HR must be a business driven function with a thorough understanding of the organization's big picture and be able to influence key decisions and policies. In general, the focus of today's HR Manager is on strategic personnel retention and talents development. HR professionals will be coaches, counselors, mentors, and succession planners to help motivate organization's members and their loyalty. The HR manager will also promote and fight for values, ethics, beliefs, and spirituality within their organizations, especially in the management of workplace diversity.

This chapter will highlight on how a HR manager can meet the challenges of workplace diversity, how to motivate employees through gain-sharing and executive information system through proper planning, organizing, leading and controlling their human resources.

Workplace Diversity

According to Thomas (1992), dimensions of workplace diversity include, but are not limited to: age, ethnicity, ancestry, gender, physical abilities/qualities, race, sexual orientation, educational background, geographic location, income, marital status, military experience, religious beliefs, parental status, and work experience.

The Challenges of Workplace Diversity

The future success of any organizations relies on the ability to manage a diverse body of talent that can bring innovative ideas, perspectives and views to their work. The challenge and problems faced of workplace diversity can be turned into a strategic organizational asset if an organization is able to capitalize on this melting pot of diverse talents. With the mixture of talents of diverse cultural backgrounds, genders, ages and lifestyles, an organization can respond to business opportunities more rapidly and creatively, especially in the global arena (Cox, 1993), which must be one of the important organisational goals to be attained. More importantly, if the organizational environment does not support diversity broadly, one risks losing talent to competitors. This is especially true for multinational companies (MNCs) who have operations on a global scale and employ people of different countries, ethical and cultural backgrounds. Thus, a HR manager needs to be mindful and may employ a 'Think Global, Act Local' approach in most circumstances.

The challenge of workplace diversity is also prevalent amongst Singapore's Small and Medium Enterprises (SMEs). With a population of only four million people and the nation's strive towards high technology and knowledge-based economy; foreign talents are lured to share their expertise in these areas. Thus, many local HR managers have to undergo cultural-based Human Resource Management training to further their abilities to motivate a group of professional that are highly qualified but culturally diverse. Furthermore, the HR professional must assure the local professionals that these foreign talents are not a threat to their career advancement (Toh, 1993). In many ways, the effectiveness of workplace diversity management is dependent on the skilful balancing act of the HR manager.

One of the main reasons for ineffective workplace diversity management is the predisposition to pigeonhole employees, placing them in a different silo based on their diversity profile (Thomas, 1992). In the real world, diversity cannot be easily categorized and those organizations that respond to human complexity by leveraging the talents of a broad workforce will be the most effective in growing their businesses and their customer base.

The Management of Workplace Diversity

In order to effectively manage workplace diversity, Cox (1993) suggests that a HR Manager needs to change from an ethnocentric view ("our way is the best way") to a culturally relative perspective ("let's take the best of a variety of ways"). This shift in philosophy has to be ingrained in the managerial framework of the HR Manager in his/her planning, organizing, leading and controlling of organizational resources. As suggested by Thomas (1992) and Cox (1993), there are several best practices that a HR manager can adopt in ensuring effective management of workplace diversity in order to attain organizational goals. They are:

Planning a Mentoring Program

One of the best ways to handle workplace diversity issues is through initiating a Diversity Mentoring Program. This could entail involving different departmental managers in a mentoring program to coach and provide feedback to employees who are different from them. In order for the program to run successfully, it is wise to provide practical training for these managers or seek help from consultants and experts in this field. Usually, such a program will encourage organization's members to air their opinions and learn how to resolve conflicts due to their diversity. More importantly, the purpose of a Diversity Mentoring Program seeks to encourage members to move beyond their own cultural frame of reference to recognize and take full advantage of the productivity potential inherent in a diverse population.

Organizing Talents Strategically

Many companies are now realizing the advantages of a diverse workplace. As more and more companies are going global in their market expansions either physically or virtually (for example, E-commerce-related companies), there is a necessity to employ diverse talents to understand the various niches of the market. For example, when China was opening up its markets and exporting their products globally in the late 1980s, the Chinese companies (such as China's electronic giants such as Haier) were seeking the marketing expertise of Singaporeans. This is because Singapore's marketing talents were able to understand the local China markets relatively well (almost 75% of Singaporeans are of Chinese descent) and as well as being attuned to the markets in the West due to Singapore's open economic policies and English language abilities. (Toh, R, 1993).With this trend in place, a HR Manager must be able to organize the pool of diverse talents strategically for the organization. He/She must consider how a diverse workforce can enable the company to attain new markets and other organizational goals in order to harness the full potential of workplace diversity. An organization that sees the existence of a diverse workforce as an organizational asset rather than a liability would indirectly help the organization to positively take in its stride some of the less positive aspects of workforce diversity.

Leading the Talk

A HR Manager needs to advocate a diverse workforce by making diversity evident at all organizational levels. Otherwise, some employees will quickly conclude that there is no future for them in the company. As the HR Manager, it is pertinent to show respect for diversity issues and promote clear and positive responses to them. He/She must also show a high level of commitment and be able to resolve issues of workplace diversity in an ethical and responsible manner.

Control and Measure Results

A HR Manager must conduct regular organizational assessments on issues like pay, benefits, work environment, management and promotional opportunities to assess the progress over the long term. There is also a need to develop appropriate measuring tools to measure the impact of diversity initiatives at the organization through organization-wide feedback surveys and other methods. Without proper control and evaluation, some of these diversity initiatives may just fizzle out, without resolving any real problems that may surface due to workplace diversity.

Motivational Approaches

Workplace motivation can be defined as the influence that makes us do things to achieve organizational goals: this is a result of our individual needs being satisfied (or met) so that we are motivated to complete organizational tasks effectively. As these needs vary from person to person, an organization must be able to utilize different motivational tools to encourage their employees to put in the required effort and increase productivity for the company. Why do we need motivated employees? The answer is survival (Smith, 1994). In our changing workplace and competitive market environments, motivated employees and their contributions are the necessary currency for an organization's survival and success. Motivational factors in an organizational context include working environment, job characteristics, and appropriate organizational reward system and so on.

The development of an appropriate organizational reward system is probably one of the strongest motivational factors. This can influence both job satisfaction and employee motivation. The reward system affects job satisfaction by making the employee more comfortable and contented as a result of the rewards received. The reward system influences motivation primarily through the perceived value of the rewards and their contingency on performance (Hickins, 1998).

To be effective, an organizational reward system should be based on sound understanding of the motivation of people at work. In this paper, I will be touching on the one of the more popular methods of reward systems, gain-sharing.

Gain-Sharing

Gain-sharing programs generally refer to incentive plans that involve employees in a common effort to improve organizational performance, and are based on the concept that the resulting incremental economic gains are shared among employees and the company.

In most cases, workers voluntarily participate in management to accept responsibility for major reforms. This type of pay is based on factors directly under a worker's control (i.e., productivity or costs). Gains are measured and distributions are made frequently through a predetermined formula. Because this pay is only implemented when gains are achieved, gain-sharing plans do not adversely affect company costs (Paulsen, 1991).

Managing Gain-Sharing

In order for a gain-sharing program that meets the minimum requirements for success to be in place, Paulsen (1991) and Boyett (1988) have suggested a few pointers in the effective management of a gain-sharing program. They are as follows:

A HR manager must ensure that the people who will be participating in the plan are influencing the performance measured by the gain-sharing formula in a significant way by changes in their day-to-day behavior. The main idea of the gain sharing is to motivate members to increase productivity through their behavioral changes and working attitudes. If the increase in the performance measurement was due to external factors, then it would have defeated the purpose of having a gain-sharing program.

An effective manager must ensure that the gain-sharing targets are challenging but legitimate and attainable. In addition, the targets should be specific and challenging but reasonable and justifiable given the historical performance, the business strategy and the competitive environment. If the gain-sharing participants perceive the target as an impossibility and are not motivated at all, the whole program will be a disaster.

A manager must provide useful feedback as a guidance to the gain-sharing participants concerning how they need to change their behavior(s) to realize gain-sharing payouts the feedback should be frequent, objective and clearly based on the members' performance in relation to the gain-sharing target.

A manager must have an effective mechanism in place to allow gain-sharing participants to initiate changes in work procedures and methods and/or requesting new or additional resources such as new technology to improve performance and realize gains. Though a manager must have a tight control of company's resources, reasonable and justifiable requests for additional resources and/or changes in work methods from gain-sharing participants should be considered.

Executive Information Systems

Executive Information System (EIS) is the most common term used for the unified collections of computer hardware and software that track the essential data of a business' daily performance and present it to managers as an aid to their planning and decision-making (Choo, 1991). With an EIS in place, a company can track inventory, sales, and receivables, compare today's data with historical patterns. In addition, an EIS will aid in spotting significant variations from "normal" trends almost as soon as it develops, giving the company the maximum amount of time to make decisions and implement required changes to put your business back on the right track. This would enable EIS to be a useful tool in an organization's strategic planning, as well as day-to-day management (Laudon, K and Laudon, J, 2003).

Managing EIS

As information is the basis of decision-making in an organization, there lies a great need for effective managerial control. A good control system would ensure the communication of the right information at the right time and relayed to the right people to take prompt actions. When managing an Executive Information System, a HR manager must first find out exactly what information decision-makers would like to have available in the field of human resource management, and then to include it in the EIS. This is because having people simply use an EIS that lacks critical information is of no value-add to the organization. In addition, the manager must ensure that the use of information technology has to be brought into alignment with strategic business goals (Laudon, K and Laudon, J, 2003).

1.8.   ROLE OF HUMAN RESOURCE MANAGER IN AN ORGANISATION

In the era of globalization, organizations are becoming increasingly competitive, dynamic, innovative and productive. It is in this context, the organizations need to innovate HR practices to prepare employees to meet the challenges of open market economy and to respond the technology and work environment.In most of the big enterprises, human resource department is set up under the leadership of personnel manager who has specialised knowledge and skills. The human resource manager performs managerial as well as operative functions. Since he is a manager, he performs the basic functions of management like planning, organising, directing and controlling to manage his department. HR manager has to perform certain operative functions of recruitment, selection, training, placement, etc., which the problems to management, the human resource managers attach highest priority to the settlement of industrial disputes than anything else. The role of the HR manager must parallel the needs of the changing organization. Successful organizations are becoming more adaptable, resilient, quick to change directions, and customer-centered. Within this environment, the HR professional must learn how to manage effectively through planning, organizing, leading and controlling the human resource and be knowledgeable of emerging trends in training and employee development.

Dave Ulrich has come out with four roles for HR to play within a business. They are:

- HR professionals have to play a strategic partner role by working to align HR and business strategy.
- HR as an administrative expert working to improve organizational processes and deliver basic HR service
- HR as an employee champion listening and responding to employees need
- HR as a change agent managing change process to increase the effectiveness of the organization.

A critical role for every HR manager comprises.

Staffing

1. Identifying work requirements within an organization.
2. Determining the numbers of people and the skills needed to do the work.
3. Recruiting, Selecting and promoting qualified candidates.

Retention

1. Rewarding employees.
2. Ensuring good working relations.
3. Maintaining a safe, healthy work environment.

Development

To preserve and enhance employees competence by improving their knowledge, skills, abilities etc.

Adjustment

1. Investigation of employee complaints.
2. Providing outplacement services.
3. Retirement Counseling.

Managing Change

To enable employees at all levels to cope with the changes. Other roles include:

Internal Customer Services

HR manager has to provide just in time Internal Customer Services by properly doing recruitment, placement, training & development, transfer & separation etc for other departments.

Managing Outsourcing

As per Hewitt survey 30% to 35% cost savings can be achieved by outsourcing HR service delivery. Therefore HR manager has to properly subcontract (outsource) various activities by identifying the agency, analyzing the work done by them and handle legal problems related with it.

Networking with Stakeholders

Stakeholders are people who share the companies' profit and loss. HR department has to network on a regular basis through meetings and visits, sending reports, newsletters etc. Proper networking will help in brand positioning and image building.

Transmission of Business Goals

Business goals which are set by the top people should be attained with the help of HR personnel. HR manager should act as a liaison by transferring and insisting the corporate goals to employees through Workshops.

Building Learning Organization

Organizations of tomorrow will be staffed by knowledge employees only. HR department has to plan purposefully in Knowledge – Creation, Knowledge - acquisition, Knowledge-integration and Knowledge-sharing. Acting as business partners, the HR manager advises and offers solutions which results in positive impact on the organisation's effectiveness. Furthermore, she/he proposes best practices and provides state-of-the-art support and counseling to her/his colleagues. Together they act as co-responsible partners for all HR matters.

1.9. JOBS AND CAREERS IN HRM

HR positions in organizations can be divided into three categories.

- **HR Specialist:** HR Specialist jobs are usually the entry-level positions for an HRM career. Included would be such roles as interviewer, compensation analyst, job analyst and trainer.

- **HR Manager:** The HR manager is usually a top ranking person and is expected to know about all areas of HRM.

- **HR Executive:** The top level HR Executive, usually the vice president of a company, has the responsibility of linking the firm's corporate policy and strategy with HRM.

1.10. QUALITIES OF HR MANAGER

HR managers need good 'people' skills and require the confidence and communication skills to deal in a calm and tactful manner with a variety of situations, balancing the needs of the individual employee against the business interests of the organization.

Good spoken and written communication skills are essential to avoid errors and misunderstandings when dealing with employees' personal details.

Natural leadership qualities, a good memory, love for detail, ability to speak and write well, ability to understand people, power to persuade, ability to make decisions and solve problems -these are a few of the characteristics of a successful person in the field of Human Resource Management.

Also helpful are skills in negotiating, coordinating work with others, assessing situations, explaining issues, answering questions, interviewing, advising, keeping records, gathering information, training in various personnel functions to name a few.

HR Manager must have the ability to deal with people.

1. **Fairness/ Firmness**: HR manager should be fair in matters which includes promotion, demotion, transfer, layoff, enforcing discipline etc

2. **Tact & Resourcefulness**: HR Manager must be tactful in dealing different and critical situations. He should be open minded, objective and adjustable.

3. **Sympathy & Consideration**: HR Manager should extend sympathy towards employees demand and consider others.

4. **Social outlook**: HR Manager must have a social outlook which benefits the society and the employees.

5. **Insight in human nature**: HR Manager must be able to understand various kinds of people. He should have knowledge about various disciplines like anthropology, sociology, psychology, economics etc. which helps to know the behaviour of people.

6. **Freedom from bias**: HR Manager should not be unfair. He should be a man of honesty, integrity, strength, just & fair and a patience listener.

7. **Knowledge of labour and other terms**: HR Manager should have a basic knowledge about the various acts and government policy towards labours.

8. **Zeal for anonymity**: HR Manager should not be proud of any success. He should pass the credit to the employees. He should avoid using words like' I, My, Me'.

1.11. HR POLICIES

HR policies provide an organization with a mechanism to manage risk by staying up to date with current trends in employment standards and legislation. Policies are general statement of a company. It gives guidelines which helps for decision making and specifies the broad strategies to be implemented by adopting a particular tactics. Human resource policies are systems of codified decisions, established by an organization, to support administrative personnel functions, performance management, employee relations and resource planning. Each company has a different set of circumstances, and so develops an individual set of human resource policies.

Purposes

HR policies allow an organization to be clear with employees on:

- The nature of the organization.
- What they should expect from the company.
- What the company expects of them.

- How policies and procedures work at your company.
- What is acceptable and unacceptable behavior.
- The consequences of unacceptable behavior.

Benefits of Policy

1. Policy   serves as a standard of performance. Actual result can be compared with the policy.
2. All personnel treated equally. Favoritism and discrimination are minimized.
3. Sound policies help to increase employee's motivation and loyalty.
4. Policy helps to solve interpersonal, intrapersonal and group conflict.

Personnel Policies are Made in the Following Areas

- Policy of hiring people with respect to reservation, gender, marital status, experience and qualification.
- Policy on terms and conditions of employment like compensation policy, hours of work, overtime, promotion, transfer etc.
- Policy regarding housing, transport, uniform etc.
- Policy regarding medical assistance- ESI, sickness benefits.
- Policy regarding training and development.
- Policy regarding industrial relations- trade union recognition, grievance procedure, collective bargaining, participative management.

Formulating and Implementing HR Policies

There are five principle sources for any company to determine their HR policy. They are:

1. Past practice of the company.
2. Prevailing practices of the rival firm.
3. The attitudes and philosophies of the founders, board of directors and the top Management people.
4. The attitudes and philosophies of the lower and middle level management.
5. The day to day problems.

A policy must be implemented skillfully to obtain desired results. It should be communicated in written form to maintain exactness.

Attempts should be made to conduct education programme to teach the managerial personnel on how to solve different personnel problems when new policies are introduced.

Principles for Policy-Making

- Policy should be definite, clear and understandable.
- Policy should be flexible and not as a rule.
- Policy should be in writing.
- Policy must contribute to the company's objective.
- Policy should guide Decision Making.

Types of Policies

- Formulated Policy.
- Appealed Policy.
- Externally imposed Policy
- Written Policy.
- Implied Policy.
- Originated Policy.
- General Policy.
- Specific Policy.

Few Company Examples

- The Nestlé policy is to hire staff with personal attitudes and professional skills enabling them to develop a long-term relationship with the Company. Each new member joining Nestlé is to become a participant in developing a sustainable quality culture which implies a commitment to the organization and a sense for continuous improvement leaving no room for complacency.
- **Toyota accepts suggestions from the employees.**
  GM has a policy of placing right people in the right job. Also has the policy of providing security with opportunity, incentive and recognition.
- TCS HR strategy depends on two policies. They are accountability and ownership. The company expects the employees to be performance focused and goal oriented and sending the non-performers out and making them the shareholders of the company.
- Indian Railways follow reservation policy in HR.
- Telco has the policy of Promotion open to all.
- GE and McDonald's have framed a latest policy in hiring, to hire those people who are environmentally sensitive ie people who are towards the protection of the environment.

1.12. HUMAN RESOURCE AUDIT

Introduction to the Human Resources Audit

A human resources audit is a tool for evaluating the personnel activities of an industry or a company. This audit is an overall quality control check on all human resources activities in an industry and an evaluation of how these activities support the strategies of industries. The Human Resources (HR) Audit is a process of examining policies, procedures, documentation, systems, and practices with respect to an organization's HR functions. The purpose of the audit is to reveal the strengths and weaknesses in the nonprofit's human resources system, and any issues needing resolution. The audit works best when the focus is on analyzing and improving the HR function in the organization. The audit itself is a diagnostic tool, not a prescriptive instrument. It will help you identify what you are missing or need to improve, but it can't tell you what you need to do to address these issues. It is most useful when an organization is ready to act on the findings, and to evolve its HR function to a level where it's full potential to support the organization's mission and objectives can be realized.

Scope of Audit

Generally, no one can measure the attitude of human being and also their problems are not confined to the HR department alone. So it is very much broad in nature. It covers the following HR areas:

- Audit of all the HR function.
- Audit of managerial compliance of personnel policies, procedures and legal provisions.
- Audit of corporate strategy regarding HR planning, staffing, IRs, remuneration and other HR activities.
- Audit of the HR climate on employee motivation, morale and job satisfaction.

Benefits of HR Audit

It provides the various benefits to the organization. These are:

- It helps to find out the proper contribution of the HR department towards the organization.
- Development of the professional image of the HR department of the organization.
- Reduce the HR cost.
- Motivation of the HR personnel.
- Find out the problems and solve them smoothly.
- Provides timely legal requirement.

- Sound Performance Appraisal Systems.
- Systematic job analysis.
- Smooth adoption of the changing mindset.

Approaches to Human Resources Audit

Prof. K. Aswathappa has identified the following approaches, which are adopted for purpose of evaluation:

- Comparative approach.
- Outside authority approach.
- Statistical approach.
- Compliance approach.
- Management by objectives (MBO) approach.

Comparative Approach

In this, the auditors identify Competitor Company as the model. The results of their organization are compared with that of the Model Company/ industry.

Outside Authority Approach

In this, the auditors use standards set by an outside consultant as benchmark for comparison of own results.

Statistical Approach

In this, Statistical measures are performance is developed considering the company's existing information.

Compliance Approach

In this, auditors review past actions to calculate whether those activities comply with legal requirements and industry policies and procedures.

Management by Objectives (MBO) Approach

This approach creates specific goals, against which performance can be measured, to arrive at final decision about industry's actual performance with the set objectives.

Conclusions

The main functions of human resources audit are to take specific actions that will help minimize employee turnover orientation training, working conditions, remuneration and benefits and opportunities for advancement. Therefore, quality of turnover is more important than the quantity of people leaving and joining the industry. Human resources management should create a work environment to make employee realize that it makes a sense to work in the factory rather than staying at home and waste their time.

1.13. HUMAN RESOURCE ACCOUNTING

What is HRA?

The American Accounting Association's Committee on Human Resource Accounting(1973) has defined ***Human Resource Accounting*** as "the process of identifying and measuring data about human resources and communicating this information to interested parties". HRA, thus, not only involves measurement of all the costs/investments associated with the recruitment, placement, training and development of employees, but also the quantification of the economic value of the people in an organisation.

Why HRA?

According to Likert (1971), HRA serves the following purposes in an organisation:

- It furnishes cost/value information for making management decisions about acquiring, allocating, developing, and maintaining human resources in order to attain cost-effectiveness.
- It allows management personnel to monitor effectively the use of human resources.
- It provides a sound and effective basis of human asset control, that is, whether the asset is appreciated, depleted or conserved.
- It helps in the development of management principles by classifying the financial consequences of various practices.

1.14. BENEFITS OF HRA

- HRA is a management tool which is designed to assist senior management in understanding the long term cost and benefit implications of their HR decisions so that better business decisions can be taken.
- HRA also provides the HR professionals and management with information for managing the human resources efficiently and effectively. Such information is essential for performing the critical HR functions of acquiring, developing, allocating, conserving, utilizing, evaluating and rewarding in a proper way.
- HRA also enables critical external decision makers, especially the investors in making realistic investment decisions. Investors make investment decisions based on the total worth of the organisation.

- HRA reflects the extent to which organisation contributes to society's human capital by investing in its development.

Finally, in a modern era where performance is closely linked to rewards and, therefore, the performance of all groups/departments/functions needs to be quantified to the extent possible, HRA helps in measuring the performance of the HR function as such.

1.15. MEASUREMENTS IN HRA

The biggest challenge in HRA is that of assigning monetary values to different dimensions of HR costs, investments and the worth of employees. The two main approaches usually employed for this are:

1. The ***cost approach*** which involves methods based on the costs incurred by the company, with regard to an employee.

2. The ***economic value approach*** which includes methods based on the economic value of the human resources and their contribution to the company's gains. This approach looks at human resources as assets and tries to identify the stream of benefits flowing from the asset.

Whatever the tool or approach to HRA, much of the potential for developing human resource accounting capability and gaining its advantage depends upon the availability of and accessibility to the required data. In those organizations, where the data is not readily available or routinely maintained, the first step towards HRA will have to be HRIS.

UNIT 2

THE CONCEPTS OF BEST FIT EMPLOYEES

Objective of the Unit 2

- Understand need and importance of Human Resource. Planning
- Know the objectives of HR Planning.
- Factors Affecting HRP.
- Process of HRP.
- Demand Forecasting & its Techniques.
- Recruitment/Sources of recruitment.
- Selection & its process.
- Job analysis – Methods & its Types.
- Process of Socialization.

2.1. HUMAN RESOURCE PLANNING

Human Resource Planning is concerned with the planning the future manpower requirements is the organisation. HR manager ensures that the company has the right type of people in the right number at the right time and place, who are trained and motivated to do the right kind of work at the right time. Obviously, human resource planning primarily makes appropriate projections for future manpower needs of the organisation envisages plan for developing the manpower to suit the changing needs of the organisation from time to time, and foresees how to monitor and evaluate the future performance. It also includes the replacement plans and managerial succession plans. Human Resource planning is the process by which a management determines how an organisation should move from its current manpower position to its desired manpower position. Through planning a management strives to have the right number and the right kinds of people at the right places, at the right time, to do things which result in both the organisation and the individual receiving the maximum long-range benefit.

Definitions of Human Resource Planning

Coleman has defined Human Resource Planning as — the process of determining manpower requirements and the means for meeting those requirements in order to carry out the integrated plan of the organisation. According to **Wikstrom,** Human Resource Planning consists of a series of activities, viz, **Forecasting** future manpower requirements, either in terms of mathematical projections of trends in the economic environment and developments in industry, or in terms of judgemental estimates based upon the specific future plans of a company;

Making an inventory of present manpower resources and assessing the extent to which these resources are employed optimally;

Anticipating manpower problems by projecting present resources into the future and comparing them with the forecast of requirements to determine their adequacy, both quantitatively and qualitatively; and

Planning is the necessary programme of requirements selection, training, development utilisation, transfer, promotion, motivation and compensation to ensure that future manpower requirements are properly met.

Human resource planning is a double-edged weapon. If used properly, it leads to the maximum utilisation of human resources, reduces excessive labour turnover and high absenteeism; improves productivity and aids in achieving the objectives of an organisation. Faultily used, it leads to disruption in the flow of work, lower production, less job satisfaction, high cost of production and constant headaches for the management personnel. Therefore, for the success of an enterprise, human resource planning is a very important function, which can be neglected only at its own peril.

2.2.   IMPORTANCE OF HUMAN RESOURCE PLANNING

Human Resource planning is the process by which a management determines how an organisation should move from its current manpower position to its desired manpower position. Through planning a management strives to have the right number and the right kinds of people at the right places, at the right time, to do things which result in both the organisation and the individual receiving the maximum long-range benefit.

Human resource planning is a double-edged weapon. If used properly, it leads to the maximum utilisation of human resources, reduces excessive labour turnover and high absenteeism; improves productivity and aids in achieving the objectives of an organisation. Faultily used, it leads to disruption in the flow of work, lower production, less job satisfaction, high cost of production and constant headaches for the management personnel. Therefore, for the success of an enterprise, human resource planning is a very important function, which can be neglected only at its own peril.

2.3.   NEED FOR HUMAN RESOURCE PLANNING

Human resource planning is needed for foreseeing the human resource requirements of an organization and supply of human resources. Its need can be accessed from the following points:

1. **Replacement of Persons**: A large number of persons are to be replaced in the organization because of retirement, old age, death, etc. There will be a need to prepare persons for taking up new position in such contingencies

2. **Labour Turnover:** There is always labour turnover in every organization. The degree of labour turnover may vary from concern to concern but it cannot be eliminated altogether. There will be a need to recruit new persons to take up the positions of those who have left the organization. If the concern is able to forecast turnover rate precisely, then advance efforts are made to recruit and train persons so that work does not suffer for want of workers.

3. **Expansion Plans**: Whenever there is a plan to expand or diversify the concern then more persons will be required to take up new positions. Human resource planning is essential under these situations.

4. **Technological Changes:** The business is working under changing technological environment. There may be a need to give fresh training to personnel. In addition, there may also be a need to infuse fresh blood into the organization. Human resource planning will help in meeting the new demands of the organization.

5. **Assessing Needs:** Human resource planning is also required to determine whether there is any shortage or surplus of persons in the organization. If there are less persons than required, it will adversely affect the work. On the other hand, if more persons are employed than the requirement, then it will increase labour cost, etc. Human resource planning ensures the employment of proper workforce

Objectives of HR Planning

The major objectives of Human Resource Planning in an organisation are:

- Ensure optimum use of human resources currently employed.
- Avoid balances in the distribution and allocation of human resources.
- Assess or forecast future skill requirements of the organisation's overall objectives.
- Provide control measure to ensure availability of necessary resources when required.
- Control the cost aspect of human resources.
- Formulate transfer and promotion policies.

2.4. FACTORS AFFECTING HUMAN RESOURCE PLANNING

In most developing countries the development of human resources has been regarded as one amongst many objectives of long-term economic growth. As a result even the objectives of economic planning and the priorities thereof began to be shifted away from purely growth-oriented development strategies to those that recognise and partly remedy the past neglect of such social sectors like population planning, health, education, housing, social security and other social services.

The Government of India has spelt out the human resources/manpower planning objectives at the macro level in successive five-year economic plans. The prime concern, throughout, has been to find a solution to the problem of unemployment and the poverty that goes with it. The key issues involved relate to questions on the rate and pattern of growth. A data base is created to facilitate the formulation of sound policies and programmes.

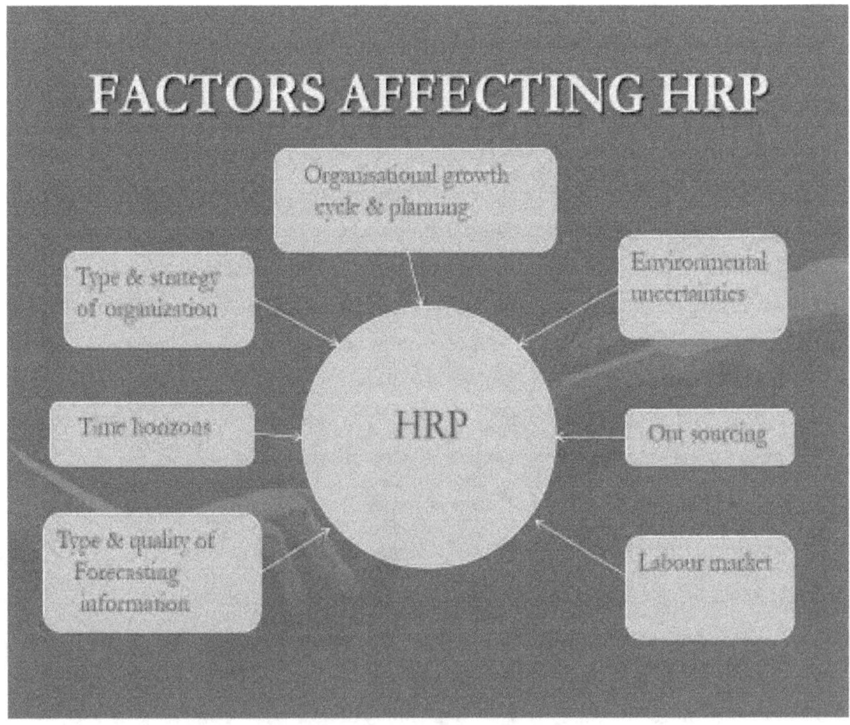

There are several factors that affect HRP. These factors or determinants can be classified into external factors and internal factors.

EXTERNAL FACTORS

- ***Government Policies:*** Policies of the government like labour policy, industrial relations policy, towards reserving certain jobs for different communities and sons-of-the soils, etc. affects the HRP.

- ***Level of Economic Development***: Level of economic development determines the level of HRD in the country and there by the supply of human resources in future in the country.

- ***Business Environment***: External business environmental factors influences the volume and mix of production and thereby the future demand for human resources.

- ***Level of Technology***: Level of technology determines the kind of human resources required.

- ***International Factors***: International factors like the demand for the resources and supply of human resources in various countries.

INTERNAL FACTORS

- ***Company Policies and Strategies:*** Company's policies and strategies relating to expansion diversification, alliances, etc. determines the human resource demand in terms of quality and quantity.

- ***Human Resource Policies:*** Human resources policies of the company regarding quality of human resource, compensation level, quality of worklife, etc. influences human resource plan.

- ***Job Analysis:*** Fundamentally, human resource plan is based on job analysis. Job description and job specification determines the kind of employees required.

- ***Time Horizons***: Companies with stable competitive environment can plan for the long run whereas the firms with unstable competitive environment can plan for only short-term range.

2.5. HUMAN RESOURCE PLANNING PROCESS

HRP is the process of forecasting, developing and controlling human resources in an organization. It identifies what must be done to ensure the availability of human resources needed by the organization to meet its goal. According to French "HRP is the process of assessing the organization's human resources need in light of organizational goals and making phase to ensure that a competent stable workforce is employed." It ensures that the organization has the right number of employee at the right place at the right time so that human resource e problem will be solved when it occur. It provides information about the existing strength and weakness of the people in the organization as well as the kinds of skills to be developed.

HUMAN RESOURCE (HR) PLANNING IN SERVICES

- Human resource planning deals in
- Having right number of people
- Representing right mix of people
- Located at right places & right time
- Aligned with organization's objectives & customer's expectations

Planning in advance to strike a balance between human required and human acquired. It is the process of forecasting the future demand for employees and supply of potential employees and bridges the gap between supply and demand to address issue of shortages and surpluses of human personnel.

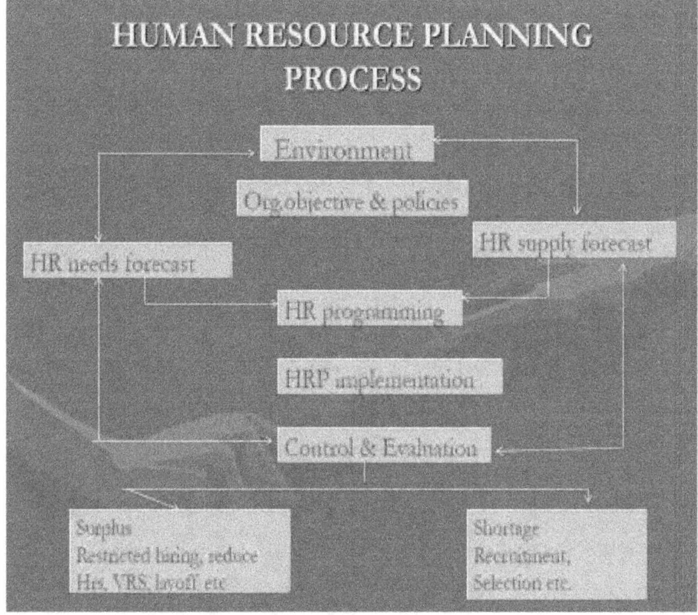

Human resource planning refers to a process by which companies ensure that they have the right number and kinds of people at the right place, at the right time; capable of performing different jobs efficiently. Planning the use of human resources is an important function in every organisation. A rational estimate to various categories of personnel in the organisation is an important aspect of human resource planning.

HRP involves the following steps:

Analysis of Organisational Plans and Objectives: Human resource planning is a part of overall plan of organisation. Plans concerning technology, production, marketing, finance, expansion and diversification give an idea about the volume of future work activity. Each plan can further be analysed into sub-plans and detailed programmes. It is also necessary to decide the time horizon for which human resource plans are to be prepared. The future organisation structure and job design should be made clear and changes in the organisation structure should be examined so as to anticipate its manpower requirements.

2.6.   DEMAND FORECASTING

The existing job design and analysis may thoroughly be reviewed keeping in view the future capabilities, knowledge and skills of present employees. The job generally should be designed and analyzed reflecting the future human resources and based on future organizational plans. The factors for manpower requirements on demand side can be analyzed by making demand forecasting.

Demand forecasting is the process of estimating the future requirements of manpower, by function and by level of skills. It has been observed that demand assessment for operative personnel is not a problem but projections regarding supervisory and managerial levels are difficult. Two kinds of forecasting techniques are commonly used to determine the organization's projected demand for human resources. These are:

    (i)   Judgemental forecasts, and

    (ii) Statistical projections.

1. **Judgemental forecasts** are also known as the conventional method. The forecasts are based on the judgement of those managers and executives who have intensive and extensive knowledge of human resource requirement. Judgemental forecasts could be of two types:

    a) **Managerial Estimate :** Under this method, the managers or supervisors who are well-acquainted with the workload, efficiency and ability of employees, think about their future workload, future capabilities of employees and decide on the number and type of human resources to be required. An estimate of staffing needs is done by the lower level managers who make estimates and pass them up for further revision.

    b) **Delphi Method:** A survey approach can be adopted with the Delphi technique. The Delphi process requires a large number of experts who take turns to present their forecast statement and underlying assumptions to the others, who then make revisions in their forecasts. Face-to-face contact among the experts is avoided.

2. **Statistical Projection**: Some forecasting techniques are based on statistical methods. Some of them are given below:

a) **Ratio-Trend Analysis**: The ratio-trend analysis is carried out by studying the past ratios and the forecasting ratios for the future. The components of internal environmental changes are considered while forecasting the future ratios. Activity level forecasts are used to determine the direct human resource requirements. This method depends on the availability of past records and the internal environmental changes likely to occur in future.

b) **Econometric Model:** Under the econometric model, the previous data is analyzed and the relationship between different variables in a mathematical formula is developed. The different variables affecting the human resource requirements are identified. The mathematical formula so developed is then applied to the forecasts of movements in the identified variables to produce human resource requirements.

c) **Work-Study Techniques**: Work-study techniques are generally used to study work measurement. Under the workload analysis, the volume of workload in the coming years is analyzed. These techniques are more suitable where the volume of work is easily measurable. If the planners forecast expansion in the operations, additional operational workers may be required. If the organization decides to reduce its operations in a particular area, there may be decreased demand for the workers. The work study method also takes into account the productivity pattern for the present and future, internal mobility of the workers like promotion, transfer, external mobility of the workers like retirement, deaths, voluntary retirements, etc.

FORECASTING SUPPLY OF HUMAN RESOURCES

One of the important areas of human resources planning is to deal with allocation of persons to different departments depending upon the work-load and requirements of the departments. While allocating manpower to different departments, care has to be taken to consider appointments based on promotions and transfers. Allocation of human resource should be so planned that available manpower is put to full use to ensure smooth functioning of all departments.

1. **Human Resource Audits**: These are analysis of each employee's skills and abilities. This analysis facilitates the human resource planners with an understanding of the skills and capabilities available in the organization and helps them identify manpower supply problems arising in the near future. These inventories should be updated

periodically otherwise it can lead to present employees being ignored for job openings within the organization.

2. **Employee Wastage**: The second step of supply forecasting is estimation of future losses of human resources of each department and of the entire organization. This is done to identify the employees who leave the organization and to forecast future losses likely to occur due to various reasons. Employees may leave the organization for reasons like retirements, layoffs, dismissals, disablement, ill health, death, etc. Reasons for high labour turnover and absenteeism should be analyzed and remedial measures taken.

3. **Internal Promotions**: Analysis is undertaken regarding the vacancies likely due to retirements and transfer and the employees of particular groups and categories who are likely to be promoted. The multiple effect of promotions and transfers on the total number of moves should be analyzed and taken into consideration in forecasting changes in human resource supply of various departments. For example, if the personnel officer is promoted as personnel manager, 2 more employees will also get promotion. The senior clerk in the personnel department will become personnel officer and the junior clerk will become senior clerk. Thus, there are 3 moves for one promotion.

Estimating Manpower Gaps: Net human resource requirements or manpower gaps can be identified by comparing demand and supply forecasts. Such comparison will reveal either deficit or surplus of human resources in future. Deficits suggest the number of persons to be recruited from outside whereas surplus implies redundant to be redeployed or terminated. Similarly, gaps may occur in terms of knowledge, skills and aptitudes. Employees deficient in qualifications can be trained whereas employees with higher skills may be given more enriched jobs.

Matching Demand and Supply: It is one of the objectives of human resource planning to assess the demand for and supply of human resources and match both to know shortages and surpluses on both the side in kind and in number. This will enable the human resource department to know overstaffing or understaffing. Once the manpower gaps are identified, plans are prepared to bridge these gaps.

Plans to meet the surplus manpower may be redeployment in other departments and retrenchment in consultation, with the trade unions. People may be persuaded to quit through voluntarily retirement. Deficit can be met through recruitment, selection, transfer, promotion, and training plans. Realistic plans for the procurement and development of manpower should be made after considering the macro and micro environment which affect the manpower objectives of the organisation.

2.7. RECRUITMENT AND SOURCES OF RECRUITMENT

Recruitment means search of the prospective employee to suit the job requirements as represented by job specification–a technique of job analysis. It is the first stage in selection which makes the vacancies known to a large number of people and the opportunities that the organisation offers. In response to this knowledge, potential applicants would write to the organisation. The process of attracting people to apply in called recruitment.

MEANING

Recruitment is the activity that links the employers and the job seekers. A process of finding and attracting capable applicants for employment

- **Dale S. Beach** has defined-Recruitment as the development and maintenance of adequate manpower resources. It involves the creation of a pool of available labour upon whom the organisation can depend when it needs additional employees.
- **According to Edwin B. Flippo:** Recruitment is the process of searching for prospective employees and stimulating them to apply for jobs in the organisation

SOURCES OF RECRUITMENT

The various sources of recruitment are generally classified as internal source and external source.

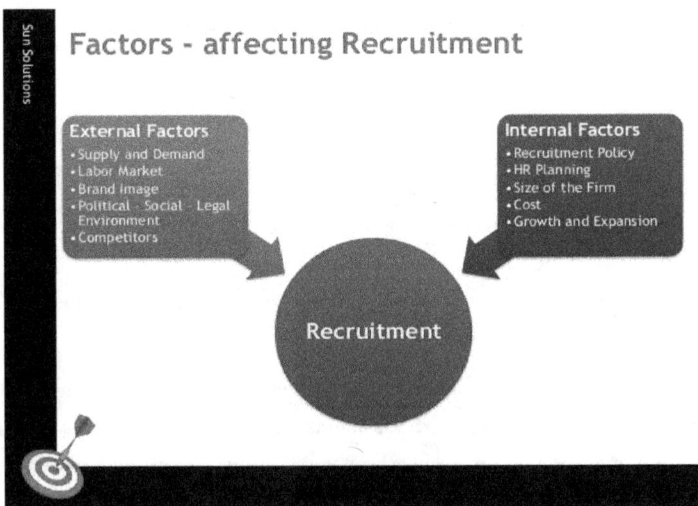

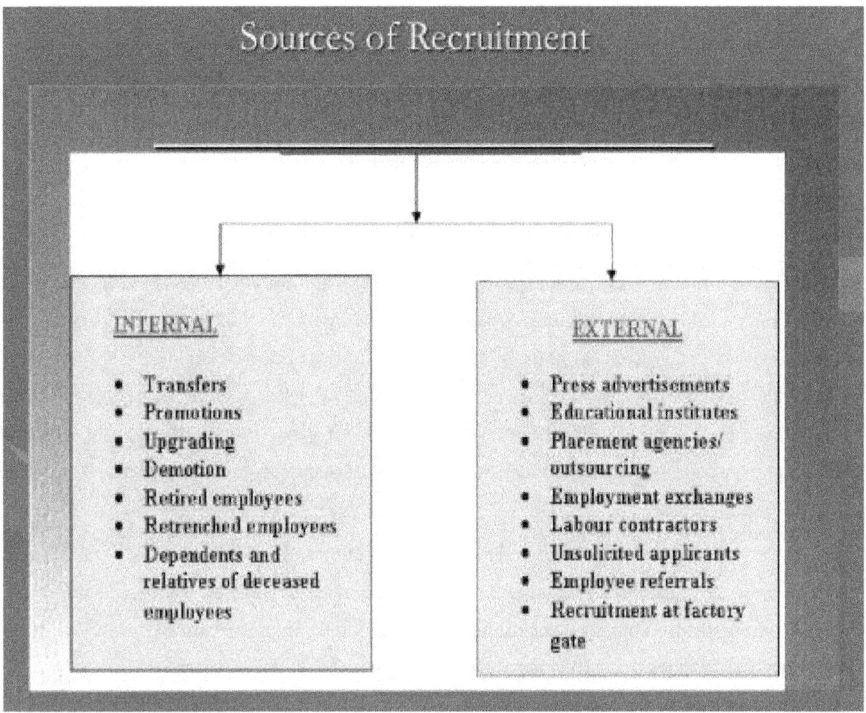

1. INTERNAL SOURCES

This refers to the recruitment from within the company. The various internal sources are promotion, transfer, past employees and internal advertisements.

2. EXTERNAL SOURCES

External sources refer to the practice of getting suitable persons from outside. The various external sources are advertisement, employment exchange, past employees, private placement agencies and consultants, walks-ins, campus recruitment, trade unions, etc.

The following external sources of recruitment are commonly used by the big enterprises

Direct Recruitment: An important source of recruitment is direct recruitment by placing a notice on the notice board of the enterprise specifying the details of the jobs available. It is also known as recruitment at factory gate. The practice of direct recruitment is generally followed for filling casual vacancies requiring unskilled workers. Such workers are known as casual or badli workers and they are paid remuneration on daily-wage basis. This method of recruitment is very cheap as it does not involve any cost of advertising vacancies.

Casual Callers or Unsolicited Applications: The organisations which are regarded as good employers draw a steady stream of unsolicited applications in their offices. This serves as a valuable source of manpower. If adequate attention is paid to maintain pending application folders for various jobs, the personnel department may find the unsolicited applications useful in filling the vacancies whenever they arise. The merit of this source of recruitment is that it avoids the costs of recruiting workforce from other sources.

Media Advertisement: Advertisement in newspapers or trade and professional journals is generally used when qualified and experienced personnel are not available from other sources. Most of the senior positions in industry as well as commerce are filled by this method. The advantage of advertising is that more information about the organization job descriptions and job specifications can be given in advertisement to allow self-screening by the prospective candidates. Advertisement gives the management a wider range of candidates from which to choose. Its disadvantage is that it may bring in a flood of response, and many times, from quite unsuitable candidates.

Employment Agencies: Employment exchanges run by the Government are regarded as a good source of recruitment for unskilled, semi-skilled and skilled operative jobs. In some cases, compulsory notification of vacancies to the employment exchange is required by law. Thus, the employment exchanges bring the jobs givers in contact with the job seekers.

However, in the technical and professional area, private agencies and professional bodies appear to be doing most of the work. Employment exchanges and selected private agencies provide a nation-wide service in attempting to match personnel demand and supply.

Management Consultants: Management consultancy firms help the organisations to recruit technical, professional and managerial personnel they specialize middle level and top level executive placements. They maintain data bank of persons with different qualifications and skills and even advertise the jobs on behalf their clients to recruit right type of personnel.

Educational Institutions or Campus Recruitment: Jobs in commerce and industry have become increasing technical and complex to the point where school and college degrees are widely required. Consequently big organisations maintain a close liaison with the universities, vocational institutes and management institutes for recruitment to various jobs. Recruitment from educational institutional is a well-established practice of thousands of business and other organisations. It is also known as campus recruitment. Reputed industrial houses which require management trainees send their officials to campuses of various management institutes for picking up talented candidates doing MBA.

Recommendation: Applicants introduced by friends and relatives may prove to be a good source of recruitment. In fact, many employers prefer to take such persons because something about their background is known. When a present-employee or a business friend recommends someone for a job, a type of preliminary screening is done and the person is placed on a job.

Labour Contractors: Labour contractors are an important source of recruitment in some industries in India. Workers are recruited through labour contractors who are themselves employees of the organisation. The disadvantage of this system is that if the contractor leaves the organisation all the workers, employed through him will also leave that is why this source of labour is not preferred by many businesses, organizations. Recruitment through labour contractors has been banned for the public sector units.

Telecasting: The practice of telecasting of vacant posts over T.V. is gaining importance these days. Special programmes like Job Watch 'Youth Pulse', Employment News etc, over the T.V have become quite popular in recruitment for various types of jobs. The detailed requirements of the job and the qualities required to do it are publicized along with the profile of the organisation where vacancy exists. The use of T.V. as a source of recruitment is less as compared to other sources.

Raiding: Raiding is a technical term used when employees working elsewhere are attracted to join organisations. The organisations are always on the lookout for qualified professionals, and are willing to offer them a better deal if they make the switch. There are always some employees who are professionally very competent, but dissatisfied with something or the other in the organisation. They form the easy' group to attract. The other group is formed of those who are equally competent but are quite satisfied with their present position. To attract them, the organisation has to offer a very lucrative package of perquisites. Whatever may be the means used to attract, often it is seen as an unethical practice and not openly talked about.

2.8.   RECRUITMENT PROCESS

1. Identify vacancy
2. Prepare job description and person specification
3. Advertising the vacancy
4. Managing the response
5. Short-listing
6. Arrange interviews
7. Conducting interview and decision making

2.9. SELECTION

INTRODUCTION

In simple words, It is the functions perform by the management of selecting the Right employees at the right time after identifying the sources of Human resources, searching for prospective employees and stimulating them to apply for jobs in an organization .The objective of the selection decision is to choose the individual who can most successfully perform the job from the pool of qualified candidates.

Selection is a part of the recruitment function. It is the process of choosing people by obtaining and assessing information about the applicants (age, qualification, experience and qualities) with a view of matching these with the job requirements and picking up the most suitable candidates. The choices are made by elimination of the unsuitable at successive stages of the selection process.

IMPORTANCE OF SELECTION
- Helps to get a proper candidate.
- Help to increase success rate.
- Help to reduce the probability.
- Helps to get organizations legal and social obligations.
- Helps to increase organization and individual effectiveness.

CRITERIA OF SELECTION

Selection decisions are usually based on how an applicant is rated (rather, predicted) in terms of the likelihood of success on the job. The information used found in the application blanks, performance in one or more tests and the interview(s). The criteria of selection needs to be critical to the job. The key job dimensions identified in job analysis and job description provide the basis for determining relevant criteria.

Frequently educational qualifications, technical skills and achievements are used as the basis for selection. But is there a statistical relationship between such requirements and job performance? It appears that certain job requirements can be measured more easily and accurately than certain others. The core job skills like sensory motor skills and manipulative skills and achievement can be measured relatively more accurately than one's aptitude, interest and personality traits. Integrity loyalty, initiative/drive/resourcefulness and intelligence/mental alertness are the key attributes influencing the selection of managerial employees. All these attributes being subjective are hard to assess accurately, yet are widely attempted. Perhaps it is so because managements and employers in India have relatively less pressure to defend the criteria.

2.10. SELECTION PROCESS

The selection process begins with the job specification. The more dearly and precisely it is done the less would be the number of qualified applicants. Suppose the purpose is to select management trainees. If the qualification prescribed is MBA, the number of applicants may be in hundred. If the qualification is graduation in any discipline, the number of applicants may be in thousand. Of course, the reputation of the firm, the job content, compensation package, location, etc. also influence the response to any, recruitment drive. But Job specification does plays an important role m deciding the quantity and, quality of response from prospective applicants.

The selection process covers the period from the job specification and initial contact with the applicant to his final acceptance or rejection. The successive stages in the selection process are referred to as hurdles that the applicants should cross. Not all selection processes, however, include all these stages. The complexity of the selection process usually increases with the increase in the skill level and job level (responsibility and accountability) of the position for which selection is being made. The sequencing of the hurdles also may vary from job to job and organization to organization.

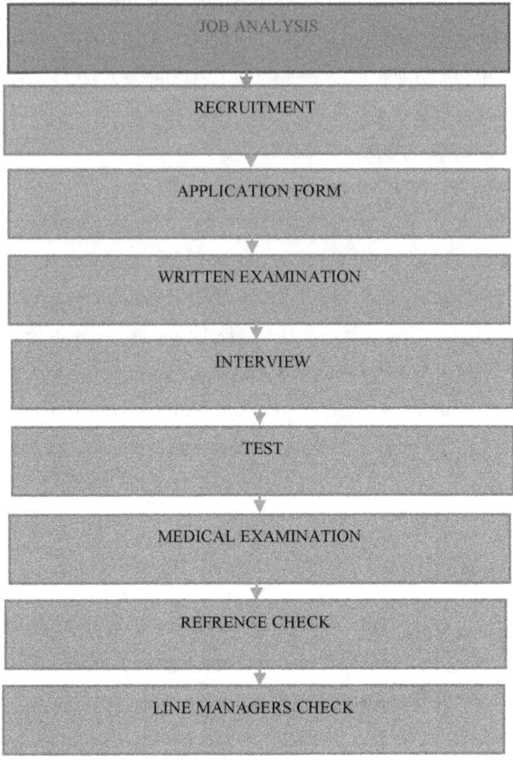

Initial Screening: The initial screening and/or preliminary interview is done to limit the costs of selection by letting only suitable candidates go through the further stages in selection. At this stage, usually a junior executive either screens all enquiries for positions against specified norms (in terms of age, qualifications and experience) through preliminary interview where information is exchanged about the job, the applicant and the, mutual expectations of the individual and the organization. If the organization finds the candidate suitable, an application form, prescribed for the purpose, is given to these candidates to fill in and submit.

Application Form: The application form is usually designed to obtain information on various aspects, of the applicant's social, demographic, academic and work-related background and references. The forms may vary for different positions some organizations may not have any form specially designed instead, ask the candidates to write applications on a plain sheet.

Tests: A test is a sample of an aspect of an individual's behaviour, performance or attitude. It also provides a systematic basis for comparing the behaviour, performance or attitude of two or more persons. Tests serve as a screening device and provide supplementary inputs in selection decisions. Their value lies in the. Fact that they serve additional predictors intended to make selection decision more apt and accurate.

- **Intelligence Tests:** These are tests to measure one's intellect or qualities of understanding. They are also referred to as tests of mental ability. The traits of intelligence measured include: Reasoning, verbal and non-verbal fluency, comprehension, numerical, memory and spatial relations ability. Binet-Simon; Standford-Binet and Weshier-Bellevue Scale are some examples of standard intelligence tests.

- **Aptitude Tests:** Aptitude refers to one's natural propensity or talent or ability to acquire a particular skill. While intelligence is a general trait, aptitude refers to a more specific capacity or potential. It could relate to mechanical dexterity, clerical, linguistic, musical academic etc.

- **Achievement Tests:** These are proficiency tests to measure one's skill or acquired knowledge. The paper and pencil tests may seek to test a person's knowledge about a particular subject. But there is no guarantee that a person who knows most also performs best. Work sample tests or performance test using actual task and working conditions (then simulated one's) provide standardized measures of behaviours to assess the ability to perform than merely the ability to know. Work sample tests are most appropriate for testing abilities in such skills as typing, stenography and technical trades. Work sample tests bear demonstrable relationship between test content and job performance.

- **PIP Tests:** PIP tests are those which seek to measure one's personality, interest and preferences. These tests are designed to understand the relationship between any one of these and certain types of jobs.

- **Interest tests** are inventories of likes and dislikes of people towards occupations, hobbies, etc. These tests help indicate which occupation (e.g. artistic, literary, technical, scientific, etc.) are more in tune with a person's interests. Strong Vocational Interest Blank and Kuder Preference Records are examples of interest tests. These tests do not help in predicting on the job performance. Besides, they leave room for faking and the underlying assumptions in the tests could be belied.

- **Projective Tests:** These tests expect the candidates to interpret problems or situations. Responses to stimuli will be based on the individual's values, beliefs and motives. Thematic Apperception Test and Rorschach Ink Blot Test are examples of projective tests. In Thematic Apperception Test a photograph is shown to, the candidate who is then asked to interpret it. The test administrator will draw inferences about the candidate's values, beliefs and motives from an analysis of such interpretation.

- **Other Tests:** A wide variety of other tests also are used thoughless frequently and in rare instances. These include polygraph (literally mean many pens), graphology (handwriting analysis), non-verbal communication tests (gestures, body movement, eye-contact, etc. a lie-detector tests.

The following could be considered as thumb rules of selection tests: (a) Tests are to be used as a screening device; (b) Tests scores are not precise measures. Use tests as supplements than standalone basis. Each test can be assigned a weightage; (c) Norms have to be developed for each test; and their validity and reliability for a given purpose is to be established before they are used; (d) Tests are better at predicting failure than success; (e)Tests should be designed, administered assessed and interpreted only by trained and competent persons.

2.11. INTERVIEWS

According to Scott "Interview is a purposeful exchange of ideas, the answering of questions and communication between two or more persons". Interview is an oral examination of candidates for employment. No selection process is complete without one or more interviews. Interview is the most common and core method of both obtaining information from job-seekers, and decision-making on their suitability or otherwise. Organizations may seek to make their selection process as objective as possible. But interview which is an essential element of the process, by and large still remains subjective. Interviews usually take place at two crucial stages in the selection process, i.e., at the beginning and in the end. Interviews can differ in terms of their focus and format. Usually several individuals interview one applicant, this is called panel interview. Such panels usually consist of representatives from-personnel and concerned operating units/line functions. In this method, usually, applicants get screened from one stage to another, at least in the initial stages.

The interviews can be structured or unstructured general or in-depth. Sometimes where the job requires the job holder to remain claim and composed under pressure, the candidates are intentionally objected to stress and strains in the interview by asking some annoying or embarrassing questions. This type of interview called the stress interview. The interview should be based on a checklist of what to look for in a candidate. Such checklist could be based on proper job analysis. Each critical attribute which the interview seeks to evaluate may be assigned a specific weightage.

JOB INTERVIEWS

In the interview, the interviewer & applicant exchange information in order to achieve a goal through conversation. The employment interviews are conducted during the selection process through proper planning. The pleasant location of the interviewing place is selected and the interviewer has the good personality with empathy & ability to communicate & listen effectively. A job profile must be prepared on the basis of job description before conducting interview.

TYPES OF INTERVIEWS

The interviews are generally categorized into the following three types.

1. **Unstructured Interview:** In unstructured interviews open ended questions are asked from the applicant in order to perform probing. It is generally non-directive in nature and applicant is encouraged to give lengthy answers.

2. **Structured Interview:** In structured interview, a list of job related questions associated to particular job are asked from each applicant in a consistent manner. It is directive or patterned in nature and includes the following four kinds of questions.
   - Situational Questions
   - Job Knowledge Questions
   - Job-sample simulation Questions
   - Worker Requirement Questions

3. **Mixed Interview**

   It is a special kind of structured interview in which specially designed questions are asked from the applicant to probe his past behavior in specific situations. It does not include the self-evaluative & hypothetical questions & inhibits to judge the personality of the applicant. The candidates are rated on the basis of their responses in the light of the bench-marked answer of successful employees.

4. **Behavioral Interview:** In behavioral interviews, applicants are required to give specific example of how they have performed a certain procedure or handled a problem in the past.

METHODS OF INTERVIEWING

Following are the main ways of conducting interviews.

01- One-on-One Interview

02- Group Interview

03- Board Interview

04- Stress Interview

2.12. BACKGROUND INVESTIGATION

The background investigation in selection process may include verification of reference from past teachers, employers or public men; public men; police verification; and, medical examination. Background verification is sought to guard oneself against possible falsification by applicant. But given the acute skill shortages and competitive pirating strategies of employers it is possible for some of them to give clean chit to those whom they wish to get rid of and be unfair to those whom they are not prepared to lose. Therefore, employers in-private sector generally find that they get more accurate information when they track the actual past performance than when they merely ask for references reflecting opinion about the candidate.

Medical and Physical Examinations are usually resorted to by employers as part of the selection process mainly to determine whether the applicant has the physical ability to carry on the duties arid responsibilities effectively; ascertain whether the applicant has a record of health problems, which can potentially affect his behaviours and performance on the job adversely know whether the applicant is more sensitive to certain aspects of work-place environment such as chemicals.

2.13. DISTINCTION BETWEEN RECRUITMENT AND SELECTION

RECRUITMENT	SELECTION
Searching for employees	It involves in series of steps in selecting
Basic purpose of recruitment is to create talent pool of candidates to enable the selection best	Basic purpose is to select right person for the right job
It is positive process	It is negative process
It is tapping HR	Selecting suitable through tests
It involves no contract	It involves contract between employer & employee

2.14. JOB ANALYSIS

A job analysis is the process used to collect information about the duties, responsibilities, necessary skills, outcomes, and work environment of a particular job. Process of defining a job in terms of its component tasks or duties and the knowledge or skills required to perform. Job Analysis is a procedure by which pertinent information is obtained about a job, i.e., it is a detailed and systematic study of information relating to the operation and responsibilities of a specific job. An authority has defined job analysis as-the process of determining, by observation and study, and reporting pertinent information relating to the nature of a specific job... It is the determination of the tasks which comprise the job and of the skills, knowledge, abilities and responsibilities required of the worker for a successful performance and which differentiate one job from all others.

Definition of Job Analysis

Job analysis is the systematic method of jobs to identify work activities, tasks, and responsibilities, KSAs, working conditions to perform the job.

Purpose

The main purpose of conducting job analysis is to prepare job description and job specification which in turn helps to hire the right quality of workforce into the organization.

It helps to understand the qualities needed by employees, defined through behavioral descriptors, to provide optimum work performance.

SOURCES OF INFORMATION FOR JOB ANALYSIS

According to **George R. Terry**, -the make-up of a job, its relation to other jobs, and its requirements for competent performance are essential information needed for a job analysis‖. Information on a job may be obtained from three principal sources: from the employees who actually perform a job; from other employees such as supervisors and foremen who watch the workers doing a job and thereby acquire knowledge about it; and from outside observers specially appointed to watch employees performing a job. Such outside persons are called the trade job analysts. Sometimes, special job reviewing committees are also established.

Steps in Job Analysis

- Select jobs for analysis.
- Determine what information to collect.
- Determine how to collect the information.
- Determine who collects the information.

- Process the information.
- Write job descriptions and job specifications

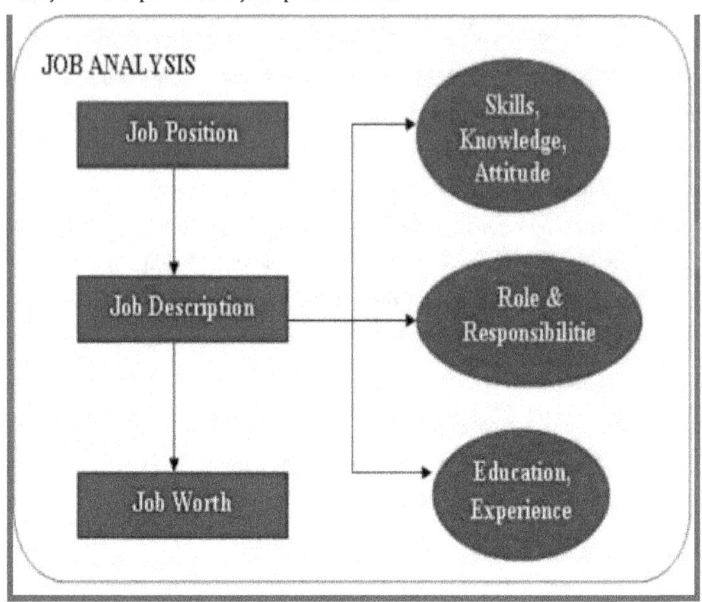

2.15. METHODS OF JOB ANALYSIS

1. *OBSERVATION METHODS*

Methods of observation include direct observation, work methods analysis, critical incident technique.

- **Direct observation**

Direct Observation is a method of job analysis to observe and record behavior / events / activities/tasks/duties while something is happening.

- **Work methods analysis**

Work methods analysis is used to describe manual and repetitive production jobs, such as factory or assembly-line jobs. Work methods analysis includes time and motion study and micro-motion analysis.

- **Critical incident technique(CIT model)**

Critical incident technique is a method of job analysis used to identify work behaviors that classify in good and poor performance.

2. INTERVIEW METHOD

Interview method is a useful tool of job analysis to ask questions to both incumbents and supervisors in either an individual or a group setting. Interview includes structured Interviews, unstructured interview, open-ended questions.

- *Questionnaire Method*

Position Analysis Questionnaire (PAQ). The Position Analysis Questionnaire (PAQ) was developed by McCormick and associates (1972) on the assumption that there is an underlying taxonomy to all jobs. That is, in contract to the other methods, the PAQ approach focuses on broad categories common to all jobs rather than on individual elements of specific jobs.

3. OTHER METHODS

- **Task Inventory**

A task inventory is a list of the discrete activities that make up a specific job in a specific organization.

- **Job element method**

This method is same the critical incident technique. It focuses on work behaviors and the results of this behavior rather than more abstract characteristics. Job element method developed by Ernest Primoff.

- **Diary method**

This method is a useful tool of job analysis to ask worker maintaining and keeping daily records or list of activities they are doing on every day

- **Checklists and rating scales**

Checklist is job analysis method base on an inventory of job elements. Questions can be asked question about purpose of position; key responsibility areas; organization; relationships; decision making; authority; Skills, knowledge, experience; working conditions

- **Competency profiling**

Competency modelling is the activity of determining the specific competencies that are characteristic of high performance and success in a given job. Contents of competency modelling include skills, knowledge, abilities, values, interests, personalities.

- **Examining Manuals/reference materials**

Manuals/reference materials such as quality manual, human resource manual, procedures, instruction, forms and job description are useful for analyst in job analysis. These documents are available for organizations applied to ISO 9000 standard.

- **Technical conference**

Technical conference is a useful tool of job analysis base on Subject Matter Experts (SMEs). SMEs conduct brainstorming sessions to identify job elements. SMEs can use all job analysis methods in here.

- **Threshold Traits Analysis System (TTAS model)**

Threshold Traits Analysis System (TTAS model) is a method of job analysis, was developed in 1970 by Felix Lopez. Threshold traits analysis system include a standard set of 33 traits: ability traits are "can do" factors and attitudinal traits are "willing to do" factors.

PURPOSES AND USES OF JOB ANALYSIS

A comprehensive job analysis programme is an essential ingredient of sound personnel management. It is fundamental to manpower management programmes because the results of job analysis are widely used throughout the programmes.

The information provided by job analysis is useful, if not essential, in almost every phase of employee relations.

- **Organisation and Manpower Planning**: It is helpful in organisational planning for it defines labour needs in concrete terms and coordinates the activities of the work force, and clearly divides duties and responsibilities.

- **Recruitment and Selection**: By indicating the specific requirements of each job (i.e., the skills and knowledge), it provides a realistic basis for hiring, training, placement, transfer and promotion of personnel.

- **Wage and Salary Administration**: By indicating the qualifications required for doing specified jobs and the risks and hazards involved in its performance, it helps in salary and wage administration. Job analysis is used as a foundation for job evaluation.

- **Job Re-engineering**: Job analysis provides information which enables us to change jobs in order to permit their being manned by personnel with specific characteristics and qualifications. This takes two forms :

- **Industrial Engineering Activity:** which is concerned with operational analysis, motion study, work simplification methods and improvements in the place of work and its measurement, and aims at improving efficiency, reducing unit labour costs, and establishing the production standard which the employee is expected to meet; and

- **Human Engineering Activity:** which takes into consideration human capabilities, both physical and psychological, and prepares the ground for complex operations of industrial administration, increased efficiency and better productivity.

- **Employee Training and Management Development:** Job analysis provides the necessary information to the management of training and development programmes. It helps it to determine the content and subject-matter of in-training courses. It also helps in checking application information, interviewing, weighing test results, and in checking references.

- **Performance Appraisal:** It helps in establishing clear-cut standards which may be compared with the actual contribution of each individual.

- **Health and Safety:** It provides an opportunity for identifying hazardous conditions and unhealthy environmental factors so that corrective measures may be taken to minimise and avoid the possibility of accidents.

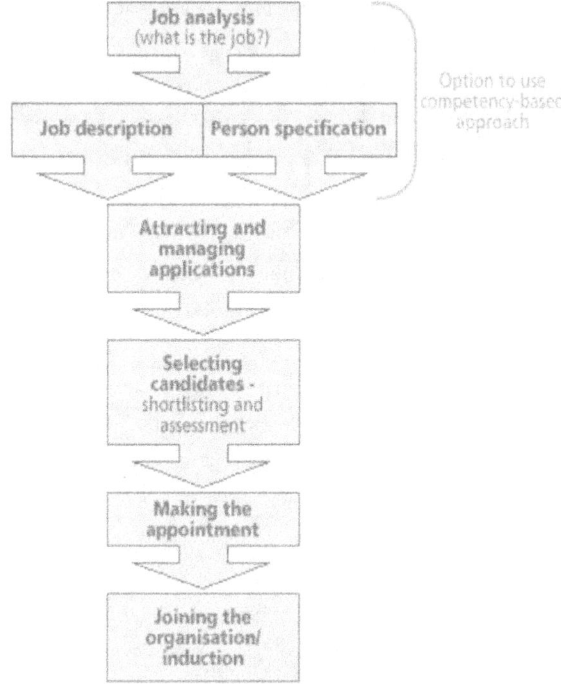

JOB DESCRIPTION

Job description is a written record of the duties, responsibilities and requirements of a particular job. It is concerned with the job itself and not with the work. It is a statement describing the job in such terms as its title, location, duties, working conditions and hazards.

In other words, it tells us what is to be done and how it is to be done and why. It is a standard of function, in that it defines the appropriate and authorized contents of a job. Job description helps top executives, especially when they jointly discuss one another's responsibilities. Overlapping or confusion can then be pointed out questions can be raised about the major thrust of each position, and problems of structure can be identified. A job description becomes a vehicle for organisational change and improvement. A job description contains the following aspects:

- **Job identification**, which includes the job title, alternative title, department, division, plant and code number of the job. The job title identifies and designates the job properly. The department division, etc. indicate the name of the department where it is situated-whether it is the maintenance department, mechanical shop etc. The location gives the name of the place.

- **Job Summary** serves two important purposes. First it provides a short definition which is useful as an additional identification information when a job title is not adequate. Second, it serves as a summary to orient the reader toward an understanding of detailed information which follows. It gives the reader a quick capsule explanation of the content of a job usually in one or two sentences.

- **Job duties** give us a comprehensive listing or the duties together with some indication of the frequency of occurrence or percentage of time devoted to each major duty. It is regarded as the heart of a job.

- **Relation to other jobs:** This helps us to locate the job in the organisation by indicating the job immediately below or above it in the job hierarchy. It also gives us an idea of the vertical relationships of work flow and procedures.

- **Supervision:** Under it is given the number of persons to be supervised along with their job titles, and the extent of supervision involved general, intermediate or close supervision.

- **Working conditions** usually give us information about the environment in which a job holder must work. These include cold, heat, dust, wetness, moisture, fumes, odour, oily conditions, etc. obtaining inside the organisation. Information about jobs can be had from

  a. Observation of employees while on work

  b.   Study of specially maintained diaries

  c. A review of Critical incidents; and

  d. Discussions with departmental heads and outside experts or consultants.

A job description enables us to frame suitable questions to be asked during an interview. It is particularly helpful when the application from is, used as a tool for eliminating the unfit personnel. A job description helps manager to analyse and choose right person for the suitable job.

- Job grading and classification
- Transfers and promotions
- Adjustments of grievances
- Defining and outlining promotional steps
- Establishing a common understanding of a job between employers and employees
- Investigating accidents
- Indicating faulty work procedures or duplication of papers
- Maintaining, operating and adjusting machinery
- Time and motion studies
- Defining the limits of authority
- Indicating case of personal merit
- Facilitating job placement
- Studies of health and fatigue
- Scientific guidance
- Determining jobs suitable for occupational therapy
- Providing hiring specifications; and
- Providing performance indicators.

JOB SPECIFICATION

Job Specification is a standard of personnel and designates the qualities required for an acceptable performance. It is a written record of the requirements sought in an individual worker for a given job. In other words, it refers to a summary of the personal characteristics required for a job. It is a statement of the minimum acceptable human qualities necessary for the proper performance of a job.

Job specifications translate the job description into terms of the human qualifications which are required for a successful performance of a job. They are intended to serve as a guide in hiring and job evaluation. As a guide in hiring, they deal with such characteristics as are available in an application bank, with testing, interviews, and checking of references.

JOB SPECIFICATIONS RELATE TO

- **Physical characteristics**, which include health, strength, endurance, age-range, body size height, weight, vision, voice, poise, eye, hand and foot co-ordination, motor co-ordination, and colour discrimination.

- **Psychological characteristics** or special aptitudes which include such qualities as manual dexterity, mechanical aptitude, ingenuity, judgment, resourcefulness, analytical ability, mental concentration and alertness.

- **Personal characteristics** traits of temperament such as personal appearance, good and pleasing manners, emotional stability, aggressiveness or submissiveness, extroversion; or, introversion, leadership, co-cooperativeness, initiative and drive, skill in dealing with others unusual sensory qualities of sight, smell, hearing, adaptability, conversational ability, etc. Responsibilities which include supervision of others, responsibility for production, process and equipment; responsibility for the safety of others; responsibility for generating confidence and trust; responsibility for preventing monetary loss. Other features of a demographic nature, which are age, sex education, experience and language ability.

JOB DESIGN

Job analysis helps in developing appropriate design of job to improve efficiency and satisfaction. Job design is the process of deciding on the contents of a job in terms of its duties and responsibilities, on the methods to be used in carrying out the job, in terms of techniques, systems and procedures and on the relationships that should exist between the jobholder and his superiors, subordinates and colleagues. It is a deliberate and systematic attempt to structure the technical and social aspects of work so as to improve technical efficiency and job satisfaction. Job design is an attempt to create a match between job requirements and human attributes. It involves both organizing the components of the job and the interaction patterns among the members of a work group.

The main objective of job design is to integrate the needs of the individual and the requirements of the organisation. Needs of employees include job satisfaction in terms of interest, challenge and achievements. Organizational requirements refer to high productivity, technical efficiency and quality of work. Today, educated and creative employees demand well-designed jobs. Therefore, increasing attempts are being made to redesign jobs so as to improve the quality of working life. A systematic body of knowledge on the designing of jobs has been developed after the Industrial Revolution and the large scale enterprises.

2.16. APPROACHES TO JOB DESIGN

The main approaches to job design are described below:

- **CLASSICAL APPROACH:** Also known as engineering approach, it was developed by F.W. Taylor and his associates. The principles of scientific management formed the basis for designing jobs in most Organizations. These principles focus on planning, standardizing and improving human effort at the operative level in order to maximize productivity. In the words of Taylor the work of every workman is fully planned out by the management at least one day in advance and each man receives in most cases complete written instructions, describing in detail the task which he is to accomplish. This task specifies not only what is to be done but how it is to be done and the exact time allowed for doing it.

Jobs designed on the basis of classical approach are not appropriate in the modern environment characterized by increased awareness, improved education and rising expectations of workforce.

- **BEHAVIOURAL APPROACH:** The findings of Elton Mayo, Frederick Herzberg and other human relations experts led to search for alternative ways of designing jobs so as to avoid the dysfunctional consequences of standardization and simplification. Job redesign, work structuring, job enrichment, participative system and other similar strategies were developed to improve the quality of work life. The aim of all these attempts is to design jobs which will not only ensure technical efficiency but will satisfy social and psychological needs of workers. The most popular behavioural approach to job redesign is the Job characteristics model of Hackman and Oldham. This model is based on the assumption that three key psychological stats of a jobholder determine his motivation, satisfaction and performance on the job.

Behavioural approach to job design is a socio-technical approach as it deals with both the technical and social aspects of a job. It is, therefore, an improvement over the classical approach which considered only the technical side of jobs. Tailstock Institute of Human Relations, London has carried out several experiments in the application of the socio-technical approach to job design.

The job characteristics model, however, suffers from some limitations. It is probabilistic and has an intuitive appeal. But there is little empirical evidence to support it. In one study of bank employees in India growth need has not been found coaching, counselling etc., are examples of corrective actions that help to improve performance.

- **NEGATIVE APPROACH:** Performance appraisal loses most of its value when the focus of management is on punishment rather than on development of employees.
- **MULTIPLE OBJECTIVES:** Rates may get confused due to too many objectives or unclear objective of performance appraisal.
- **RESISTANCE:** Trade unions may resist performance appraisal on the ground that it involves discrimination among its members. Negative ratings may affect interpersonal relations and industrial relations particularly when employees/unions do not have faith in the system of performance appraisal.
- **LACK OF KNOWLEDGE:** The staff appraising performance of employees might not be trained and experienced enough to make correct appraisal.

2.17. VARIOUS TECHNIQUES OF JOB DESIGN

- Job Enrichment
- Job Enlargement
- Job Rotation
- Job Engineering and
- Socio technical systems
- Ergonomics

Job Enrichment - which focuses on increasing the number of tasks a job holder is responsible for performing, additional tasks are not the focus for the goal, but an increase in tasks could be a result of giving the job holder more authority, discretion, and responsibility for decision making in their current role.

Job Enlargement - It increases job scope or job diversity. The number of different operations required in a job and the frequency with which the job cycle is repeated. It decreases some boredom but it is not enough to motivate as nature of work.

Job Rotation - Job rotation is the systematic and planned rotation of individuals in pre-determined jobs (other than their own) so they can gain additional knowledge or skills. It is for managers because they need to be familiar with operations.

Job engineering – focuses on the tasks to be performed, methods used, and workflows among employees, layout of workplace, performance standards and interdependencies among machines and people.

Socio–technical systems – focus on organizations as being made up of people with various competencies who use tools, machines and techniques to create goods and services valued by customers and other stakeholders.

Ergonomics – focuses on minimizing the physical demands and risks of work. It involves in designing the aids ranging from computer software to instruments used to perform tasks.

2.18. SOCIALIZATION

When new employees enter an organization they feel out of place because of the new surroundings, new boss and new co-workers. Hence, it is the responsibility of the management to orient the employees and to make the process of socialization smooth. This will ensure that the new employees adapt to the organizational culture as soon as possible. The process of adaptation is commonly termed induction or socialization.

The socialization process is not confined to employees entering new organizations. It is also important for employees moving within the organization as a result of lateral transfers and promotions. Orientation is only a small part of the overall socialization program. The process of orientation includes introduction of the new employee to the organization and to his work unit and supplementing the information given to him during recruitment and selection.

An organization's orientation program should make a new employee familiar with the organization's history, philosophy, objectives, procedures and rules. To understand the concept of socialization, a look at organization culture and its underlying concepts–roles, values, and norms–is necessary. A new employee, to fit into the organization, must understand the role he has to play in that particular job, the values of the organization that he has to uphold and the norms set by his peer group that he has to conform to.

MEANING

It is a long term of planned & unplanned activities through which an individual acquires attitudes, behaviors, and knowledge needed to successfully participate as a member of an organization and learns firm's culture.

DEFINITION

According to Mc.Shane -"Socialization is the process by which organizational members become a part of or absorbed into the culture of an organization"

2.19. PROCESS OF SOCIALIZATION

The socialization process is based on some general assumptions. They are: The process of socialization has an influence on the performance of an employee; an effective socialization process ensures that a new employee fits well into the organization, socialization helps to handle new employee anxiety and the process of socialization requires the involvement of co-workers and the work environment. Socialization can be conceptualized as a process consisting of three stages – Pre-arrival, Encounter, and Metamorphosis.

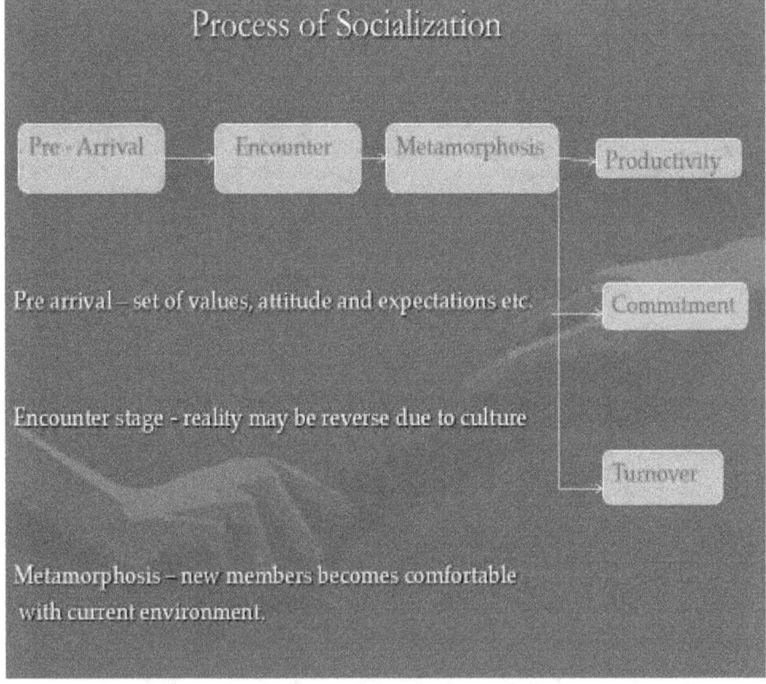

The process of socialization affects the new employee's work productivity, commitment to the organization's objectives and his decision to stay with the organization. They are various alternatives that a manager can consider when designing effective socialization strategies. They are Formal or Informal, Individual or Collective, Sequential or Non-sequential, Fixed or Variable, Tournament or Contest, Serial or Disjunctive, Investiture or Divestiture Socialization Strategies. The human resource manager must consider the various alternatives and their influence while designing the appropriate program for the organization. Socialization is an ongoing process and should not be stopped after the initial orientation program. Given the changing business environment it is always important to equip employees with the right skills to perform effectively.

METHODS OF SOCIALIZATION WITHIN ORGANIZATION

Stories – narration events about organization

Rituals – repetitive sequence of activities

Material symbols – material symbols used by the organization convey specific meanings indicating status.

Languages – to identify the culture and sub culture of people.

Review Questions

1. What do you understand by human resource planning? Describe its characteristics.
2. Discuss the objectives of human resource planning. How the planning is carried at various levels in the organization?
3. Briefly discuss the steps involved in manpower planning in an industry.
4. Define HRP or manpower planning. Review its benefits and limitations. What steps can be taken by an organization to make manpower planning more effective?
5. What is manpower or HR planning? Why is it necessary? Discuss the various steps involved in integrated strategic planning and HR.
6. What are the bases of HR planning?
7. Describe the various steps in conducting HRP.
8. What is recruitment and selection in human resource management?
9. What are the different methods of recruitment?
10. What are the steps in recruitment?
11. Why recruitment and selection is important to HR?
12. Explain selection and its process.

13. What is interview?

14. Discuss types of Interviews with suitable examples

15. List out different types of Tests.

16. What is Job analysis? Explain in detail various methods of Job analysis.

17. Elaborate various techniques of Job Design.

18. Write short notes on Ergonomics.

19. What is Socialization? Explain the methods of Socialization in organization.

20. Explain the process of Socialization.

UNIT 3

TRAINING AND EXECUTIVE DEVELOPMENT

Objective of the Unit 3

- Understand Meaning and Nature of Training and Development
- The Objectives of Training & Development
- The Needs assessment and importance of Training & Development
- Methods of Training
- Understanding the importance of Executive Development Programme & its common practices
- Self-Development
- Knowledge Management, its types & process.

3.1. TRAINING AND DEVELOPMENT

INTRODUCTION

Training and Development is a continuous process. In a rapidly changing work profile, employee training and development is not only desirable, but it has become essential to cope up with the changes in environment, Technology and know-how. Training is corner-stone of sound management and it makes employees more effective, productive and competitive. Training has acquired a significant position across the developed and developing countries. Training plays an important role in enhancing productivity and improving organizational functioning. Training improves behavior and makes performance of trainee more useful and productive for him and for organization. Training improves operative skills, inter-personal skills as well as decision-making skills. Training is the act of increasing the knowledge and skills of the employee for doing a job. It is nothing but imparting specific skill for doing particular job. Education is increasing general knowledge and understanding of an employee's total environment. Learning provides access to better opportunities in life and also improves quality. Development is improving or growing the overall personality of an individual.

We can calculate the Training and Development needs as follows:

Training and Development = Standard Performance – Actual Performance

Training and Development offers Competitive Advantage to a firm by removing performance deficiencies and makes employees stay long, minimize accidents and damages and meets future employee needs. It also helps to reduce Complaints, Absenteeism and

Turnover. The Optimum Utilization of Human Resources can be improved through training and development that further helps the employee to achieve the organizational goals as well as their individual goals.

Development of Human Resources: Training and Development helps to provide an opportunity and broad structure for the development of human resources' technical and behavioral skills in an organization. It also helps the employees in attaining personal growth. Development of skills of employees – Training and Development helps in increasing the job knowledge and skills of employees at each level. It helps to expand the horizons of human intellect and an overall personality of the employees.

DEFINITIONS

1. **According to Edwin B. Flippo** – "Training is the act of increasing the knowledge and skills of an employee for doing a particular job".
2. **Training – Dale s Beach** – defines "the training as the organized procedure by which people learn knowledge and or skill for a definite purpose"
3. **Training** is a short term educational process and utilizing a systematic and organized procedure by which employees learn technical knowledge and skills for a definite purpose.

Training involves the development of skills that are usually necessary to perform a specific job. Its purpose is to achieve a change in the behavior of those trained and to enable them to do; their jobs better. Training makes newly appointed workers fully productive in the minimum of time. Training is equally necessary for the old employees whenever new machines and equipment are introduced and/or there is a change in the techniques of doing the things. In fact, training is a continuous process. It does not stop anywhere. The managers are continuously engaged in training their subordinates. They should ensure that any training programme should attempt to bring about positive Changes in the (i) Knowledge, (ii) skills, and (iii) attitudes of the workers. The purpose of training is to bring about improvement in the performance of work. It includes the learning of such techniques as are required for the better performance of definite tasks.

3.2.   TRAINING OBJECTIVES

- To prepare employee both new & old to meet present requirements
- To prevent obsolescence
- To prepare employees for higher tasks
- To assist employees to perform effectively

- To broaden the minds of senior managers by providing them with opportunities
- To develop potentialities of people
- To ensure smooth working environment
- To promote individual & collective morale, sense of responsibility, cooperative attitudes & good relationships among each other.
- **Productivity** – Training and Development helps in increasing the productivity of the employees that helps the organization further to achieve its long-term goal.
- **Team spirit** – Training and Development helps in inculcating the sense of team work, team spirit, and inter-team collaborations. It helps in inculcating the zeal to learn within the employees.
- **Organization Culture** – Training and Development helps to develop and improve the organizational health culture and effectiveness. It helps in creating the learning culture within the organization.
- **Organization Climate** – Training and Development helps building the positive perception and feeling about the organization. The employees get these feelings from leaders, subordinates, and peers.
- **Quality** – Training and Development helps in improving upon the quality of work and work-life.
- **Healthy work environment** – Training and Development helps in creating the healthy working environment. It helps to build good employee, relationship so that individual goals aligns with organizational goal.
- **Health and Safety** – Training and Development helps in improving the health and safety of the organization thus preventing obsolescence.
- **Morale** – Training and Development helps in improving the morale of the work force.
- **Image** – Training and Development helps in creating a better corporate image.
- **Profitability** – Training and Development leads to improved profitability and more positive attitudes towards profit orientation.

Training enables the employees to get acquainted with jobs and also increase, their aptitudes and skills and knowledge. It makes newly recruited employees fully productive in the minimum of time. Even for the old workers, it is necessary to refresh them and to enable them to keep up with new methods and techniques as well as new machines and equipment's for doing the work. Thus, training is not a one-step process but it is a continuous or never-ending process because it increases the knowledge and skills of new employees in performing their jobs and serves as a refresher course for the old employees. Training job will never be finished as long as the organization remains in operation. At any given time, the different phases of training programme will be found at practically every stage of progress. Men may be learning by their own experiences and by trial and error methods. Training does not disappear from any organisation merely because its presence is ignored. The purpose of training is to bring about improvement in the performance of workers. It includes the learning of such techniques as are required for the intelligence performance of definite task.

There is a growing realisation about the importance of training in Indian organisations, especially after globalisation. This has posed a lot of challenges to Indian industries. Without efficiency, effectiveness and competency, it would be impossible to survive and to be internationally competitive, all out efforts are required. Quality innovation, technology up gradation, cost reduction and productive work culture, have thus become the slogans of every industry, which no organisation will be able to achieve without continuously training its human resources. Justifiably, therefore, there is an upward trend in investment in training in many organisations. But increasing the investment in training and hiking training budgets is not going to achieve desired results. There are certain fundamentals and basic in training which must be given due importance if investments have to bring in returns.

3.3.   NATURE OF TRAINING AND DEVELOPMENT

Training is the most important component of Human Resource Development (HRD) but HRD is training plus. An organisation which aspires to grow must be in tune with the changing needs of the society. Training becomes relevant in the context since it is only through training that the gap between performance of the organization and the felt need of a changing society can be neutralised Training reduces the gap by increasing employees knowledge, skill, ability and attitude.

Training makes a very important contribution to the development of the organisation's human resources and hence to the achievement of its aims and objectives. To achieve its purpose, training needs to be effectively managed so that the right training is given to the right people, in the right form, at the right time and at the right costs.

Training is a vital phase of management control. It helps in reducing accidents, eliminating wastages and increasing, the quality of work.

Training and Development are terms which are sometimes used interchangeably. Development was seen as an activity associated with managers, In contrast training has a more immediate concern and has been associated with improving the knowledge and skill of non-managerial employees in the present job.

Training and development may be regarded interactive, each complementing the other. The logical step for the organisation is to produce a plan for human resource development (i.e. training and development) which will dovetail into the employee resourcing plan (i.e. selection) and the organisation's overall strategic plan.

3.4. IMPORTANCE OF TRAINING

- **Increasing Productivity:** Instruction can help employees increase their level of performance on their present job assignment. Increased human performance often directly leads to increased operational productivity and increased company profit. Again, increased performance and productivity, because of training, are most evident on the part of new employees who are not yet fully aware of the most efficient and effective ways of performing their jobs.

- **Improving Quality:** Better informed workers are less likely to make operational mistakes. Quality increases may be in relationship to a company product or service, or in reference to the intangible organisational employment atmosphere.

- **Helping a Company Fulfil its Future Personnel Needs:** Organisations that have a good internal educational programme will have to make less drastic manpower changes and adjustments in the event of sudden personnel alternations. When the need arises, organisational vacancies can more easily be staffed from internal sources if a company initiates and maintains and adequate instructional programme for both its non-supervisory and managerial employees.

- **Improving Organisational Climate:** An endless chain of positive reactions results from a well-planned training programme. Production and product quality may improve; financial incentives may then be increased, internal promotions become stressed, less supervisory pressures ensue and base pay rate increases result. Increased morale may be due to many factors, but one of the most important of these is the current state of an organisation's educational endeavour.

- **Improving Health and Safety:** Proper training can help prevent industrial accidents. A safer work environment leads, to more stable mental attitudes on the part of employees. Managerial mental state would also improve if supervisors now that they can better themselves through company-designed development programmes.

- **Obsolescence Prevention:** Training and development programmes foster the initiative and creativity of employees and help to prevent manpower obsolescence, which may be due to age, temperament or motivation, or the inability of a person to adapt himself to technological changes.

- **Personal Growth:** Employees on a personal basis gain individually from their exposure to educational experiences. Again the Management development programmes seem to give participants a wider awareness, an enlarged skin, an enlightened altruistic philosophy, and make enhanced personal growth possible.

It may be observed that the need for training arises, an increased use of technology in production; Labour turnover arising from normal separations due to death or physical incapacity, from accidents, disease, superannuation, voluntary retirement, promotion within the organisation and change of occupation or job.Need for enabling employees to do the work in a more effective way, to reduce learning time, reduce supervision time reduce waste and spoilage of raw material and produce quality goods, and develop their potential to achieve both individual and organizational goals.

3.5. TRAINING NEED ASSESSMENT &ITS PROCESS

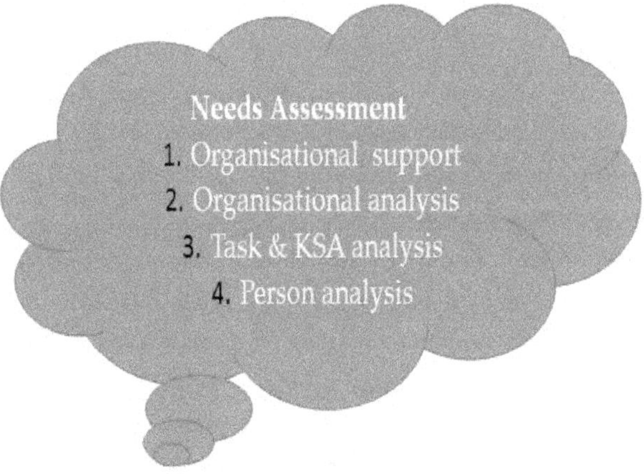

WHY DO A TRAINING NEEDS ASSESSMENT?

A TNA provides information on the training and skills development requirements of all members of your network. It is one of the key steps in preparing a training plan and will provide you with information on which to base your networks training plan. It enables you to:

- Identify the gap between current and required levels of knowledge, skills and attitude
- Identify what the general content of training should be
- Form the foundation of a training plan

- Provide a baseline for the evaluation of a training plan
- Ensure that appropriate and relevant training is delivered
- Maximize use of scarce resources

BENEFITS OF A TRAINING NEEDS ASSESSMENT

- Identifies performance goals and the knowledge, skills and abilities needed by a company's workforce to achieve those goals
- Identifies gaps in training provision in sectors and or regions
- Helps direct resources to areas of greatest priority
- Addresses resources needed to fulfill the organisational mission, improve productivity, and provide quality products and services

According to many training experts, attaining the objectives of the business should be the ultimate concern of any training and development effort. Therefore, conducting an organizational needs analysis should be the first step in effective needs assessment. It begins with an examination of the short and long-term objectives of the organization and the trends that are likely to affect these objectives. It can include a human resource analysis, analysis of efficiency indexes, and an assessment of the organizational climate.

THE ORGANIZATIONAL NEEDS ANALYSIS should translate the organization's objectives into an accurate estimate of the demand for human resources. Efficiency indexes including cost of labor, quantity of output (productivity), quality of output, waste, and equipment use and repairs can provide useful information. The organization can determine standards for these indexes and then analyze them to evaluate the general effectiveness of training programs.

Job Needs Analysis

The specific content of present or anticipated jobs is examined through job analysis. For existing jobs, information on the tasks to be performed (contained in job descriptions), the skills necessary to perform those tasks (drawn from job qualifications), and the minimum acceptable standards (obtained from performance appraisals) are gathered. This information can then be used to ensure that training programs are job specific and useful.

Person Needs Analysis

After information about the job has been collected, the analysis shifts to the person. A person needs analysis identifies gaps between a person's current capabilities and those identified as necessary or desirable. Person needs analysis can be either broad or narrow in scope. The broader approach compares actual performance with the minimum acceptable standards of performance. The narrower approach compares an evaluation of employee proficiency on each required skill dimension with the proficiency level required for each skill. The first method is based on the actual, current job performance of an employee; therefore, it can be used to determine training needs for the current job. The second method, on the other hand, can be used to identify development needs for future jobs.

Distinction between Training and Development

Training	Development
Training means learning's skills and knowledge for doing a particular job. It increases job skills	Development means the growth of an employee in all respects. It shapes attitudes.
The term 'training' is generally used to denote imparting specific skills among operative Workers and employees.	The term 'development' is associated with the overall growth of the executives.
Training is concerned with maintaining and improving current job performance. Thus, it has a short-term perspective.	Executive development seeks to develop competence and skills for future performance. Thus, it has a long-term perspective.
Training is job-centered in nature	Development is career-centered in nature
The role of trainer or supervisor is very important in training.	All development is 'self-development'. The executive has to be internally motivated for self-development

3.6. BENEFITS OF TRAINING

- It helps in improving the quality and quantity of a worker's output
- It enables the worker to make the most economical and best use of materials and equipment
- It provides opportunities for Self Awareness, Self-Exploration and Growth
- It helps to increase the market value of employees, their earning power and job security
- It improves the Morale of employees by reducing dissatisfaction, complaints, grievances and absenteeism
- It gives a sense of satisfaction to the worker and makes him feel that he is being properly cared for
- It makes the worker committed and loyal to the Company

Factors Which Motivate Participants to Attend Training

- Desire for personal growth and development
- Incentives or benefits arising out of attending training
- Consistency between personal learning objectives and programme objective
- Self-image and level of self –esteem
- Previous training experiences
- Inadequate learning skills
- Programme content or the topic
- Training methodology, methods or techniques

Causes for the Failure of Training

- Lack of whole-hearted support and commitment for training by management
- The benefits of training are not clear to the top management
- The top management do not appreciate and reward in house trainers for effective training
- The top management rarely plans and budgets systematically for training
- Lack of cohesive group of trainees
- Timely information about external programmes may be difficult to obtain

Improving Effectiveness of Training

1. Specific training objectives should be outlined on the basis of the type of performance required to achieve organizational goals and objectives. An audit of personal needs
2. Compared with operational requirements will help to determine the specific training needs of individual employees.
3. Attempt should be made to determine if the trainee has the intelligence, maturity and motivation to successfully complete the training programme.
4. The trainee should be helped to see the need for training by making him aware of the personal benefits he can achieve through better performance.
5. If necessary a combination of training methods should be selected
6. The trainee should be provided with regular, constructive feedback concerning their progress in training
7. As the trainee acquires new knowledge, skills or attitudes and applies them in work situation he should be significantly rewarded.

3.7. TRAINING METHODS

There are various methods of training, which can be divided in to cognitive and behavioral methods. Trainers need to understand the pros and cons of each method, also its impact on trainees keeping their background and skills in mind before giving training.

Cognitive methods are more of giving theoretical training to the trainees. The various methods under Cognitive approach provide the rules for how to do something, written or verbal information, demonstrate relationships among concepts, etc. These methods are associated with changes in knowledge and attitude by stimulating learning.

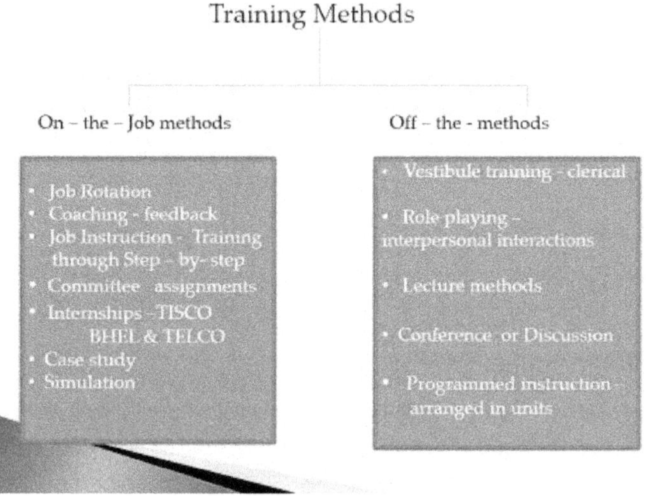

I. OFF THE JOB TRAINING METHODS

1. **Case Study method**: Case study method presents a trainee with a written description of an organisational problem. The person then analyzes the case, diagnoses the problem and presents his or her findings and solutions in discussion with other trainees.

2. **Management Games**: With management games trainees are dividend in to give or six persons group, each of which competes with the others in a stimulated marketplace. Management games can be good development tools. People learn best by getting involved, and the games can be useful for gaining such involvement. They help trainee develop their problem solving skills, as well as to focus attention on planning rather than just putting out fires. The group also usually elects their own officers and organize themselves; they can thus develop leadership skills and faster cooperation and team work.

3. Transactional Analysis

In every social interaction, there is a motivation provided by one person and a reaction to that motivation given by another person. This motivation-reaction relationship between two persons is a transaction. Transactional analysis can be done by the ego states of an individual.

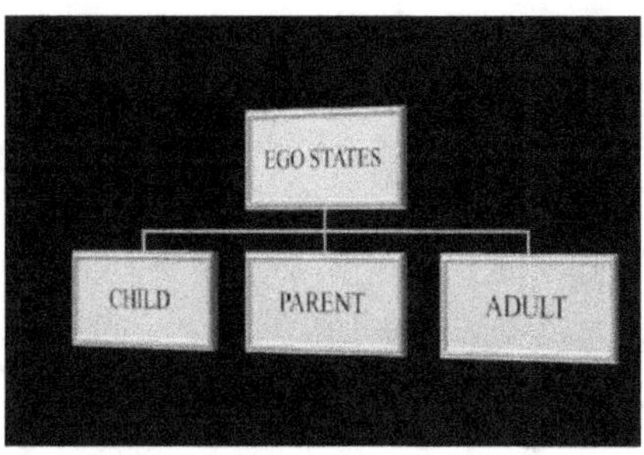

An ego state is a system of feelings accompanied by a related set of behaviors. There are basically three ego states:

Child: It is a collection of recordings in the brain of an individual of behaviors, attitudes, and impulses which come to her naturally from her own understanding as a child. The characteristics of this ego are to be spontaneous, intense, unconfident, reliant, probing, anxious, etc. Verbal clues that a person is operating from its child state are the use of words like "I guess", "I suppose", etc. and non verbal clues like, giggling, coyness, silent, attention seeking etc.

Parent: It is a collection of recordings in the brain of an individual of behaviors, attitudes, and impulses imposed on her in her childhood from various sources such as, social, parents, friends, etc. The characteristics of this ego are to be overprotective, isolated, rigid, bossy, etc. Verbal clues that a person is operating from its parent states are the use of words like, always, should, never, etc and non-verbal clues such as, raising eyebrows, pointing an accusing finger at somebody, etc.

Adult: It is a collection of reality testing, rational behavior, decision making, etc. A person in this ego state verifies, updates the data which she has received from the other two states. It is a shift from the taught and felt concepts to tested concepts.

4. Lecturer Method

Lecture is telling someone about something. Lecture is given to enhance the knowledge of listener or to give him the theoretical aspect of a topic. When the trainer begins the training session by telling the aim, goal, agenda, processes, or methods that will be used in training that means the trainer is using the lecture method.

Main Features of Lecture Method

Less expensive can be reached large number of people at once

Knowledge building exercise

Less effective because lectures require long periods of trainee inactivity

5. **Simulation Method:** Simulation is creating computer versions of real-life games. It is about imitating or making judgment or opinion how events might occur in a real situation.

6. **Behavior Modeling Method** uses the innate inclination for people to observe others to discover how to do something new. It is more often used in combination with some other techniques.

Procedure of Behavior Modeling Technique

In this method, some kind of process or behavior is videotaped and then is watched by the trainees. The trainee first observes the behavior modeled in the video and then reproduces the behavior on the job

7. **In-Basket Technique** – It provides trainees with a log of written text or information and requests, such as memos, messages, and reports, which would be handled by manger, engineer, reporting officer, or administrator.

In this technique, trainee is given some information about the role to be played such as, description, responsibilities, general context about the role.

The trainee is then given the log of materials that make up the in-basket and asked to respond to materials within a particular time period.

After all the trainees complete in-basket, a discussion with the trainer takes place. In this discussion the trainee describes the justification for the decisions. The trainer then provides feedback, reinforcing decisions made suitably or encouraging the trainee to increase alternatives for those made unsuitably.

Training Techniques Focuses on

- Building decision making skills.
- Assess and develops Knowledge,
- Skills and Attitudes (KSAs).
- Develops of communication and interpersonal skills.
- Develops procedural knowledge.
- Develops strategic knowledge

8. **Role Play Method** is a simulation in which each participant is given a role to play. Trainees are given with some information related to description of the role, concerns, objectives, responsibilities, emotions, etc. Then, a general description of the situation, and the problem that each one of them faces, is given. For instance, situation could be strike in factory, managing conflict, two parties in conflict, scheduling vacation days, etc. Once the participants read their role descriptions, they act out their roles by interacting with one another.

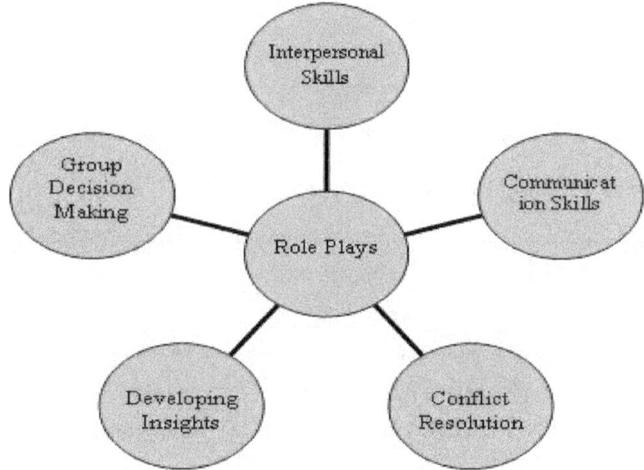

Role Plays helps in developing interpersonal skills and communication skills, Conflict resolution, Group decision making, developing insight into one's own behavior and its impact on others.

There are various types of role plays, such as:

Multiple Role Play – In this type of role play, all trainees are in groups, with each group acting out the role play simultaneously. After the role play, each group analyzes the interactions and identifies the learning points.

Single Role Play – One group of participants plays the role for the rest, providing demonstrations of situation. Other participants observe the role play, analyze their interactions with one another and learn from the play.

Role Rotation – It starts as a single role play. After the interaction of participants, the trainer will stop the role play and discuss what happened so far. Then the participants are asked to exchange characters. This method allows a variety of ways to approach the roles.

Spontaneous Role Play – In this kind of role play, one of the trainees plays herself while the other trainees play people with whom the first participant interacted before.

II. ON THE JOB TRAINING METHODS

This method of training uses more knowledgeable, experienced and skilled employees, such as managers, supervisors to give training to less Knowledgeable, skilled, and experienced employees.

This type of training often takes place at the work place in informal manner.

It is done on ad-hoc manner with no formal procedure, or content at the start of training, or during the training, no specific goals or objectives are developed

Trainers usually have no formal qualification or training experience for training

Procedure of on-the-job Training Program

1. The participant observes a more experienced, knowledgeable, and skilled trainer
2. The method, process, and techniques are well discussed before, during and after trainer has explained about performing the tasks
3. When the trainee is prepared, the trainee starts performing on the work place
4. The trainer provides continuing direction of work and feedback the trainee is given more and more work so that he accomplishes the job flawlessly.

The Various Methods of on the Job Training

1. **Vestibule Training:** This method involves the creation of a separate training center within the plant itself for the purpose of providing training to the new employees. Machines and tools are arranged so as to create working conditions similar to those in the workshop. In this method the trainee remains free from the confusion and the pressure of the work situation and concentrates more on learning.

2. **Apprenticeship Training:** This training helps to give knowledge and skill in those trades and crafts. The trainee work as apprentice under the direct supervision of experts for two to seven years. This method provides actual work experience in the actual job as well as imparting theoretical knowledge through classroom lectures. This method is an expensive one.

3. **Sensitivity Training:** Sensitivity training is the most controversial laboratory training method. Many of its advocates have an almost religious zeal in their enhancement with the training group experience. Some of its critics match this favour in their attacks on the technique. As a result of criticism and experience, a somewhat revised approach, often described as team development training has appeared. National Training Laboratories at Bethel U.S.A. The training groups themselves called T GROUP first used it. Since then its use has been extended to other organizations, universities and institutes.

    Training is essential for the smooth, economic, timely and efficient production, work or service in any organization. To get work accomplished well from a worker or employee, it is a must that he is given proper training in methods of work. Training is the organized producer by which people learn knowledge and skill for a definite purpose management can't make a choice as between training or no training. On the other hand, it is a must. The only choice lies in the method of training.

4. **Internship Training:** This method involves a joint programme of training in which enterprises and the vocational and the training institutes cooperate. This is done to bring about a balance between theoretical and practical knowledge.

5. **Coaching** is one of the training methods, which is considered as a corrective method for inadequate performance. According to a survey conducted by International Coach Federation (ICF), more than 4,000 companies are using coach for their executives. These coaches are experts most of the time outside consultants. A coach is the best training plan for the CEO's because it is one to one interaction. It can be done at the convenience of CEO. It can be done on phone, meetings, through e-mails, chat. It

provides an opportunity to receive feedback from an expert. It helps in identifying weaknesses and focus on the area that needs improvement

6. **Job Rotation** Under this method the trainee rotated among different managerial jobs. Some of the major benefits of job rotation are: It provides the employees with opportunities to broaden the horizon of knowledge, skills, and abilities by working in different departments, business units, functions, and countries Identification of Knowledge, skills, and attitudes (KSAs) required. It determines the areas where improvement is required. Assessment of the employees who have the potential and caliber for filling the position can be traced

7. **Simulation:** An increasing popular technique of management development is simulation of performance. In this method, instead of taking participants into the field, the field can be simulated in the training session itself Simulation is the presentation of real situation of organisation in the training session. It covers situations of varying complexities and roles for the participants. It creates a whole field organisation, relates participants, through key roles in it, and has them deal with specific situations of a kind they encounter in real life. There are two common simulation methods of training: role-playing is one and business game is the other.

8. **Role-playing:** Role-playing is a laboratory method, which can be used rather easily as a supplement of conventional training methods. Its purpose is to increase the trainee's skill in dealing with other people. One of its greatest use, in connection with human relations training, but it is also used in sales training as well. It is spontaneous acting of a realistic situation involving two or more persons, under classroom situations. Dialogue spontaneously grows out of the situation, as the trainees assigned to it develop it. Other trainees in the group serve as observers or critics. Since people take rules every day, they are somewhat experienced in the art, and with, a certain amount of imagination they can project themselves into roles other than their own. Since a manager is regularly acting roles in his relationship with other it is essential for him to have role awareness and to do role thinking so that they can size up each size up each relationship and develop the most effective interaction position.

9. **Gaming:** Gaming has been devised to simulate the problems of running a company or even a particular department. It has been used for a variety of training objectives from investment strategy, collective bargaining techniques to the morale of clerical personnel. It has been used at all the levels, from the executives for the production supervisors. Gaming is a laboratory method in which role-playing exists but its

difference is that it focuses attention on administrative problems, while role-playing tend to emphasis mostly feeling and tone between people in interaction.

Gaming involves several terms, each of which given a firm to operate for a number of periods. Usually the periods is short one year or so. In each period, each-team makes decisions on various matters such as fixation of price, level of production inventory level, and so forth.

Since each team is competing with others, each firm's decisions win affect the results of all others. All the firm's decisions are fed into a computer, which is programmed to know real market.

10. **Serving on Committees:** Under this method the trainee is made to serve in a committee. Thereby he can learn various organizational problems and the views of others. Also the trainees learn to adjust to the overall needs of the company.

11. **Observation Assignment:** In this method the newly recruited executive called "understudy" is made an assistant to the current job holder. He learns by experience, observation and imitation.

SELECTION OF A TRAINING METHOD

The selection of the appropriate training method depends on the following factors:

1. Nature of Problem area
2. level of trainees in the organization's hierarchy
3. Methods ability to hold and arouse the interest of trainees
4. Availability of competent trainers
5. Availability of Finance
6. Availability of time

3.8. EVALUATION OF TRAINING AND DEVELOPMENT

Training and Development in BPO Industry

BPO is Business Process Outsourcing. It is an agreement between two parties for specific business task. The BPO industry is growing at an annual growth rate of 14% and is expected to cross $310 billion by 2008. Job seekers prefer BPO's over other sectors because it is providing high paying jobs to graduates/undergraduates. To deliver desired services to customer, who is 10,000 miles away, it is important to have good amount of business knowledge and required expertise.

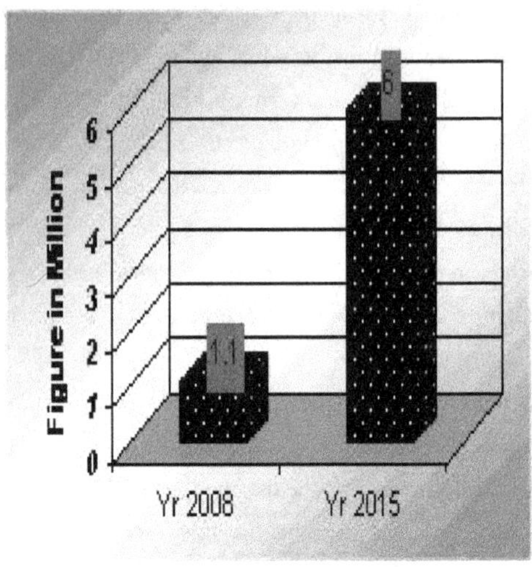

The various reasons behind the increasing training need in the BPO industry are:

1. BPO industry is expected to generate 1.1 million jobs by 2008, and 6 million jobs by 2015, which is why training need has increased more than ever before.

2. High attrition rate in this sector reason being unsatisfied employee, monotonous work, neglected talent, inadequate know-how, etc

3. Coming up of high profile BPOs

Training has become a major tool to retain employees. People working in BPO sector face the problem of night shift, job stress that results in de motivation. Well-designed training program with clear career path increases the job satisfaction among the young professionals and help them in becoming efficient and effective at the work place. Therefore, organizations have to handle such challenges of meeting training needs, although, the sector is taking a lot of initiatives in conducting training for new joiners. Companies are now aligning business goals with training costs. But what more important is, is the development of the skills of middle management. Various BPO's have an elaborate training infrastructure that includes Computer-Based Training rooms, and specially trained and qualified in-house trainers. The companies are now busy designing training programs for their employees. These companies try identifying the strengths and weaknesses and are emphasizing more on their personalities, problem-solving skills, and leadership skills. With constant change in processes, technologies, techniques, methods, etc, there is a constant need of updation, training and development the BPO employees to consistently deliver customer goals.

Training in Banking and Insurance Sector

Favorable economic climate and number of other factors such as, growing urbanization, increasing consumerism, rise in the standard of living, increase in financial services for people living in rural areas, etc has increased the demand for wide range of financial products that has led to mutually beneficial growth to the banking sector and economic growth process. This was coincided by technology development in the banking operations. Today most of the Indian cities have networked banking facility as well as Internet banking facility. Some of the major players in the banking sector are State Bank of India, HDFC Bank, Citibank, ICICI Bank, Punjab National Bank, etc.

In the Insurance sector also, rapid expansion has created about 5 lakh job opportunities approximately in the past five years. These openings are mainly in the field of insurance advisors or marketing agents. The eligibility criteria for these jobs is graduation with some experience in marketing or become insurance agents after completing school but this needs some relevant training.

Earlier there were no training programs as such for insurance agents but on-the-job training only that was given once the new agent was appointed. But now the scenario has been changed, with the coming up of big players like ICICI Life Insurance, ICICI Lombard, HDFC Life Insurance, Tata AIG General Insurance, etc in this sector, people who've had some formal training are preferred while recruitment because it can be helpful in the insurance field. However, only the insurance degree in this field does not guarantee success. To be successful an agent must have strong interpersonal, networking, and communication skills. Number of opportunities in Banking and Insurance sector has increased than ever before. With this rapid expansion and coming up of major players like ICICI, HDFC, UTI, Bajaj Allianz, etc in the sector, the need of human resource development has increased.

TECHNIQUES OF EVALUATION OF TRAINING

Several techniques of evaluation are being used in organisations. One approach towards evaluation is to use **experimental and control groups.** Each group is randomly selected, one to receive training (experimental) and the other not to receive training (control).

The random selection helps to assure the formation of groups quite similar to each other. Measures are taken of the relevant indicators of success (e.g. words typed per minute, quality pieces produced per hour, wires attached per minute) before and after training for both groups. If the gains demonstrated by the experimental group are better than those by the control group, the training programme is labelled as successful.

Another method of training evaluation involves **longitudinal or time-series analysis.** Measurements are taken before the programme begins and are continued during and after the programme is completed. These results are plotted on a graph to determine whether changes have occurred and remain as a result of the training effort. To further validate that change has occurred as a result of training and not due to some other variable, a control group may be included.

One simple method of evaluation is to send a **questionnaire to the trainees** after the completion of the programme to obtain their opinions about the programme's worth. Their opinions could also be obtained through interviews. A variation of this method is to measure the knowledge and/or skills that employees possess at the commencement and completion of training. If the measurement reveals that the results after training are satisfactory, then the training may be taken as successful. In order to conduct a thorough evaluation of a training programme, it is important to assess the costs and benefits associated with the programme. This is it difficult task, but· is useful in convincing the management about the useful-ness of training.

3.9.   EXECUTIVE DEVELOPMENT

Executive Development Program

Today, it is the growth that makes one person stay at the company. The opportunity and challenges is what keeps a person satisfied and charmed with his job. Companies have understood this fact and therefore are forming policies and procedures to develop their employees.

Process of executive Development program

Executive development Program (EDP) is one such program. With Human resource making a move from a welfare department to a strategic partner, more and more companies are undertaking this program. There are four major steps to be covered during the EDP:

1. Problem Assessment: the experts along with the concerned employees and CEO shall begin with an assessment of the company's current problem and owner's plans of the future.

2. Management Audit and Appraisal: there shall be regular feedback sessions to check as to whether we are reaching where we are supposed to reach.

3. Analysis of Development Needs: here the problem that has been uncovered shall be tried to and remedied via a development program.

4. Identify Replacement needs: the assessment may uncover a need to recruit and select new management talent. The format of EDP will vary with company's size and nature of operation so as to provide optimum result.

Succession Planning is a corporate favorites these days but to make it really beneficial and not just a passing flavor, help of professionals is needed. Career Solutions also provides you with the option of helping you, your company's heir is a much more objective and rational manner. A continuous interaction with our experts shall enable you to pick the Best Person who then shall take the baton from your hands and march towards the Future.

Meaning of EDP

The executive development is a planned, systematic and continuous process of learning and growth designed to induce behavioral change in individuals by cultivating their mental abilities and inherent qualities through the acquisition, understanding and use of new knowledge, insights and skills as they are needed for more effective performance of the work of managing.

Managers develop not only by participating in formal courses of instruction drawn by the organisation but also through actual job experience in the organisation. It should be recognised that it is for the organist ion to establish the development opportunities for its managers and potential managers. But, an equal rather more important counterpart to the efforts of organisation are those of the individuals.

It should be accepted as discipline of self-education. The individuals must have the motivation and the capacity to learn and develop. As the individuals differ from one another in aptitudes, attitudes, talents, aspiration, needs and motivation, they should be provided an effective organizational climate to develop themselves and change their behaviour in managing the people and resources.

Objectives

- Enhancing managerial skills of executives to enable them to shoulder higher responsibilities in the future.
- Enable participants to understand managerial concepts and techniques relevant for formulating and implementing strategies in different functional areas.
- Enable participants to communicate effectively with subordinates and top management people.

3.10. METHODS OF EXECUTIVE DEVELOPMENT PROGRAMME

A great variety of management development techniques are used by different organizations to develop their executive manpower. The selection of techniques rests on philosophy of development. There are two principal methods of executive development which are generally used by the firms. One is on-the-job development and the other is off-the job development. We shall discuss here under the various one-the-job and off-the-job executive development technologic. There are two various methods:

1. **On-the-job Method**
2. **Off-The-Job-Method**

OFF THE JOB METHOD

The main techniques under this method are

a. **Special Courses:** The method of special courses requires the trainee to leave the work place and to devote is entire time to developmental objectives. The prime object of such special courses is to provide an opportunity to the trainee is to acquire knowledge with full devotion. Development is primary and work is secondary. These courses may be conducted in a number of ways-Firstly, the organisation establishes such courses to be taught to the trains by the members of the firm or by the regular instructor appointed by the firm or by the regular instructor appointed by the firm or by the specialists (professors and lecturers from other outside institutions. The second approach to this technique is to send the personnel to programmes established by the colleges or universities. The organisation sponsors some of its members to the courses and bears the expenses. The third approach to the technique is to work with a college or other institutions in establishing a course or a series of courses to be taught by faculty members. A big organisation may starts its own training school.

b. **Role Playing:** Under this method, two or more trainees are assigned different roles to play by creating an artificial conflict situation. No dialogued is given beforehand. The role players are provided with the written or oral description of the situation and the role to play. Sufficient time is given to the role players to plan tier actions and they must act their parts before the class. For instance role playing situation may be a supervisor discussing grievances with is subordinate.

c. **Case Study:** Case study technique is extensively used in teaching law, business management, human relation, etc., to let the trainee understand that there may be different solutions to a particular problem. Under this method, the trainees are given a realistic problem to discuss, which is more or less related to the principles already taught. This method provides an opportunity to the trainee to apply his skill to the solution of realistic problems.

    Cases may be used in either of the two ways:

    (i) They can be used after exposing the formal theory under which the trainee applies their skill to specific situation, or

    (ii) They may be assigned to the trainees for written analysis or oral discussion without any prior discussion of the theory.

d. **Conference:** A conference is a group meeting conducted according to an organized plan is which members participate in oral discussion of a particular problem and thus develop their knowledge and understanding. It is an effective training device for conferences members and conference leaders. Both learns a lot from others view point and compare his opinions with others. The conference leaders may also learn how to develop his skill to motivate people through his direction of discussion. Conferences may of three types: (i) The directed or guided conference, (ii) Consultative conference, and (ii) Problem solving conference. However guided conference is generally used for training purposes.

e. **Multiple Management:** Under this system, a permanent advisory board or committee of executives study the problems of organisation and make recommendations to the higher management for final decision. There is another device, constituting a junior board of directors in a company for training the executives. The board is given power to discuss any problem which the senior board of directors (constituted by shareholders) could discuss. The utility of junior board is only to train the junior executives. Thus junior board discuss wide variety of subjects which a senior board can discuss or in other way, it is an advisory body.

f. **Managements Games:** It is a classroom exercise, in which teams of students compete against each other to achieve common objective. The game is designed to be a close representations of real life conditions. The trainees are asked to make decisions about production, cost, research and development, etc., for an organisation. Since they are often divided into teams as competing companies, experience is obtained in team work. Under this method, the trainees learn by analysing problems by using some intention and by making trial and error type of decisions. Any wrong is corrected by the trainer or sometimes a second chance is given to something all other again.

g. **Syndicate Method:** Under this method, 5 or 6 groups consisting of about 10 members are formed. Each group (Syndicate) is composed of carefully selected men who, on the one and, represents fair cross section of the executive life of t country, i.e. men from public sector and private sector undertakings, civil and defense services, banking, insurance, etc., and on the other hand, a good well balance team of management from different fields, i.e., production, marketing, personnel, finance, etc. The groups are given assignments, made up before hand to be submitted within a specified date and time. Each man in t group is appointed leader of the group for the performance of the given task by rotation and so for the secretary for the subdivision of the course. Each task is assigned in the form of a 'Brief', a document prepared by the experts on the faculty with meticulous care. It also fixes the time by which the study is to be completed. Lecturers by experts are also arranged to supplement the study. The report prepared and submitted by a group is circulated among the members of the other groups for comparative study and critical evaluation. The leader or chairman of the group is required to present the views of his group in the joint session and justify his group's view in case of criticism or questions.

h. **Sensitivity Training or T-Group:** In sensitivity training, the executives spends about two work-hours attending the lectures on the subject such as leadership and communication. The members, under this method, sit around a table and discuss. The trainer, usually a psychologist, neither leads the discussion nor suggests what should be discussed but only guides the discussion. The members freely discuss and criticize the behaviour of each other thereby giving a feedback positive or negative.

i.   **Programmed Instruction:** Programmed instruction as gained a lot of importance both in training and in industry in modern times it includes teaching machines, auto instruction, automatic instruction and programmed learning. It is an application of science of learning to the task of training and education.

The core feature of programmed instruction is the participation by the trainee and immediate fed back by him. Programmed instruction machines include films, tapes, programmed books, illustrations, printed material, diagrams, etc. It performs two functions: (i) provides information to the learner, and, (ii) provides feedback whether the response is correct or wrong.

j.   **Selective Readings:** Many executives find it very difficult to do much reading other than that absolutely required in the performance of their jobs. Some organizations provide some time for reading which will advance the general knowledge and background of the individuals. Many organizations purchase some high level journals like the Commerce, the Capitalist, the Management in Govt., etc. And dailies like the Economic Times, the Financial Express, etc.

On The Job Method

It is most popular method of developing the executive talent. The main techniques are:

a.   **Coaching:** Under this technique, the superior coaches the job knowledge and skill, to his subordinates. He briefs the trainees what is expected of them and guides how to get it. He also watches their performance and directs them to correct the mistakes. The main objective of this training is to provide them diversified knowledge. Coaching is recognised as one of t managerial responsibilities, and the manger as an obligation to train and develop the subordinates working under him. He delegates his authority to the subordinates to prepare them to handle the complex situations.

b.   **Understudy:** This system is quite different from the system discussed above. Under this system, a person is specifically designated as their apparent who is called the understudy. The understudy's future depends on what happens to his superior leaves his post due to promotion, retirement or transfer. The department manager picks up one individual from the department to become his understudy. He guides him to learn his job and tackle the problems that confront the manger.

c.   **Job Rotation:** Under this system, an individual is transferred one job to another or from open department all to another in the coordinated and planned manager with a view to broaden the general background of the trainee in the business. The trainees is rotated from one job to another and thus acquires a considerable degree of specialized knowledge and skill but a man can never acquire t diversified skill needed for promotion unless is deliberately put in different types of situations.

    d.   **Special Project:** A special assignment is a highly useful training device, under which a trainee is assigned a project that is closely related to his job. He will study the problem and submit the written recommendations upon it. It will not only provide the trainee a valuable experience in tackling the problem but would also have the other values of educating the trainees about t importance of t problem but would also have the other values of educating the trainees about the importance of the problem and to understand the organizational relationship of the problem with different angles.

    e.   **Committee Assignments:** This system is similar to special project. Under this system an ad-hoc committee is constituted and is assigned a subject related to the business to discuss and make recommendations. The committee will study the problem, discuss it and submit to be report containing the various suggestions and recommendations to the departmental manager. With a view to avoid the unnecessary hardships in studying the problem, the members of the committee should be selected from different departments, having specialized knowledge in different fields but connecting to the problem.

3.11. PURPOSE OF INDUCTION FOR NEW EMPLOYEES

The new employee may have some difficulty in settling down to his new job and in developing a sense of belonging. He can easily adjust himself to his new job if he is given a clear explanation of the work of the department to which he is attached. This introduction of the employee to the job is known as induction. The purpose of induction and orientation is to help the new employee and the organization to accommodate each other. Included in this process may be financial assistances for expenses of travel filling out of pay roll and other forms, introduction to colleagues and explanation of the policies and practices of the organization, many other factors which serve to integrate the new employee into the enterprise.

The need for security, belonging, esteem and knowledge is met through proper induction and orientation. Haphazard procedures, casual greetings, and lack of information can precipitate anxiety, discouragement, disillusionment or defensive behavior, including quitting. A successful induction is that which reduces the anxiety of the new employee. Therefore, such methods which bring this about are explained to company workers.

3.12. SELF-DEVELOPMENT

INTRODUCTION

The organisation should create a climate for Self-development. Self-Development should not be left to chance it should be a planned effort. All organization may not be in position to provide opportunities for development. It is the individual's responsibility to constantly strive for his self-development. Every employee should formulate an action plan for Self-development. This plan has to be related to the career goal of the individual.

Meaning

Self-development means self-desire to improve through an individual's attempt to embark on study and practical explosive that are independent of organizational role.

6 Stages of Approach in Self-development

1. Self-assessment
2. Diagnosis
3. Action planning
4. Monitoring & review
5. Adopting skills for self-development
6. Developing self-awareness

Joe Luft and Harry Ingram originally developed the "Johari window" in the 1950's to help people better understand their relationship with themselves and others. At the outset it had a simple but powerful goal – to provide a model for better communication and was therefore used as a simple reflection exercise at the beginning of many management training workshops.

The four areas of the model (or mental "rooms" as the management writer Charles Handy called them) are described below and shown in the diagram that follows these descriptions:

The **Open** or **Arena** area: This so-called "room" on the chart below at top left represented traits of the subjects that both they and their peers are completely aware of.

The **Hidden** or **Façade** area: This room representing information about the person that a person's colleagues are unaware of (because they have not been shared and have been deliberately concealed).

The **Blind** area: This room represented information that the subject is not aware of, but others are, and they can decide whether and how to inform the individual about these "**blind spots**".

The **Unconscious** or **Unknown** area: This room representing the participant's behaviors or motives that were not recognized by anyone participating. This may be because they do not apply or because there is collective ignorance of the existence of these traits.

JOHARI WINDOW (Knowing self)

	Known to Self	Unknown to Self
Known to Others	**Open** (Public knowledge; what I show to you)	**Blind** (Feedback - your gift to me)
Unknown to Others	**Hidden** (Private; mine to share if I trust you)	**Unconscious** (Unknown; new awareness can emerge)

For many years this model enjoyed widespread use in many circles to aid better communication, and it was made great use of in business training to enable leaders to give better feedback and build team relationships. But while the use of Johari's window has inevitably lessened over time as it has got older and more familiar.

The following three factors helps us to evaluate where we stand and this evaluation will be a good starting point for making plans for success.

1. **Job Responsibility:** We have to list some 6-8 major job responsibilities like Punctual to the work, Meeting the target, handling Grievances, Reporting to the Top Management, Ability to coordinate etc. and we can rate our self on five point scale- excellent, very good, average and poor depending on the responsibilities we are discharging.

2. **Leadership Qualities:** The following are some of the leadership qualities and one can rate on each of these qualities.

    a. Technical Competence

    b. Effective Intelligence

    c. Innovator

    d. Motivator

    e. Intrapreneur

f.   Decision Maker

g.   Good Communicator

h.   Administrative Skills

3. **Relationships:** The growth of many people has been held back because of poor relationships with the boss, peers, subordinates, clients, union leaders and customers. Proper analysis of relationships with others should be made.

Self-evaluation balance sheet can be prepared on the basis of the above three evaluation. Everybody has some assets and some liabilities.

All factors rated excellent and very good constitutes asset of an individual and average and poor represent the liabilities.

Based on the Self-Evaluation Balance Sheet, We have to build our career on our assets and work on the liabilities. Effort must be made in a systematic manner to progressively move towards the aim with the help of a time bound schedule.

SELF-EVALUATION-BALANCE SHEET

ASSETS	LIABILITIES
Job Responsibilities	
Maintain good Communication	Handling Grievances
Punctual to the work	Reporting to the Top Management
Meeting the target	Ability to coordinate
Leadership Qualities	
Technical Competence	Intrapreneur
Effective Intelligence	Decision Maker
Innovator	Administrative Skills
Motivator	Good Communicator
Relationship Qualities	
Boss	Peers
Subordinates	Clients
Union leadership	Government, Public

3.13. KNOWLEDGE MANAGEMENT

Organizations are facing ever increasing challenges, brought on by market place pressures or the nature of the workplace. Many organizations are now looking to KM to address these challenges. Such initiatives are often started with the development of Knowledge Management Strategy.

- Knowledge Management is a correct mix of people, processes and technology in an organization.
- It is the systematic leveraging of information and expertise to improve organizational and operational innovation, responsiveness, productivity and competency.
- Knowledge management refers to an enterprise that consciously and comprehensively gathers, organizes, shares and analyzes its knowledge to achieve its goals.

3.14. IMPORTANCE OF KNOWLEDGE MANAGEMENT IN ORGANIZATIONS

- Knowledge has become increasingly relevant for organizations because of the shift from an industrial economy to knowledge-based economy.
- Knowledge management has gained in importance because companies have discovered that people, their skills and knowledge are essential to gain competitive advantage.
- Innovation in products and processes becomes more and more important in both manufacturing as well as service sectors.
- Knowledge management provides the enterprise-wide discipline and a sustainable process for growth at all times.

Types of Knowledge

- Explicit Knowledge
- Tacit Knowledge

Explicit Knowledge

Expressed in words and numbers and shared in the form of data, scientific formulae, product specifications, articles and manuals, universal principles, reports, patents, pictures, video images, software, and so forth.

Tacit Knowledge

Deeply rooted in an individual's action and experience. Subjective and personal insights, intuitions, etc.

Dimensions of Tacit Knowledge

a) Technical Dimension : Informal and hard-to-pin-down skills or crafts

b) Cognitive Dimension: Beliefs, perceptions, ideals, values, emotions and mental models

Elements of Knowledge Management

Knowledge creation – generating facts, information, techniques that are relevant to organization.

Knowledge sharing – involves sharing, communicating & distributing the knowledge in organization wide.

Knowledge utilization – using knowledge to solve problems for which it has been acquired.

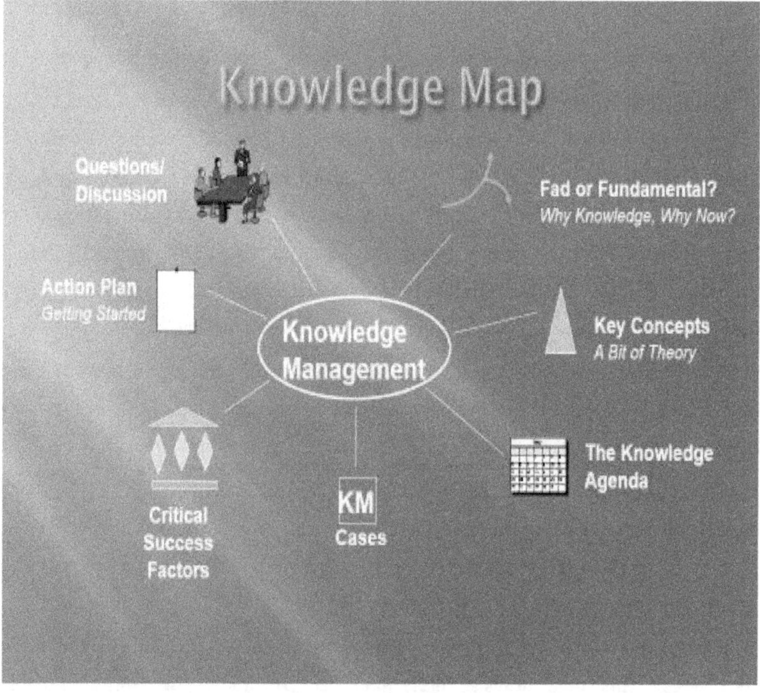

3.15. APPROACHES OF KNOWLEDGE MANAGEMENT

Knowledge mgt. is acquiring & storing information

a. Establishing database & retrieval system

b. Gathering information from customers

c.   Maintaining employee skill profile & talents

d.   Maintaining platform for sharing & disseminating information

Implementation of Knowledge Management

1.   Strategy contains – why, whom, what of knowledge sharing

2.   Organizing KM program – provides budget for knowledge sharing, choose technology for K sharing, communicating to others (workshops, conferences), adopting methods of KS and measuring the performance.

3.   Reinforcement for KM – which induces the behaviour of persons thru introducing new incentive schemes, motivating them to protect the family values.

3.16. KNOWLEDGE MANAGEMENT PROCESS

Knowledge Management Process

Beckman has proposed a comprehensive eight-stage process for knowledge management.

The **identify** stage determines which core competencies are critical to success. Then the related strategic capabilities and knowledge domains are identified. Knowledge domains are specialized subject matter areas where recognized experts can demonstrate superior performance. Next the existing levels of expertise in the workforce are assessed for each knowledge domain. Once the gaps between existing and needed expertise are determined, domain experts, together with training and IT professionals, can begin constructing education programs and Performance Support Systems to improve expertise levels.

The **collect** stage deals with acquiring existing knowledge, skills, theories, and experience needed to create the selected core competencies and knowledge domains. In order to be useful, knowledge, expertise, and experience must be formalized by making it explicit.

In addition, practitioners should know where and how to purchase needed knowledge and expertise in the form of databases and expert systems. In order to acquire expertise, valid knowledge sources should be identified. For example, employee suggestion programs, domain experts, and best practices databases might provide valuable sources of knowledge.

The **select** stage takes the continuous stream of collected, formalized knowledge and assesses its value. This stage serves as filter, quality control, and summarizer of knowledge. Is there insight within the acquired information? Is this piece of knowledge already in the organizational memory? Is the acquired knowledge a new plausible domain theory that needs to be added to the knowledge Repository? Clearly, domain experts must assess and select the knowledge to be added to the organizational memory. Without a strong filtering mechanism, the corporate memory will be nothing more than a Tower of Babel, where the valuable nuggets of knowledge are lost in a sea of information and data. However, it is important that a diversity of viewpoints from multiple domain experts be represented where appropriate. Initially, one framework should be selected as the basis for organizing and classifying knowledge to be stored in the Knowledge Repository.

The **store** stage takes the nuggets of knowledge and classifies them and adds them to the organizational memory. This corporate memory resides in three different forms: in human minds, on paper, and electronically. Knowledge in human minds needs to be made explicit and formalized in order to be useful. What does this mean? Knowledge must be organized and represented into differing knowledge structures within a Knowledge Repository, just as data and information are organized and represented in differing types of databases. Much of this knowledge can be represented in electronic form as Expert Systems.

The **share** stage retrieves knowledge from the corporate memory and makes it accessible to users. The workforce makes their needs and personal interests known to the corporate memory, which then automatically distributes any incoming new knowledge to its "subscribers" either electronically or, by paper. In addition, individuals, teams, and departments often share ideas, opinions, gossip, knowledge, and expertise in meetings held in person or through groupware. It is crucial that the potentially valuable portions of these communications, discussions, arguments, and collaborations are made available to the Capture stage of the Knowledge Management process. For example, differing points of view and their rationales should be captured as part of any decision-making process, as well as the method used to reach the final decision.

The **apply** stage retrieves and uses the needed knowledge in performing tasks, solving problems, making decisions, researching ideas, and learning. In order to easily access, retrieve, and apply the right pieces of knowledge at the right time in the right form, more than a query language is needed. First, to ease access, natural classification and navigation systems need to be built for browsing or retrieving knowledge. To retrieve just the right knowledge requires that the system understand the user's purpose and context. To receive the knowledge at the right time requires a proactive system that monitors the user's actions and determines when it is appropriate to intervene with help in the form of a job aid or training module. Users can also customize the format in which knowledge is presented. Finally, users can request reference, advisory, testing, and certification modules.

The **create** stage uncovers new knowledge through many avenues, such as observing customers, customer feedback and analysis, causal analysis, benchmarking and best practices, lessons learned from business reengineering and process improvement projects, research, experimentation, creative thinking, and automated knowledge discovery and data mining. This stage also covers how to elicit nonverbal, unconscious knowledge from domain experts and turn it into documented formal knowledge. The key here is to make sure that these valuable new sources of knowledge and insight are formalized and captured by the Knowledge Management process, and made available to users who need the knowledge.

The eight stage may be added, the **sell** stage, in which new products and services are crafted from the intellectual capital that can be marked external to the enterprise. Before this stage is possible, considerable maturity should be attained in the other seven stages. Clearly, there can be some risk to this if the new product involves substantial portions of strategic core competences.

The Future of KM

- Change is inevitable in an ever-changing, progressive environment.
- Developing a Knowledge Management strategy provides a unique opportunity to gain a greater understanding of the way the organization operates, and the challenges that confront it.
- A successful Knowledge Management strategy happens only when a culture of knowledge sharing is inculcated in the organization.

KM and Organizational Structure

The phenomenal growth of the Internet has resulted in radical changes in the structure of organizations from the more traditional bureaucratic and matrix type of organizational structure to a more radical virtual corporation and hypertext organization and knowledge base is an essential part of these organizational types. Virtual corporations are extensively outsourced organizations focusing on adding more value to a selected number of core competencies, which are centrally stored. Quinn, while describing this type of organization has stressed on the accumulation and leveraging of knowledge for the success of this type of organization.

The hypertext organization structure, (Monaca and Takeuchi) on the other hand consists of three layers, the central layer, project team layer and the knowledge base layer. In this knowledge base layer, the organizational know-how generated in the other two layers is categorized, rearranged and re-contextualized.

KM and Organization Culture

One of the main challenges in the implementation of knowledge management initiatives is to bring about a change in the attitude of people in the organization. In spite of the management consultants advocating team management and the spread of collaboration tools, they are faced with traditional entrenched human traits of rugged individualism. While people talk of sharing knowledge and team management, they are also aware that knowledge is power and very few are willing to give up power. The culture of the organization needs to change from one of hoarding information to sharing of information. The various tools and techniques available to convert tacit knowledge into explicit knowledge may prove ineffective in the absence of a culture, which facilitates sharing, and individuals who are willing to share this information.

Effective knowledge creation depends upon the way in which people relate to each other in the organisation. Untrustworthy behavior, constant competition, 'that's not my job' attitude are impediments to proper knowledge transfer and sharing.

The activities of the human resources department should focus on creating an appropriate culture in the organization that facilitates sharing of information and motivating individuals to make their tacit knowledge, gained through years of experience and practice, explicit.

Review Questions

1. Define Training and Development. What are the differences between training and development?
2. Examine the objectives, need and purpose of training.
3. How Training Benefits the Organisation?
4. What can be the subject matter of Executive Development Programme (EDP)?
5. What are the requisites for the success of Management Development Programmes (MDP)?
6. Elaborate on the different methods that are generally used for the training of employees.
7. Write a short note on induction training.
8. Examine the main techniques of evaluation of training of employees.
9. What is self-Development? Explain in detail with Johari window.
10. What is knowledge Management? Briefly discuss the various types of Knowledge.
11. Explain the process of Knowledge management.

UNIT 4

SUSTAINING EMPLOYEE INTEREST

Objective of Unit 4

- Compensation plans – Meaning & Definitions
- Objectives of compensation plans
- Methods of Compensation plans
- Job evaluation & its Methods
- Motivation – Definition, types of motivation
- Various Theories of Motivation
- Career management- Process of career management, Stages of career management.
- Steps in career management
- Rewards & its types
- Mentoring & its process
- Protégé Relationship

4.1.   COMPENSATION PLANS

INTRODUCTION

Compensation is a tool used by management for a variety of purpose to further the existence of the company. It is a remuneration that an employee receives in return for his or her contribution in the organisation. So, the employee compensation programs are designed to attract capable employees to the organisation, to motivate them towards superior performance and to retain their services over an extended period of time. Compensation mgt. are designed to overcome low cost pay structure that will attract, motivate and retain competent employees.

MEANING AND DEFINITION OF COMPENSATION

In layman's language the word compensation 'means something, such as money, given or received as payment for service. The word compensation may be defined as money received in the performance of work, plus the many kinds of benefits and services that organization provides their employee. It refers to wide range of financial and non-financial rewards to employee for their service rendered to the organization. It is paid in the form of wages, salaries, special allowance and employee benefits such as paid vacation, insurance, maternity leaves, free travel facility , retirement benefits etc.

According to Wendell French, Compensation is a comprehensive term which includes wages, salaries and all other allowance and benefits.

Wages are the remuneration paid for skilled, semi-skilled and unskilled operative workforce.

Salary is the remuneration of those employees who provides mental labour to the employer such as supervisor, office staff, executive etc. wages are paid on daily or hourly basis whereas salary is paid on monthly basis.

Why Employee Compensation?

1. Attract capable employees to the organization
2. Motivate them toward superior performance (better pay better performance)
3. Retainment of their services over an extended period of time

Objectives of Compensation Planning

The basic purpose or objective of establishing sound compensation is to establish and maintain an equitable rewards system. The other aim is the establishment and maintenance of an equitable compensation structure i.e. an optimal balancing of conflicting personnel interest so that the satisfaction of employees and employers is maximised and conflicts minimized, the compensation management is concerned with the financial aspect of employees need, motivation and rewards. A sound compensation structure tries to achieve these objectives:

To attract manpower in a competitive market.

- To control wages and salaries and labour costs by determining rate change and frequency of increment.
- To maintain satisfaction of employees by exhibiting that remuneration is fair adequate and equitable. To induce and improved performance, money is an effective motivator.

a) **To Employees:**
   - Employees are paid according to requirement of their jobs i.e highly skilled jobs are paid more compensation than low skilled jobs. This eliminates inequalities.
   - The chances of favouritism are minimised.
   - Jobs sequence and lines of promotion are established wherever they are applicable.
   - Employee's moral and motivation are increased because of the sound compensation structure.

b) To Employers:

- They can systematically plan for and control the turnover in the organization.
- A sound compensation structure reduces the likelihood of friction and grievance over remunerations.
- It enhances an employee morale and motivation because adequate and fairly administrative incentives are basis to his wants and need.
- It attracts qualified employees by ensuring and adequate payment for all the jobs.
- In dealing with a trade union, they can explain the basis of their wages programme because it is based upon a systematic analysis of jobs and wages facts.

4.2.   FACTORS AFFECTING COMPENSATION PLANNING

Factors determining compensation of an employee considerable amount of guess word and negotiation are involved. But following are the certain factors which have been extracted as having an important bearing upon the final decision:

a. **Supply and Demand of Labour**: Whatever the organization produces as commodity they desire services and it must pay a price that of workers acting in concert. If more the labour is required, such as at war time prosperity, there will be tendency to increase the compensation; whereas the situation when anything works to decrease the supply of labour, such as restriction by a particular labour union, there will be a tendency to increase the compensation. The reverse of each situation is likely to result in a decrease in employee compensation, provided, labour union, ability to pay, productivity, government do not intervene.

b. **Ability to Pay**: Labour Unions has often demanded an increase in compensation on the basis that the firm is prosperous and able to pay.

c. **Management's Philosophy:** Management's desire to maintain or improve moral, attract high calibre employees, reduce turnover, and improve employees standard of living also affect wages, as does the relative importance of a given position to a firm.

d. **Legislation:** Legislation related to plays a vital role in determining internal organization practices. Various acts are prescribed by government of country for wage hours laws. Wage-hour laws set limits on minimum wages to be paid and maximum hours to be worked. In India minimum wages act 1948 reflecting the wage policy for an organization and fixation of minimum rates of wages to workers in sweated industries. In 1976 equal remuneration act was enacted which prohibits discrimination in matters relating to remuneration on the basis of religion, region or gender.

4.3. VARIOUS MODES OF COMPENSATION

Various modes of compensation are as follows:

Wages and Salary- Wages represent hourly rates of pay and salary refers to monthly rate of pay irrespective of the number of hours worked. They are subject to annual increments. They differ from employee to employee and depend upon the nature of jobs, seniority and merit.

Incentives- These are also known as payment by results. These are paid in addition to wages and salaries. Incentive depends upon productivity, sales, profit or cost reduction efforts. **Incentive scheme are of two types:**

   i.   **INDIVIDUAL INCENTIVE SCHEMES.**

   ii.   **GROUP INCENTIVE SCHEMES.**

Fringe Benefits- These are given to employees in the form of benefits such as provident fund, gratuity, medical care, hospitalization, accident relief, health insurance, canteen, uniform etc.

Non-Monetary Benefits- They include challenging job responsibilities, recognition of merit, growth prospects, competent supervision, comfortable working condition, job sharing and flexi time.

INCENTIVE COMPENSATION PLANS

Incentives are monetary benefits paid to workmen in lieu of their outstanding performance. Incentives vary from individual to individual and from period to period for the same individual. They are universal and are paid in every sector.

It works as motivational force to work for their performance as incentive forms the part total remuneration. Incentives when added to salary increase the earning thus increase the standard of living.

The advantage of incentive payment are reduced supervision, better utilization of equipment, reduced scrap, reduced lost time, reduced absenteeism and turnover & increased output.

According to Burack & Smith, An incentive scheme is a plan or programme to motivate individual or group on performance. An incentive programme is most frequently built on monitory rewards (incentive pay or monetary bonus), but may also include a variety of non-monetary rewards or prizes.

KINDS OF INCENTIVES

Incentives can be classified under the following categories:

1. Individual and Organizational Incentives
2. Financial and Non-financial Incentives
3. Positive and Negative Incentives

1) *Individual and Organizational Incentives*

According to L.G. *Magginson*, Individual incentives are the extra compensation paid to an individual for all production over a specified magnitude which stems from his exercise of more than normal skill, effort or concentration when accomplished in a predetermined way involving standard tools, facilities and materials. Individual performance is measured to calculate incentive whereas organizational or group incentive involve cooperation among employees, management and union and purport to accomplish broader objectives such as an organization-wide reduction in labour, material and supply costs, strengthening of employee loyalty to company, harmonious management and decreased turnover and absenteeism.

    I.   INDIVIDUAL INCENTIVE SYSTEM IS OF TWO TYPES:

- Time based System- It includes Halsey Plan, Rowan Plan, Emerson Plan and Bedeaux Plan.
- Production based System- it includes Taylor's Differential Piece Rate System, Gantt's Task and Bonus Plan

    II.   GROUP INCENTIVE SYSTEM IS OF FOLLOWING TYPES

    a.   Scalon Plan
    b.   Priestman's Plan
    c.   Co-Partnership Plan
    d.   Profit Sharing

TIME BASED SYSTEM

a. *HALSEY PLAN*

Under this plan a standard time is fixed in advance for completing a work. Bonus is rewarded to the worker who performs his work in less than the standard time and paid wages according to the time wage system for the saved time.

The total earnings of the worker = wages for the actual time + bonus

Bonus = 33.5% of the time saved (standard time set on past experience)

Or

50% of the time saved (standard are scientifically set)

Example: Time required to complete job (S) = 20 hours

Actual Time taken (T) = 15 hours Hourly Rate of Pay (R) = Rs 1.5

Calculate the wage of the worker. Solution: T X R + (S-T) X R

15 X 1.5 + (20-15) X 1.5 = 22.5 + 3.75 = 26.25 Rs 2

In this equation 3.75 Rs are the incentives for saving 5 hours.

b. ROWAN PLAN

Under this method minimum wages are guaranteed given to worker at the ordinary rate for the time taken to complete the work. Bonus is that proportion of the wages of the time taken which the time saved bears to the standard time allowed.

Incentive = Wages for actual time for completing the work + Bonus where,

Bonus   =   S-T X T X R

c. EMERSON PLAN

Under this system, wages on the time basis are guaranteed even to those workers whose output is below the standard. The workers who prove efficient are paid a bonus. For the purpose of determining efficiency, either the standard output per unit of time is fixed, or the standard time for a job is determined, and efficiency is determined on the basis of a comparison of actual performance against the standard.

d. BEDEAUX PLAN

It provides comparable standards for all workers. The value of time saved is divided both to the worker and his supervisor in the ratio of ¾ and ¼ respectively. A supervisor also helps a worker in saving his time so he is also given some benefit in this method. The standard time for each job is determined in terms of minutes which are called Bedeaux points or B's. each B represents one minute through time and motion study. A worker is paid time wages upto standard B'sor 100% performance. Bonus is paid when actual performance exceeds standard performance in terms of B's.

PRODUCTION BASED SYSTEM

a. TAYLOR'S DIFFERENTIAL PIECE RATE SYSTEM

F.W. Taylor, founder of the scientific management evolved this system of wage payment. Under this system, there is no guarantee of minimum wages. Standard time and standard work is determined on the basis of time study. The main characteristics of this system are that two rates of wage one lower and one higher are fixed. Those who fail in attaining the standard, are paid at a lower rate and those exceeding the standard or just attaining the standard get higher rate. Under this system, a serve penalty is imposed on the inefficient workers because they get the wages at lower rates. The basic idea underlying in this scheme is to induce the worker at least to attain the standard but at the same time if a worker is relatively less efficient, he will lose much. For example, the standard is fixed at 40 units per day and the piece rate are 40 P. and 50 P. per unit. If a worker produces 40 units or more in a day, he will get the wages at the rate of 50 P per unit and if he produces 39 units will get the wages at 40 paise per unit for the total output.

b. GANTT'S TASK AND BONUS PLAN

In this, a minimum wage is guaranteed. Minimum wage is given to anybody, who completes the job in standard time. If the job is completed in less time, then there is a hike in wage-rate. This hike varies between 25% to 50% of the standard rate.

c. PROFIT SHARING

It is a method of remuneration under which an employer pay his employees a share in form of percentage from the net profits of an enterprise, in addition to regular wages at fixed intervals of time.

2) FINANCIAL AND NON-FINANCIAL INCENTIVES

Individual or group performance can be measured in financial terms. It means that their performance is rewarded in money or cash as it has a great impact on motivation as a symbol of accomplishment. These incentives form visible and tangible rewards provided in recognition of accomplishment. Financial incentives include salary, premium, reward, dividend, income on investment etc. On the other hand, non-financial incentives are that social and psychological attraction which encourages people to do the work efficiently and effectively. Non-financial incentive can be delegation of responsibility, lack of fear, worker's participation, title or promotion, constructive attitude, security of service, good leadership etc..

3) POSITIVE AND NEGATIVE INCENTIVES

Positive incentives are those agreeable factors related to work situation which prompt an individual to attain or excel the standards or objectives set for him, whereas negative incentives are those disagreeable factors in a work situation which an individual wants to avoid and strives to accomplish the standards required on his or her part. Positive incentive may include expected promotion, worker's preference, competition with fellow workers and own record etc. Negative incentives include fear of lay off, discharge, reduction of salary, disapproval by employer etc.

4.4. FRINGE BENEFITS

Employees are paid several benefits in addition to wages, salary, allowances and bonus. These benefits and services are called fringe benefits because these are offered by the employer as a fringe. Employees of the organization are provided several benefits and services by the employer to maintain and promote employee's favorable attitude towards the work and work environment. It not only increases their morale but also motivate them. These provided benefits and services forms the part of salary and are generally refereed as fringe benefits.

According to D. Belcher, Fringe benefits are any wage cost not directly connected with the employee's productive effort, performance, service or sacrifice.

According to Werther and Davis, Fringe embrace a broad range of benefits and services that employees receive as part of their total compensation, package-pay or direct compensation and is based on critical job factors and performance.

According to Cockman, Employee benefits are those benefits which are supplied by an employer to or for the benefits of an employee and which are not in the form of wages, salaries and time rated payments. These are indirect compensation as they are extended condition of employment and are not related to performance directly.

KINDS OF FRINGE BENEFITS

The various organizations in India offer fringe benefits that may be categorized as follows:

1. **Old Age and Retirement Benefits** - these include provident fund schemes, pension schemes, gratuity and medical benefits which are provided to employee after their retirement and during old age as a sense of security about their old age.

2. **Workman's Compensation** - these benefits are provided to employee if they are got ignored or die under the working conditions and the sole responsibility is of the employer.

3. **Employee Security-** Regular wage and salary is given to employee that gives a feeling of security. Other than this compensation is also given if there is lay-off or retrenchment in an organization.

4. **Payment for Time Not Worked**–Under this category of benefits, a worker is provided payment for the work that has been performed by him during holidays and also for the work done during odd shifts. Compensatory holidays for the same number in the same month are given if the worker has not availed weekly holidays.

5. **Safety and Health**–Under this benefit workers are provided conditions and requirements regarding working condition with a view to provide safe working environment. Safety and Health measures are also taken care of in order to protect the employees against unhealthy working conditions and accidents.

6. **Health Benefits**–Employees are also provided medical services like hospital facility, clinical facility by the organization.

4.5. JOB EVALUATION

INTRODUCTION

Job evaluation is an orderly and systematic technique of determining the relative worth of the various jobs within the organisation so as to develop an equitable wage and salary structure.

Job evaluation – means using job analysis information to systematically determine the value of each job in relation to all jobs within the organization (ranking all jobs)

According to International Labour Organisation (ILO) "Job evaluation may be defined as an attempt to determine and compare the demands which the normal performance of particular jobs makes on normal workers without taking into account of the individual abilities or performance of the workers concerned".

The aim of the majority of systems of job evaluation is to establish, on an agreed logical basis, the relative value of different jobs in a plant/industry."

What Is Job Evaluation?

Process of systematically determining the relative worth of jobs to create a job structure for the organization. Evaluation is based on a combination of job content, skills required, value to the organization, organizational culture and the external market.(Note: focus is the job, not the person doing a job.).

Determining Internally Aligned Job Structure

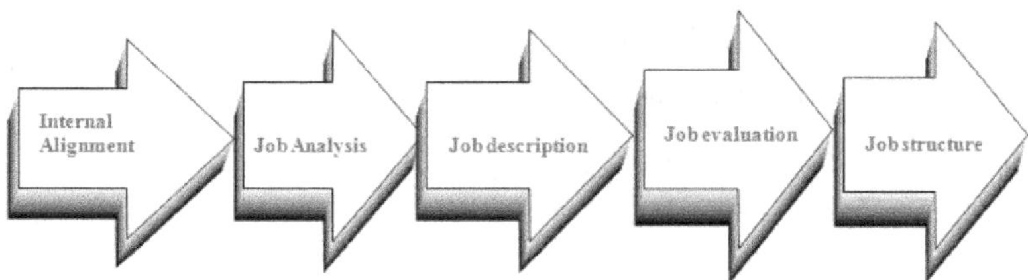

Work Relationships within Organization

Some Major Decisions in Job Evaluation

- Establish purpose of evaluation
- Decide whether to use single or multiple plans
- Choose among alternative approaches
- Obtain involvement of relevant stakeholders
- Evaluate plan's usefulness

Objectives of Job Evaluation

1. To determine equitable wage differentials between different jobs in the organisation.
2. To eliminate wage inequities.
3. To develop a consistent wage policy.
4. To establish a rational basis for incentive and bonus schemes.
5. To provide a frame work for periodic review and revision of wage rates.
6. To provide a basis for wage negotiation with Trade Unions.
7. To minimize wage discrimination on the basis of age, sex, caste, region etc.

Principles of Job Evaluation

The Principles of Job Evaluation are as Follows

a. Job evaluation must attempt to rate the job and not the man.
b. Elements of job selected for the job must be common to most of the jobs, few in number and simple to identify and easy to understand.
c. Clean definition of elements and consistency of degrees of such elements, improve accuracy of job evaluation.
d. Secure willing co-operation and support of supervisors on job evaluation. This is obtained by selling this idea among them and obtains this participation in the process.
e. Secure co-operation and participation from employees.
f. Minimize number of wage rate within each grade.

4.6. METHODS OF THE EVALUATION

There are different methods of job evaluation.

They can be classified as

1. Non-Quantitative Methods

a. Ranking or job comparison
b. Grading or job classification.

2. **Quantitative Methods**

   a. Point rating

   b. Factor comparison.

1. *NON-QUANTITATIVE METHODS*

Here a job is compared as a whole with other jobs.

(a) Ranking or Job Comparison

Ranking of job is normally done by an "expert committee" formed by the organisation. This committee consists of representatives from management and employees. This committee may also consist of a certain number of experts either as permanent members or co-opted members on as required basis. Here the jobs are ranked as a "whole job" instead of breaking them into parts. Three techniques can be used for ranking jobs.

They are as Follows

(i) Job Description

In this technique a written jobs description is prepared for every job. The job descriptions are then studied and analysed. The differences between them in terms of duties, responsibilities, skill requirements etc., are noted.

Each job is assigned a rank depending upon its relative significance. Several rates may independently rank each job. The average of these ratings is calculated to determine the final rankings.

The Following Table Illustrates the Procedure

Job	Rates X Rates Y Rates Z	Average
A BC		

In this method, the rate is required to keep in mind all the jobs being ranked. This may not be possible when the number of jobs is large. To overcome this paired comparison method can be used.

(ii) Paired Comparison

In this technique each job is paired with every other job in the series. The more difficult job in each pair is identified. Rank is then assigned on the basis of the number of times a job is rated more difficult.

This Method can be Understood by the Following Example

Pair	More difficult job	Rank
Assistant-upper division clerk	Assistant	1
Upper division clerk lower	Upper division clerk	2
Lower division clerk peon	Lower division clerk	3
Assistant – lower division clerk	Assistant	4
Assistant peon	Assistant	5
Upper Division clerk – Peon	Upper division clerk Peon	6

(iii) Ranking along a Number Line

In this technique ranks obtained through job descriptions and paired comparisons are spread along a number line. Each job is then placed along the line on the basis of its closeness to the highest ranked job.

For example, in the following number line, A is the highest ranked job; E is the lowest ranked job. Other jobs are spaced according to their closeness to the highest ranked job.

ADVANTAGES OF RANKING METHOD

1. Simple and easy to understand.
2. Faster and inexpensive.

DISADVANTAGES

1. Subjective and influenced by personal bias.
2. Specific job requirements are not taken into account.
3. Ranking does not give indications of actual differences between jobs; in terms of difficulties or responsibilities.

(b) Grading Method

This method is made popular by civil services used mostly for administrative jobs. Here different "grades" or "classes" of jobs are predetermined based on certain criteria such as skill, knowledge, responsibility etc. Even though, initially grading method is envisaged by civil service for administrative and clerical jobs, later this concept became popular and extended to defence services, marketing, sales and managerial cadre jobs. This method is applicable for workers, supervisors and managerial jobs. In India, the following classification methods are used.

Government Departments

Class I, II, III... for officers in descending order.

Public Sector Units (PSU)

Grade 1, 2, 3... for officers in ascending orders.

Civil Services

Group A, B, C... non-officers.

The Steps Involved in this Method are as Follows

a. Prefix the grade/classification.

b. Prepare job description.

c. Identify key jobs in each grade/class

d. Allocate all jobs in each grade/class based on criteria.

Advantages

1. This method is easy to understand and simple to operate.

2. It is more accurate and systematic than the ranking method.

3. It is economical and therefore suitable for small concerns.

4. It provides an opportunity to develop a systematic organisation structure.

5. This method is used in government offices.

Disadvantages

1. It is very difficult to write accurate and precise description of job grades.

2. Some job may involve tasks which overlap more than one grade. It is difficult to classify such jobs in a particular grade.

3. The system is rigid and personal judgment is involved in deciding job classes and assigning jobs to specific classes.

2. QUANTITATIVE METHODS

In quantitative methods key factors of the job are selected and measured.

(a) Point Rating

It is the most widely used method of job evaluation. Under it, jobs are divided into component factors. Points or weightage are assigned to each factor depending on the degree of its importance in a particular job. The total points for a job indicate its relative worth or value. The procedure involved is as follows:

Steps 1: Job Cluster

Group jobs into similar families having common nature and characteristics. This arrangement assists realistic assessment of factors and comparison of jobs.

Steps 2: Identification of Factors

Based on the cluster of jobs, identify relevant factors which are common to these jobs. Unlike factors comparison, there is no restriction on the number of factors. Normally number of factors does not exceed 15.

Step 3: Assigning Degrees to Factors

For the purpose of fine tuning the edifices between jobs, each factor is subdivided into various degrees like, "illiterate", "High school level", "graduate", "Post-graduate" etc.

Step 4: Fixing Relative Weightages

All factors will not carry same weightages. This weightage varies from cluster to cluster, committee of experts assign weightages.

For e.g., a manual job carry higher weightage of "physical ability" compared to "mental ability" and so on.

These weightages are then converted to percentages. These percentages are counted as points for first degree. Points for higher degrees for the same factor are obtained by multiplying the first degree points by the corresponding number 2,3,4 etc.

Step 5: Assign Money Value to Points

Expert committee work out money values in terms of rupees per hour for a range of points having grouped them into different classes/grades.

Step 6: Prepare Job Evaluation Manual

Job evaluation manual is prepared by selecting a number of "key jobs" in each Department/cluster. For each key job, identify the relevant factors, their degrees and points.

Key jobs in job-evaluation manual serve an example for future evaluation of all other jobs. Job evaluation manual become more effective if "Job description" and Job specification can be redrafted in terms of factors identified for each cluster.

Step 7: Rating Jobs

With the help of job-evaluation manual and formula pre-determined for conversion of points to money value, we can now prepare the rating for all jobs by comparing term with key jobs.

Advantages

(i) This method is the most comprehensive and accurate method of job evaluation. Factors are divided into sub factors and different degrees of a factor are considered. Wage and Salary Administration 137

(ii) Assignment of point scores and money values is consistent thereby minimizing bias and human judgment.

(iii) Systematic wage differentials according to content of the job can be determined.

Designing a Point Plan: Six Steps

- Conduct job analysis
- Determine and define the compensable factors.
- Scale the factors (define factor degrees).
- Weight the factors according to importance (and then assign points to degrees within the factors or sub factors).
- Communicate the plan, train users, prepare manual.
- Apply to non-benchmark jobs (note issue of interrater reliability).

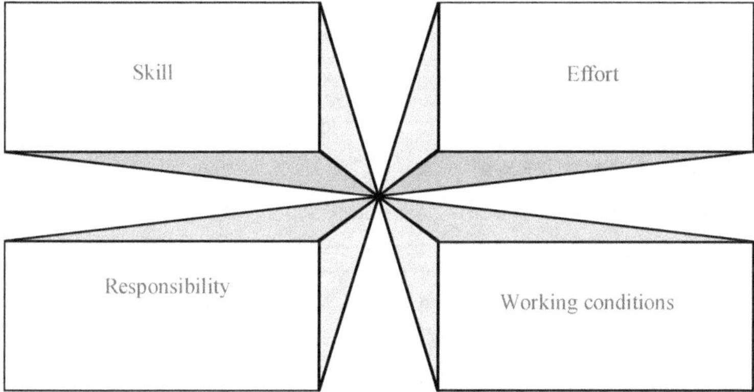

Disadvantages

a. It is expensive and time consuming.

b. Point method is complicated and an average worker cannot understand it easily.

c. Errors may occur if assigned point values are not realistic. It is difficult to determine factor levels and assigns point values.

d. It is difficult to apply this method to managerial jobs wherein the work content is not measurable in quantitative terms.

(b) Factor Comparison

Under this method, a few key jobs are selected and compared in terms of common factors. The procedure involved is as follows.

(i) Select and Define the Factors

The factors common to all jobs are selected and defined clearly. Skill, physical and mental effort, responsibility and working conditions are the main factors used.

(ii) Select Key Jobs

Key jobs serve as standards against which other jobs can be compared. A key job is one having standardised contents and well accepted pay rate, key jobs should be a cross-section of all jobs in the organisation representing all levels of pay.

(iii) Rank Key Jobs by Factors

Job descriptions are carefully analysed and the key jobs are rated in terms of the selected factors.

(iv) Decide Rates for Key Job

A fair and equitable wage rate (hourly and daily) is dimensioned for each key job.

(v) Apportion the Wage Rate

The wage rate for a job is allocated among the identified and ranked factors. A specimen rating and allocation scheme is given below.

Key job	Wage rate	Skill	Physical effort	Mental requirement	Responsibility	Working condition
Tool maker	80	25(1)	5(5)	23(1)	24(1)	3(5)
Welder	75	20(3)	15(2)	14(3)	11(4)	15(2)
Machinist	70	22(2)	7(4)	17(2)	20(2)	4(4)
Painter	65	13(4)	12(3)	10(4)	12(3)	18(1)
Labourer	50	10(5)	19(1)	5(5)	4(5)	12(3)

(vi) Evaluate the Remaining Jobs

The remaining jobs are compared with the key jobs in terms of each factor. Suppose, 'carpenter job is to be similar to tool maker in skill (Rs. 25), machinist in physical effort (Rs. -7), welder in mental requirements (Rs. 14), painter in responsibility (Rs. 12), and painters in working condition (Rs. 18). Then, the wage rate for this job would be Rs.76.

Advantages

1. Method is scientific being analytical and quantifiable.

2. Limited of factors makes this method simple and easy.

3. Jobs are compared with each other to obtain relative value.

4. Job pricing is directly obtained without intermediary point's weightage.

Disadvantages

1. Using just five factors are not realistic.

2. Direct determination of rating shift the focus of job evaluation from "job worth" to "jobwage" in money value. This creates bias.

3. Requires expertise.

Job Evaluation Form

Job _bookstore manager_

Check one: [X] Administrative   [ ] Technical

Compensable Factors	Degree	x	Weight	=	Total
Skill: (40%)	1 2 3 4 5				
Mental	4		20%		80
Experience	3		20%		60
Effort: (30%)					
Physical	1		15%		30
Mental	3		15%		60
Responsibility: (20%)					
Effect of Error	4		10%		40
Inventiveness/ Innovation	2		10%		30
Working Conditions: (10%)					
Environment	1		5%		5
Hazards	1		5%		5
					310

4.7. MOTIVATION & ITS BASIC MODEL

EMPLOYEE MOTIVATION: THEORY AND PRACTICE

The job of a manager in the workplace is to get things done through employees. To do this the manager should be able to motivate employees. But that's easier said than done! Motivation practice and theory are difficult subjects, touching on several disciplines. In spite of enormous research, basic as well as applied, the subject of motivation is not clearly understood and more often than not poorly practiced. To understand motivation one must understand human nature itself. And there lies the problem!

Human nature can be very simple, yet very complex too. An understanding and appreciation of this is a prerequisite to effective employee motivation in the workplace and therefore effective management and leadership.

Motivation - is a process which begins with a physiological or psychological need or deficiency which triggers a behavior or a desire that is aimed at goal or an incentive. Fred Luthans needs drives incentives

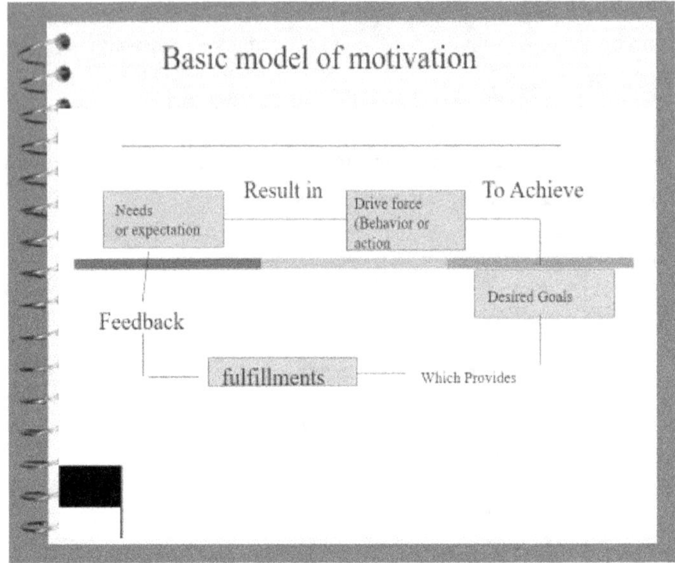

Motivation is the key to performance improvement

Performance is considered to be a function of ability and motivation, thus:

Job performance = f(ability)(motivation)

Ability in turn depends on education, experience and training and its improvement is a slow and long process. On the other hand motivation can be improved quickly.

There are many options and an uninitiated manager may not even know where to start. As a guideline, **there are broadly seven strategies for motivation**.

- Positive reinforcement/high expectations
- Effective discipline and punishment
- Treating people fairly
- Satisfying employees needs
- Setting work related goals
- Restructuring jobs
- Base rewards on job performance

These are the basic strategies, though the mix in the final 'recipe' will vary from workplace situation to situation. Essentially, there is a gap between an individual's actual state and some desired state and the manager tries to reduce this gap.

Why is Motivation Important?

- Under optimal conditions, effort can often be increased and sustained
- Delegation without constant supervision is always necessary
- Employees can become self-motivated
- Motivated employees can provide competitive advantage by offering suggestions & working to satisfy customers

Motivation is, in effect, a means to reduce and manipulate this gap. It is inducing others in a specific way towards goals specifically stated by the motivator. Naturally, these goals as also the motivation system must conform to the corporate policy of the organization. The motivational system must be tailored to the situation and to the organization.

In one of the most elaborate studies on employee motivation, involving 31,000 men and 13,000 women, the Minneapolis Gas Company sought to determine what their potential employees desire most from a job. This study was carried out during a 20 year period from 1945 to 1965 and was quite revealing. The ratings for the various factors differed only slightly between men and women, but both groups considered security as the highest rated factor. The next three factors were; advancement type of work company - proud to work for, Surprisingly, factors such as pay, benefits and working conditions were given a low rating by both groups. So after all, and contrary to common belief, money is not the prime motivator.

4.8.   MAJOR THEORIES OF MOTIVATION

I. Need Approaches

- Maslow's Hierarchy of Needs
- Alderfer's ERG Theory
- Herzberg's Two Factor Theory
- McClelland's learned Needs Theory

II. Cognitive Approaches

- Expectancy Theory
- Equity Theory/ Social Comparison
- Goal Setting Theory

III. Reinforcement Theory or Operant Conditioning

How Rewards & Reinforcements Sustain Motivation over Time (Behavior Modification)

CARROT &STICK MOTIVATION THEORY

The traditional Victorian style of strict discipline and punishment has not only failed to deliver the goods, but it has also left a mood of discontent amongst the "working class".

Punishment appears to have produced negative rather than positive results and has increased the hostility between 'them' (the management) and 'us' (the workers). In contrast to this, the 'carrot' approach, involving approval, praise and recognition of effort has markedly improved the work atmosphere, leading to more productive work places and giving workers greater job satisfaction.

Manager's Motivation 'toolkit'

The manager's main task is to develop a productive work place, with and through those he or she is in charge of. The manager should motivate his or her team, both individually and collectively so that a productive work place is maintained and developed and at the same time employees derive satisfaction from their jobs.

This may appear somewhat contradictory, but it seems to work. The main tools in the manager's kitbag for motivating the team are:

- Approval, praise and recognition
- Trust, respect and high expectations
- Loyalty, given that it may be received

Removing organizational barriers that stand in the way of individual and group performance (smooth business processes, systems, methods and resources - see outline team building program)

- Job enrichment
- Good communications
- Financial incentives

These are arranged in order of importance and it is interesting to note that cash is way down the ladder of motivators. Let's look at a couple of examples taken from real life situations. The Swedish shipbuilding company, Kockums, turned a 15 million dollar loss into a 100 million dollar profit in the course of ten years due entirely to a changed perception of the workforce brought about by better motivation. At Western Electric there was a dramatic improvement in output after the supervisors and managers started taking greater interest in their employees.

Don't Coerce-persuade!

Persuasion is far more powerful than coercion, just as the pen is mightier than the sword. Managers have a much better chance of success if they use persuasion rather than coercion. The former builds morale, initiative and motivation, whilst the latter quite effectively kills such qualities. The three basic components in persuasion are:

- Suggest
- Play on the person's sentiments; and
- Appeal to logic.

Once convinced, the person is so motivated as to deliver the 'goods'. The manager will have achieved the goal quietly, gently and with the minimum of effort. It is, in effect, an effortless achievement.

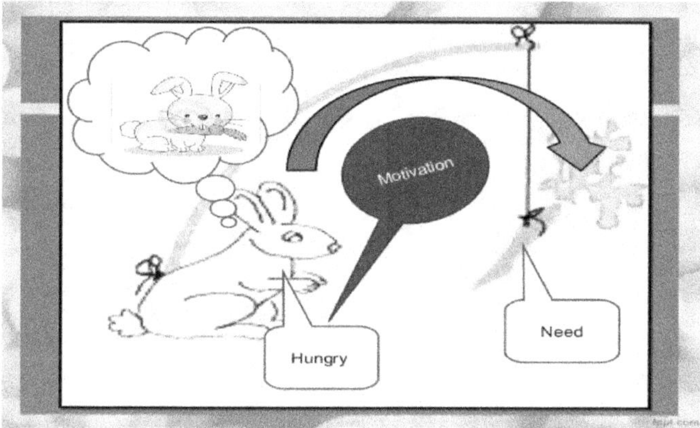

There has been a considerable amount of research into persuasion/motivation in the field of advertising and marketing. The research is entirely of the applied type, which can and has been used to great practical advantage. Some of the findings in this field were first published in the fifties in a book with the title, The Hidden Persuaders, which became a bestseller.

- More contemporary 'persuaders' used by advertising and marketing people include:
- Faster talk is found to be more effective, since it is remembered better.
- Brain emits fast beta waves when a person is really interested in a particular presentation. These waves can be detected by an instrument.

Subliminal approach using short duration presentation, whereby the message is transmitted below the level of awareness. Can these findings be used in actual work conditions? AT&T (The American Telephone and Telegraph Co.,) recognizing the importance of hidden needs, at one time succeeded in promoting long distance calls by use of the simple phrase: 'Reach out, reach out and touch someone'. Managers will need to adapt this persuasion/motivation technique to their own situation.

TRADITIONAL THEORY 'X' & 'Y'- DOUGLAS MCGREGOR

This can best be ascribed to Sigmund Freud who was no lover of people, and was far from being optimistic. Theory X assumes that people are lazy; they hate work to the extent that they avoid it; they have no ambition, take no initiative and avoid taking any responsibility; all they want is security, and to get them to do any work, they must be rewarded, coerced, intimidated and punished. This is the so-called 'stick and carrot' philosophy of management. If this theory were valid, managers will have to constantly police their staff, whom they cannot trust and who will refuse to cooperate. In such an oppressive and frustrating atmosphere, both for the manager and the managed, there is no possibility of any achievement or any creative work. But fortunately, as we know, this is not the case.

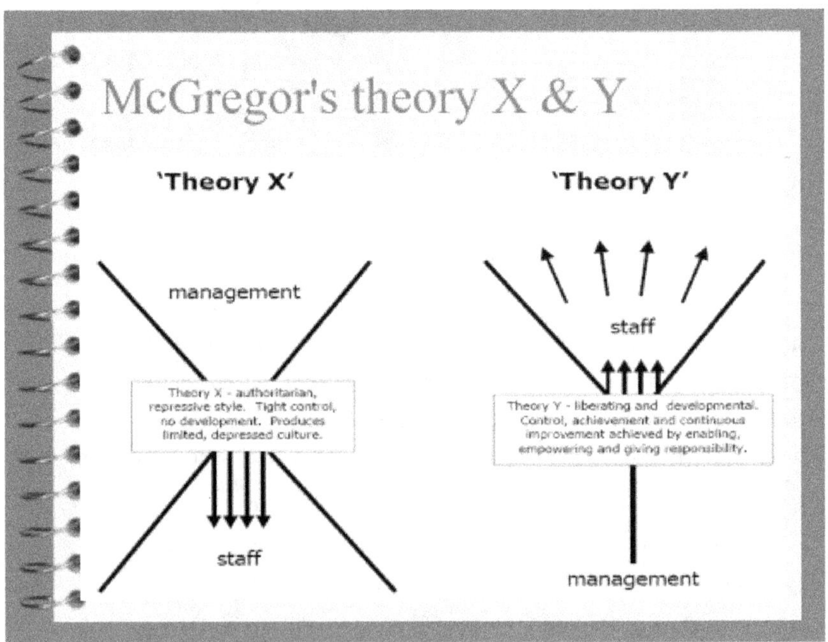

THEORY 'Y'

This is in sharp contrast to theory 'X'. McGregor believed that people want to learn and that work is their natural activity to the extent that they develop self-discipline and self-development. They see their reward not so much in cash payments as in the freedom to do difficult and challenging work by themselves.

The manager's job is to 'dovetail' the human wish for self-development into the organizations need for maximum productive efficiency. The basic objectives of both are therefore met and with imagination and sincerity, the enormous potential can be tapped.

It could be construed; by some, that Theory 'Y' management is soft and slack. This is not true and the proof is in the 'pudding', for it has already proved its worth in the USA and elsewhere. For best results, the persons must be carefully selected to form a homogeneous group. A good leader of such a group may conveniently 'absent' from group meetings so they can discuss the matters freely and help select and 'groom' a new leader. The leader does no longer hanker after power, lets people develop freely, and may even (it is hoped) enjoy watching the development and actualization of people, as if, by themselves. Everyone, and most of all the organization, gains as a result.

ABRAHAM MASLOW – HIERARCHIAL THEORY

This is a refreshing change from the theory X of Freud, by a fellow psychologist, Abraham Maslow. Maslow totally rejects the dark and dingy Freudian basement and takes us out into the fresh, open, sunny and cheerful atmosphere. He is the main founder of the humanistic school or the third force which holds that all the good qualities are inherent in people, at least, at birth, although later they are gradually lost.

Maslow's central theme revolves around the meaning and significance of human work and seems to epitomize Voltaire's observation in Candied, 'work banishes the three great evils-boredom, vice and poverty'. The great sage Yajnavalkya explains in the Brihadaranyaka Upanishad that by good works a man becomes holy, by evil works evil. A man's personality is the sum total of his works and that only his works survive a man at death. This is perhaps the essence of Maslow's hierarchy of needs theory, as it is more commonly known.

Maslow's major works include the standard textbook (in collaboration with Mittlemann), Principles of Abnormal Psychology (1941), Maslow's theory of motivation and the basis of the basic human needs, according to Maslow, various needs are:

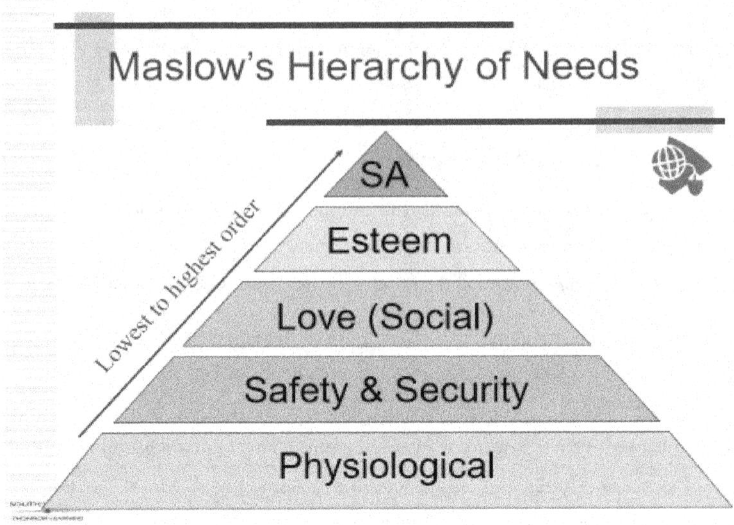

- Physiological needs (Lowest)
- Safety needs
- Social/love needs
- Esteem needs; and
- Self-actualization needs (Highest)

Man's behavior is seen as dominated by his unsatisfied needs and he is a 'perpetually wanting animal', for when one need is satisfied he aspires for the next higher one. This is, therefore, seen as an ongoing activity, in which the man is totally absorbed in order to attain perfection through self-development.

The highest state of self-actualization is characterized by integrity, responsibility, magnanimity, simplicity and naturalness. Self-actualizers focus on problems external to themselves. His prescription for human salvation is simple, but not easy: 'Hard work and total commitment to doing well the job that fate or personal destiny calls you to do, or any important job that "calls for" doing'.

FREDERICK HERZBERG-HYGIENE/MOTIVATION THEORY

According to this theory, people work first and foremost in their own self-enlightened interest, they are truly happy and mentally healthy through work accomplishment. People's needs are of two types:

Motivation–Hygiene Theory of Motivation

- Company policy & administration
- Supervision
- Interpersonal relations
- Working conditions
- Salary
- Status
- Security

Hygiene factors avoid job dissatisfaction

Motivation factors increase job satisfaction

- Achievement
- Achievement recognition
- Work itself
- Responsibility
- Advancement
- Growth

- Salary?

SOURCE: Adapted from Frederick Herzberg, *The Managerial Choice: To be Efficient or to Be Human* (Salt Lake City: Olympus, 1982). Reprinted by permission.

- Human Needs (hygiene factors)
- Supervision
- Interpersonal relations
- Working conditions
- Salary
- Human Needs (motivators)
- Recognition
- Work
- Responsibility
- Advancement

Unsatisfactory hygiene factors can act as de-motivators, but if satisfactory, their motivational effect is limited. The psychology of motivation is quite complex and Herzberg has exploded several myths about motivators such as:

- shorter working week
- increasing wages
- fringe benefits
- sensitivity/human relations training;
- Communication.

As typical examples, saying 'please' to shop-floor workers does not motivate them to work hard, and telling them about the performance of the company may even antagonize them more. Herzberg regards these also as hygiene factors, which, if satisfactory, satisfy animal needs but not human needs.

Chris Argyris

According to Argyris, organization needs to be redesigned for a fuller utilization of the most precious resource, the workers, in particular their psychological energy. The pyramidal structure will be relegated to the background, and decisions will be taken by small groups rather than by a single boss. Satisfaction in work will be more valued than material rewards. Work should be restructured in order to enable individuals to develop to the fullest extent. At the same time work will become more meaningful and challenging through self-motivation. Rensis Likert: identified four different styles of management:

- Exploitative-authoritative
- Benevolent-authoritative
- Consultative
- Participative.

The participative system was found to be the most effective in that it satisfies the whole range of human needs. Major decisions are taken by groups themselves and this results in achieving high targets and excellent productivity. There is complete trust within the group and the sense of participation leads to a high degree of motivation.

ERG THEORY

Clayton Alderfer's extended and simplified Maslow's Hierarchy into a shorter set of three needs: Existence, Relatedness and Growth (hence 'ERG'). Unlike Maslow, he did not see these as being a hierarchy, but being more of a continuum.

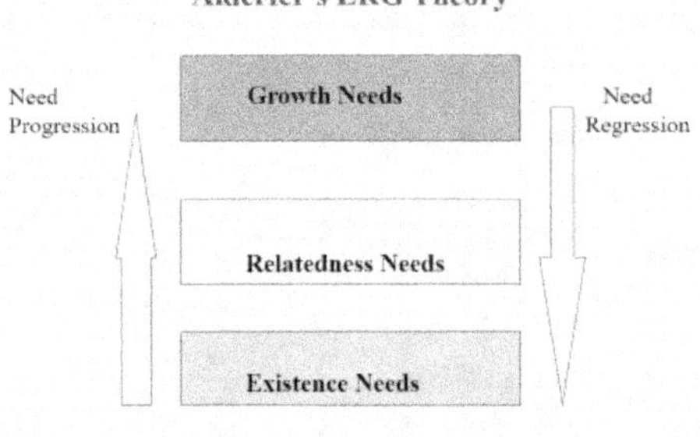

EXISTENCE

At the lowest level is the need to stay alive and safe, now and in the foreseeable future. When we have satisfied existence needs, we feel safe and physically comfortable. This includes Maslow's Physiological and Safety needs.

RELATEDNESS

At the next level, once we are safe and secure, we consider our social needs. We are now interested in relationships with other people and what they think of us. When we are related, we feel a sense of identity and position within our immediate society. This encompasses Maslow's Love/belonging and Esteem needs.

GROWTH

At the highest level, we seek to grow, be creative for ourselves and for our environment. When we are successfully growing, we feel a sense of wholeness, achievement and fulfilment. This covers Maslow's Self-actualization and Transcendence.

Luthans advocates the so-called 'contingency approach' on the basis that certain practices work better than others for certain people and certain jobs. As an example, rigid, clearly defined jobs, authoritative leadership and tight controls lead in some cases to high productivity and satisfaction among workers. In some other cases just the opposite seems to work. It is necessary, therefore, to adapt the leadership style to the particular group of workers and the specific job in hand.

VICTOR VROOM EXPECTANCY THEORY

Vroom's 'expectancy theory' is an extension of the 'contingency approach'. The leadership style should be 'tailored' to the particular situation and to the particular group. An individual should also be rewarded with what he or she perceives as important rather than what the manager perceives. For example, one individual may value a salary increase, whereas another motivation by explaining how individual goals influences individual performance. It may, instead, value the promotion. This theory contributes an insight into the study of employee performance and efforts.

Expectancy Theory

Involves 3 cognitions/perceptions:

1. Expectancy -   the perceived probability that effort will lead to task performance. E link

2. Instrumentality -   the perceived probability that performance will lead to rewards. I link

3. Valence -   the anticipated value of a particular outcome to an individual.

Effort	Performance	Rewards or Outcomes

E link   I link

Expectancy Model of Motivation

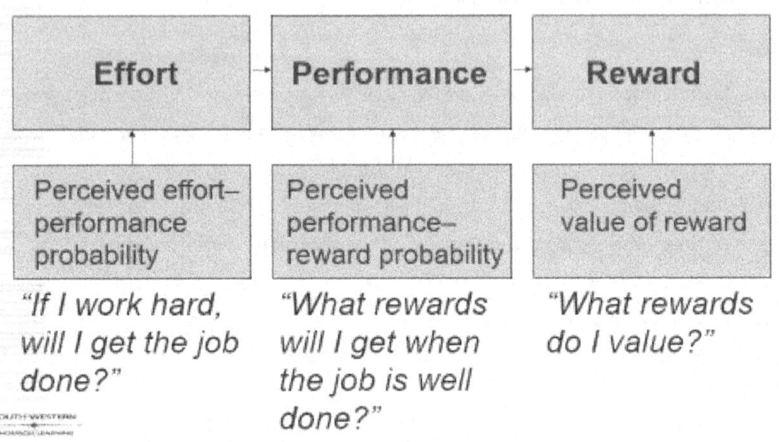

EXPECTANCY THEORY
(Text adds "Personal Goals" after Outcomes)

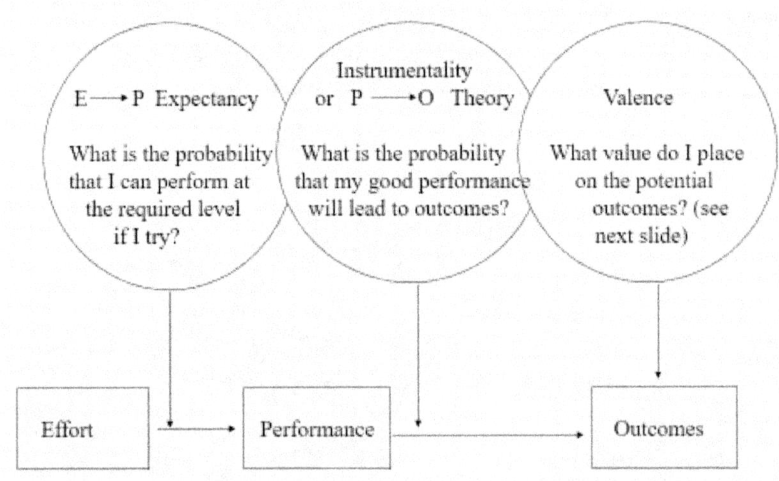

MCCLELLAND'S THEORY OF NEED (ACHIEVEMENT)

The motivation theories described so far look at the individual's primary needs and their relative importance in life. However just fulfilling of primary needs is not sufficient for one, people have secondary needs that are learned, parental style and social norms. In this theory McClelland focuses on three important aspect of motivation they are given below:

1. **Need for achievement**: it concerned with those people who have strong desire and determination to do something better or more efficiently that it has been done before. People with high need of achievement want to accomplish challenging goals effectively through their own effort. Such people want to take the risk and want to get immediate feedback also. They seek situation where they can attain personal responsibility for finding solution to problem. Thus they prefer working alone rather than in a group because of their strong need to assume personal responsibility for tasks.

2. **Need for Affiliation**: It refers to a desire to establish and maintain friendly and warm relation with other and avoid conflicts and confrontation. It is similar to Maslow's belongingness need and Alderfer's relatedness need. People having such needs prefer to work in a group which include interaction with other. They can effectively accomplish the interacting job like sales.

3. **Need for power**: Need or Power refers to a desire to control others to influence their behavior. People having such needs prefer to stay in competitive and status position. They want to maintain their prestige. They are likely to make more suggestion in meeting, evaluate situation, and communicate effectively.

In this theory McClelland proposed three needs which must be learned rather than instinct (character). As a result of life experience these needs are acquired over time. He also focuses that a respective working environment should be created for a particular people having particular needs.

EQUITY THEORY

This theory states those individuals are motivated by their desire to be treated equally in their work relationship. The motivation of employee is influenced by the extent to which they feel they are being treated fairly and equitably by the organization. Individual always want to avoid inequalities compared to other and they are motivated to resolve these inequalities. According to this theory individual in compare themselves to another in terms of their input-outcome ration. They first evaluates themselves and compare the result with other.

Input are individual's contribution to the organization such as: education, experience, effort and loyalty. Outcomes are what the individual receive in return such as: pay, recognition, social relationship etc. If the person find these ration to be equal or nearly equitable than he/she experience a feeling of equity, but if the ratio are not nearly equitable, then inequality exists and the person will be motivated to take some action to resolve such inequality

The process of equity theory can be shown as:

i) Self-evaluation

ii) Evaluation of others

iii) Comparing of self with others.

iv) Feeling of equity/ inequity

v) Action to reduce inequity.

Frustration

Frustration refers to the psychological phenomenon which may be occurred, due to the difficulties, conflicts to their goal directive activities. Thus, frustration is the feeling caused by a sense of privation (lack of something), deprivation (blocking or interfering with) or conflict in relation to their goal directive activities.

According to Richard M. Stress "Frustration refers to a psychological reaction to an obstruction or impediment to goal oriented behavior."

Causes of Frustration

i) When an individual is unable to fulfil his/her needs, frustration occurs.

ii) When a motivated drive is blocked before a person reaches a desired goal, frustration occur.

iii) It occurs due to lack of interpersonal relation.

iv) When people are assigned to job that have contrasting characteristics, unequal degree of status, and frequently foster completion.

GOAL SETTING THEORY

In 1960's, **Edwin Locke** put forward the Goal-setting theory of motivation. This theory states that goal setting is essentially linked to task performance. It states that specific and challenging goals along with appropriate feedback contribute to higher and better task performance. In simple words, goals indicate and give direction to an employee about what needs to be done and how much efforts are required to be put in.

The important **features of goal-setting theory** are as follows:

- The willingness to work towards attainment of goal is main source of job motivation. Clear, particular and difficult goals are greater motivating factors than easy, general and vague goals.

- Specific and clear goals lead to greater output and better performance. Unambiguous, measurable and clear goals accompanied by a deadline for completion avoids misunderstanding.

- Goals should be realistic and challenging. This gives an individual a feeling of pride and triumph when he attains them, and sets him up for attainment of next goal. The more challenging the goal, the greater is the reward generally and the more is the passion for achieving it.

- Better and appropriate feedback of results directs the employee behaviour and contributes to higher performance than absence of feedback. Feedback is a means of gaining reputation, making clarifications and regulating goal difficulties. It helps employees to work with more involvement and leads to greater job satisfaction.

- Employees' participation in goal is not always desirable.

- Participation of setting goal, however, makes goal more acceptable and leads to more involvement.

- Goal setting theory has certain eventualities such as:

- Self-efficiency- Self-efficiency is the individual's self-confidence and faith that he has potential of performing the task. Higher the level of self-efficiency, greater will be the efforts put in by the individual when they face challenging tasks. While, lower the level of self-efficiency, less will be the efforts put in by the individual or he might even quit while meeting challenges.

- Goal commitment- Goal setting theory assumes that the individual is committed to the goal and will not leave the goal.

  The goal commitment is dependent on the following factors:

  1. Goals are made open, known and broadcasted.

  2. Goals should be set-self by individual rather than designated.

  3. Individual's set goals should be consistent with the organizational goals and vision

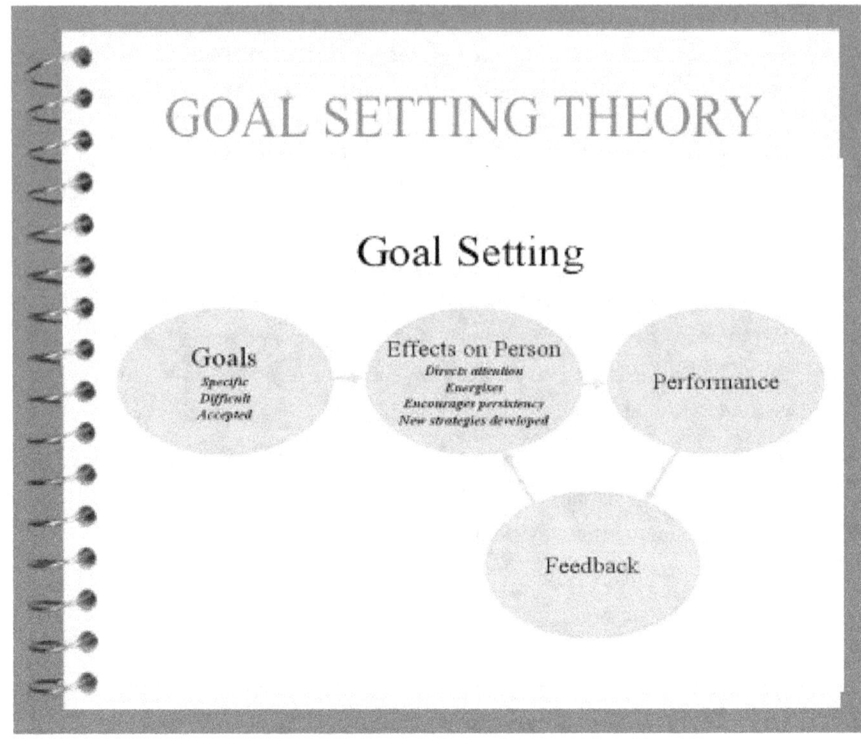

Advantages of Goal Setting Theory

- Goal setting theory is a technique used to raise incentives for employees to complete work quickly and effectively.
- Goal setting leads to better performance by increasing motivation and efforts, but also through increasing and improving the feedback quality.

Limitations of Goal Setting Theory

- At times, the organizational goals are in conflict with the managerial goals. Goal conflict has a detrimental effect on the performance if it motivates incompatible action drift.
- Very difficult and complex goals stimulate riskier behaviour.
- If the employee lacks skills and competencies to perform actions essential for goal, then the goal-setting can fail and lead to undermining of performance.
- There is no evidence to prove that goal-setting improves job satisfaction.

REINFORCEMENT THEORY OF MOTIVATION

Reinforcement theory of motivation was proposed by BF Skinner and his associates. It states that individual's behaviour is a function of its consequences. It is based on "law of effect", i.e, individual's behaviour with positive consequences tends to be repeated, but individual's behaviour with negative consequences tends not to be repeated.

Reinforcement theory of motivation overlooks the internal state of individual, i.e., the inner feelings and drives of individuals are ignored by Skinner. This theory focuses totally on what happens to an individual when he takes some action. Thus, according to Skinner, the external environment of the organization must be designed effectively and positively so as to motivate the employee. This theory is a strong tool for analysing controlling mechanism for individual's behaviour. However, it does not focus on the causes of individual's behaviour.

The managers use the following methods for controlling the behaviour of the employees:

- **Positive Reinforcement**- This implies giving a positive response when an individual shows positive and required behaviour. For example-Immediately praising an employee for coming early for job. This will increase probability of outstanding behaviour occurring again. Reward is a positive reinforce, but not necessarily. If and only if the employees' behaviour improves, reward can said to be a positive reinforce. Positive reinforcement stimulates occurrence of a behaviour. It must be noted that more spontaneous is the giving of reward, the greater reinforcement value it has.

- **Negative Reinforcement**- This implies rewarding an employee by removing negative/undesirable consequences. Both positive and negative reinforcement can be used for increasing desirable/required behaviour.

- **Punishment**- It implies removing positive consequences so as to lower the probability of repeating undesirable behaviour in future. In other words, punishment means applying undesirable consequence for showing undesirable behaviour. For instance - Suspending an employee for breaking the organizational rules. Punishment can be equalized by positive reinforcement from alternative source.

- **Extinction**- It implies absence of reinforcements. In other words, extinction implies lowering the probability of undesired behaviour by removing reward for that kind of behaviour. For instance - if an employee no longer receives praise and admiration for his good work, he may feel that his behaviour is generating no fruitful consequence. Extinction may unintentionally lower desirable behaviour.

Implications of Reinforcement Theory

Reinforcement theory explains in detail how an individual learns behaviour. Managers who are making attempt to motivate the employees must ensure that they do not reward all employees simultaneously. They must tell the employees what they are not doing correct. They must tell the employees how they can achieve positive reinforcement.

Application of Employee Motivation Theory to the Workplace

Management literature is replete with actual case histories of what does and what does not motivate people. Presented here is a tentative initial broad selection of the various practices that have been tried in order to draw lessons for the future.

Job Satisfaction-is there a Trend?

This is the title of a study carried out by the US Department of Labor among 1500 workers, who were asked to rate the job factors, from a list of 23, which they considered important starting from the most important factor. Their findings (Sanzotta (1977)) are contained in the table below. Job Satisfaction Findings

White-collar Workers	*Blue-collar Workers*
A. Interesting work	A. Good pay
B. Opportunities for development	B. Enough help and resources
C. Enough information	C. Job security
D. Enough authority	D. Enough information
E. Enough help and resources	E. Interesting work
F. Friendly, helpful co-workers	F. Friendly, helpful co-workers
G. See results of own efforts	G. Clearly defined responsibilities
H. Competent supervision	H. See results of own work
I. Clearly defined responsibilities	I. Enough Authority
J. Good pay	J. Competent supervision

It is interesting that out of the 23 job factors listed for the survey, yet with the exception of two items (white-collar workers' choice (B) and blue-collar workers' choice (C)) groups selected the same top ten factors, although with different rankings. It is significant that good pay was considered as the most important factor by the blue-collar workers, but it ranked as the least important for white-collar workers.

Individualize Motivation Policies

It is well known that individual behavior is intensely personal and unique, yet companies seek to use the same policies to motivate everyone. This is mainly for convenience and ease compared to catering for individual oddities (Lindstone (1978)). 'Tailoring' the policy to the needs of each individual is difficult but is far more effective and can pay handsome dividends. Fairness, decisiveness, giving praise and constructive criticism can be more effective than money in the matter of motivation.

Leadership is considered synonymous (Tack (1979)) with motivation, and the best form of leadership is designated as SAL, situation adaptable leadership.

In this style of leadership, one is never surprised or shocked, leadership must begin with the chief executive and it is more a matter of adaptation than of imparting knowledge. Ultimately, it is the leadership quality which leads to the success of a company through team building and motivating its people.

'The One-minute Manager'

A contemporary bestseller (Blanchard & Johnson (1983)) aimed at managers who seek to make star performers of their subordinates. To start with, the manager sets a goal, e.g. one page read in one minute, and it is seen to be achieved by 'one minute' of praising or reprimand as the case may be. But to be effective, these must be given (a) promptly, (b) in specific terms, and the behavior, rather than the person, should be praised or reprimanded.

The concept is basic and it makes sense, although the book seeks to 'dramatize' it. 'One minute' praising is seen to be the motivating force. Everyone is considered a winner, though some people are disguised as losers, and the manager is extolled not to be fooled by such appearances.

STRATEGIES FOR MOTIVATION

- Positive reinforcement
- Effective discipline
- Treating people fairly
- Satisfying employees needs
- Setting work related goals
- Restructuring jobs
- Base rewards on job performance

4.9.   CAREER MANAGEMENT

Career development is an organized approach used to match employee goals with the business needs of the agency in support of workforce development initiatives. The purpose of career development is to:

- Enhance each employee's current job performance.
- Enable individuals to take advantage of future job opportunities. Fulfil agencies 'goals for a dynamic and effective workforce.

Career development involves managing your career either within or between organizations. It also includes learning new skills, and making improvements to help you in your career. Career development is an ongoing, lifelong process to help you learn and achieve more in your career. Whether you are looking at making a career change, or moving up within a company, planning your own career development will help you succeed. By creating a personal career development plan, you can set goals and objectives for your own personal career growth. Don't make the mistake of leaving your career development future in the hands of your employer, hoping that you will get the next promotion or pay raise. This misconception can lead to job dissatisfaction and resentment. Career planning is a lifelong process, which includes choosing an occupation, getting a job, growing in our job, possibly changing careers, and eventually retiring. The Career Planning Site offers coverage of all these areas. This article will focus on career choice and the process one goes through in selecting an occupation. This may happen once in our lifetimes, but it is more likely to happen several times as we first define and then redefine ourselves and our goals.

Managers are responsible for linking the organization's needs to employee career goals, and can assist employees in the career planning process. Human Resources is responsible for designing career paths and employee development programs that help employees reach their goals. Each employee is responsible for planning and managing his/her career.

Definitions by Management Scholars

- Development of overall goals and objectives
- Development of a strategy (a general means to accomplish the selected goals/ objectives)
- Development of the specific means (policies, rules, procedures and activities) to implement the strategy, and
- Systematic evaluation of the progress toward the achievement of the selected goals/ objectives to modify the strategy, if necessary.

Objectives

Career Management is the combination of structured planning and the active management choice of one's own professional career. The outcome of successful career management should include personal fulfilment, work/life balance, goal achievement and financial assurance.

- Development of overall goals and objectives
- Development of a strategy (a general means to accomplish the selected goals/ objectives)
- Development of the specific means (policies, rules, procedures and activities) to implement the strategy, and
- Systematic evaluation of the progress toward the achievement of the selected goals/ objectives to modify the strategy, if necessary.

What is Career?

The sequence of positions that a person has held over his or her life. The word career refers to all types of employment ranging from semi-skilled through skilled, and semi-professional to professional. The term career has often been restricted to suggest an employment commitment to a single trade skill, profession or business firm for the entire working life of a person. In recent years, however, career now refers to changes or modifications in employment during the foreseeable future. There are many definitions by management scholars of the stages in the managerial process.

4.10. CAREER PLANNING PROCESS

A career pertains to all the jobs that are held during one's working life. Edwin B.Flippo defined a career as a sequence of separate but related work activities that provides continuity, order and meaning in a person's life.

Need for Career Planning Process

Career Planning is necessary due to the following reasons:

- To attract competent persons and to retain them in the organization.
- To provide suitable promotional opportunities
- To enable the employees to develop and make them ready to meet future challenges
- to increase the utilization of managerial reserves within an organization
- To correct employee placement
- To reduce employee dissatisfaction and turnover
- To improve motivation and morale.

Advantages of Career Planning and Development

- Career planning helps to pave a secure path. For example, if a person wants to become a banker, they have to possess a Bachelor's degree in finance. Preplanning can help achieve the educational targets effectively and also helps to evaluate one's personality. In short, career planning is necessary to guide towards a proper and safer future.

- Without proper planning, we may find ourselves lost - it will also be difficult to find the job we want in the future. It motivates and drives us to accomplish the task.

- A well-planned career helps us to achieve our goals and dreams. As time passes by, we grow and our needs change. Therefore, to keep pace with the future, we need to plan well ahead. It helps us to make many adjustments along the way as we keep learning throughout our lives. Successful people are those who have adopted proper career planning.

- Mentors and guides play a pivotal role in this. It is an important aspect of our lives, but we should not put too much pressure on ourselves, as that would probably discourage us from making any real, profitable choices.

Career Anchor

The distinct pattern of self-perceived talents, attitudes, motives & values that guide and stabilize a person's career after several years of world experience & feedback.

Schein's career anchors represent aspects of work that are especially valued or needed by people for their personal fulfilment.

They include:

1. Managerial competence: the individual desires opportunities to manage.
2. Technical/functional competence: the individual desires to use various technical abilities and special competencies.
3. Security: the individual is basically motivated by a need for job security or stability in the work situation.
4. Creativity: the individual is motivated by a need to create or build something.
5. Autonomy and independence: of primary interest to this person is the opportunity to work independently and without organizational constraints. Career planning and development activities allow employees to grow in any of these desired directions.

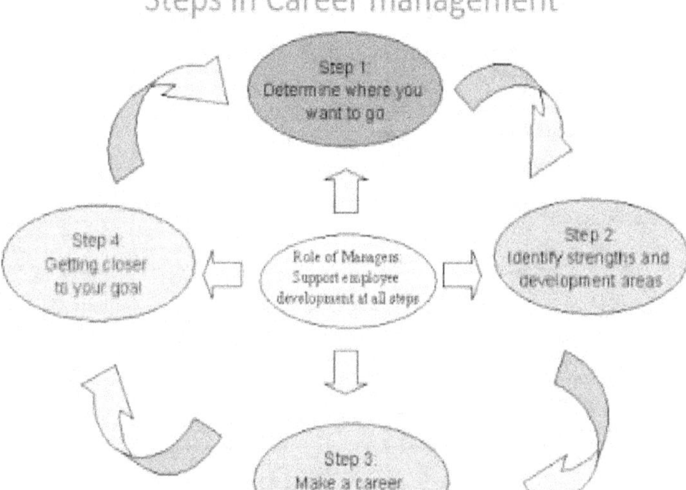

- Tell the employee that you want to meet with him or her to discuss career development plans and hopes. Ask the employee to think in advance about his or her options for growth and development and how they see their career unfolding in your company. Encourage the employee to think about how they'd really like to see their careers progress.

- Suggest that the employee think about and come prepared to discuss these questions: What professional job or career growth goals does the employee hope to achieve within three years? What would the employee like to accomplish this year? What opportunities does the employee consider options to accomplish these goals?

- What can the employee do to ensure that he or she is making progress on this career path? What resources and support can the organization provide so that the employee can accomplish his or her professional job or career growth goals?

- Hold the meeting and direct the conversation to these questions. Be flexible because the employee may have other avenues that he or she wants to discuss.

CAREER PLANNING PROCESS

Career development and the career planning process include a number of specific steps that help to identify personal skills and attributes. Finding out how those skills can be utilized in the job market is accomplished by researching a number of career fields that are of interest to you and then by gaining experience in those fields and/or speaking to people currently working in the field.

Step #1: Self-Assessment

Evaluating who you are as a person. This involves taking a personal inventory of who you are and identifying your individual values, interests, skills, and personal qualities. What makes you tick as a person? Career assessments may be required to promote a better understanding of personal attributes and skills.

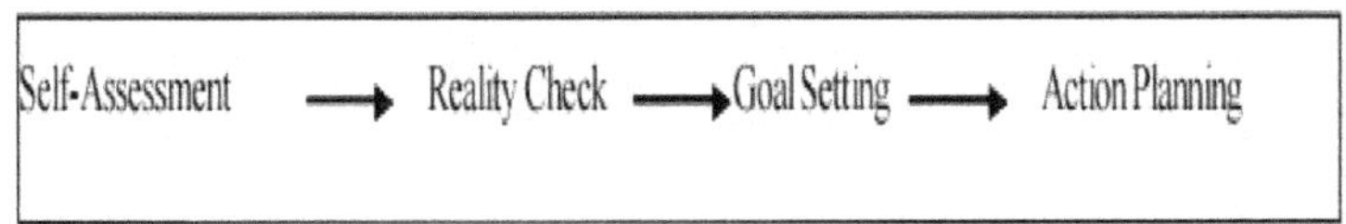

The Career Management Process

Step #2: Research (Career Exploration)

Obtain an insider's perspective about the career field you are considering. Conduct Informational Interviews in person, phone, or by email. Professionals enjoy sharing their expertise with people interested in the field. Perform informational interviews with alumni from your college to gain their perspective of the field and to listen to what they have to say. This strategy provides first-hand knowledge from someone currently working in the field and gives you an opportunity to ask about their experiences as well as potential jobs and what one might expect if just entering the field.

Gain experience through internships or by job shadowing for one to several days to see what a typical work day entails and to gain perspective of what the environment is like and the typical job responsibilities of someone working in the field. Research what types of jobs are available in your area of interest by checking out Majors to Career Converter, The Occupational Outlook Handbook and The Career Guide to Industries. The Occupational Outlook Handbook offers a wealth of information for those currently just entering the job market and for those anticipating making a career change.

Step #3: Decision-Making

Once you've made a thorough self-assessment and have done some research of career options, it's time to make a decision. This can be difficult since there may still be many unknowns and a fear of making the wrong choice. One thing for sure is that although we can do all the necessary steps to making an informed decision, there is no absolute certainty that we are unquestioningly making the right decision. This uncertainty is easier for some people than others but a key point to remember is that you can always learn from any job you have and take those skills and apply them at your next job.

Step #4: Search (Taking Action)

It's now time to look for prospective jobs and/or employers, send out cover letters and resumes, and begin networking with people in the field. Keep in mind that cover letters and resumes are designed to make a favorable impression on employers (if done properly) and the interview process is what will ultimately land you the job. In other words, make sure your cover letter and resume highlight your skills and strengths based on the employer's needs and that you are fully prepared to knock their socks off at the interview. Take time to research the employer's website prior to the interview, and be prepared to ask thoughtful questions based on your research.

Step #5: Acceptance

Wow! You've completed all of the steps above and you've been accepted into a new and exciting or different job. Congratulations! According to the Bureau of Labor Statistics, 64.1% of people change jobs between 5 and 14 times in their lifetime. Consequently, learning the skills above will increase your chances of gaining meaningful and satisfactory work as well as help you to avoid many of the stresses that occur with changing jobs. By recognizing that change is good (even advantageous), changing jobs can be viewed as a positive experience and need not be as anxiety provoking as it may initially seem. You will continue the process of self-assessment, research, decision-making, and job searching in order to make effective and fulfilling career changes throughout your lifetime.

4.11. CAREER STAGES

What people want from their careers also varies according to the stage of one's career. What may have been important in an early stage may not be important in a later one. Four distinct career stages have been identified: trial, establishment/advancement, mid-career, and late career. Each stage represents different career needs and interests of the individual

Trial Stage

The trial stage begins with an individual's exploration of career-related matters and ends usually at about age 25 with a commitment on the part of the individual to a particular occupation. Until the decision is made to settle down, the individual may try a number of jobs and a number of organizations.

Unfortunately for many organizations, this trial and exploration stage results in high level of turnover among new employees. Employees in this stage need opportunities for self-exploration and a variety of job activities or assignments.

Establishment Stage

The establishment/advancement stage tends to occur between ages 25 and 44. In this stage, the individual has made his or her career choice and is concerned with achievement, performance, and advancement. This stage is marked by high employee productivity and career growth, as the individual is motivated to succeed in the organization and in his or her chosen occupation. Opportunities for job challenge and use of special competencies are desired in this stage. The employee strives for creativity and innovation through new job assignments. Employees also need a certain degree of autonomy in this stage so that they can experience feelings of individual achievement and personal success.

Mid-Career

The period occurring between the mid-thirties and mid-forties during which people often make a major reassessment of their progress relative to their original career ambitions and goals.

Maintenance stage. The mid-career stage, which occurs roughly between the ages 45 and 64, has also been referred to as the maintenance stage. This stage is typified by a continuation of established patterns of work behavior. The person is no longer trying to establish a place for himself or herself in the organization, but seeks to maintain his or her position. This stage is viewed as a mid-career plateau in which little new ground is broken. The individual in this stage may need some technical updating in his or her field. The employee should be encouraged to develop new job skills in order to avoid early stagnation and decline.

Late-career Stage

In this stage the career lessens in importance and the employee plans for retirement and seeks to develop a sense of identity outside the work environment.

4.12. SUCCESSION PLANNING

Succession planning is a process whereby an organization ensures that employees are recruited and developed to fill each key role within the company. Through succession planning process, Company can recruit superior employees, develop their knowledge, skills, and abilities, and prepare them for advancement or promotion into ever more challenging roles.

Succession planning is a process for identifying and developing internal personnel with the potential to fill key or critical organizational positions. Succession planning ensures the availability of experienced and capable employees that are prepared to assume these roles as they become available.

Succession planning accelerates the transition of qualified employees from individual contributors to managers and leaders.

Succession planning: Prepares current employees to undertake key roles such as:

- Develops talent and long-term growth
- Improves workforce capabilities and overall performance
- Improves employee commitment and therefore retention
- Meets the career development requirements of existing employees
- Improves support to employees throughout their employment
- Counters the increasing difficulty of recruiting employees externally
- Focuses on leadership continuity and improved knowledge sharing
- Provides more effective monitoring and tracking of employee proficiency levels and skill gaps

There are four stages to developing an effective succession plan

- Identifying roles for succession
- Developing a clear understanding of the capabilities required to undertake those roles
- Identifying employees who could potentially fill and perform highly in such roles; and
- Preparing employees to be ready for advancement into each identified role.

Without the implementation of a succession plan, there can be significant impacts on an organization including:

- Loss of expertise and business knowledge
- Loss of business continuity
- Damaged client relationships
- Time and effort to recruit and train replacement employees

Advantages of Succession Planning

Succession Planning helps you take a more strategic approach to leadership development, employee skill assessment and perhaps even more important as baby boomers retire–preserving critical organizational knowledge. With incumbents ready to go any time an expected or unexpected change occurs in the organization and can ensure business continuity at all levels of the organization. Organizations use succession planning to achieve a number of objectives like:

- Improve recruitment process for key positions.

- Active development of longer-term prospective successors by ensuring their career growth and analysing work, responsibilities, skills and knowledge required for the future audit the 'talent pool' of the organization and that helps in allocation of responsibilities and development strategies and fill the identified talent gaps

- Build a 'key talent resource' of employees who share key skills, knowledge, experiences and values seen as important to the future of the organization

To summarize, the main advantage of succession planning in an organization is the active development of a strong 'talent resource' for the future which is vital to attract and retain the best and key people which will help in present and more for the future growth of the organization. Have the right people with right skills in the right jobs doing the right things. If they people are doing wrong things then you are right back where you started. The key is to match the needs of the organization to the goals of the individual. Keeping talented people in place by providing them with opportunities they may not receive elsewhere will create a stronger and more loyal group of future managers and executives thus saving the company's recruiting and hiring costs over the long-term.

4.13. MODELS OF SUCCESSION PLANNING

There are three main models that companies use to implement succession planning:

- Short-term planning or emergency replacements
- Long-term planning or managing talent
- Combination of above plans

Short-term or Emergency Replacements

This is the most common model of succession planning and serves as a crucial point for all types of businesses. Short-term replacement planning is focused on an urgent need caused by a sudden development within the organization–skilled employee leaving the company, expansion or contraction of business. Sometimes, emergency replacement planning must work to retain knowledge that is about to be lost. Emergency knowledge retention is an option to consider if the organization is about to lose specialized knowledge and does not have a successor to take the knowledge.

Long-term Planning or Managing Talent

Talent management focuses on the future needs of the organization. Working within the strategic framework for the company's future goals, senior management identifies the positions necessary for growth and the best candidates to fill those roles. Some organizations invite all employees to take part in an assessment process, while others have managers identify leadership candidates.

The advantages of this model include:

- Identifies a specialized talent pool
- Defines and builds future skills required for the success of the organization
- Motivates and retains employees by involvement in their career growth

Combination of Both the Plans

This model allows senior management to plan for the long-term growth of both the organization and employees within the organization and prepare for emergency replacements to ensure that business is not affected by knowledge loss or lack of skilled employees.

4.14. REWARD MANAGEMENT

INTRODUCTION

One-time cash or non-cash award for significant outstanding performance. Employees are motivated by both intrinsic and extrinsic rewards. To be effective, the reward system must recognize both sources of motivation. All reward systems are based on the assumptions of attracting, retaining and motivating people. Financial rewards are an important component of the reward system, but there are other factors that motivate employees and influence the level of performance.

In fact, several studies have found that among employees surveyed, money was not the most important motivator, and in some instances managers have found money to have a demotivating or negative effect on employees.

Today's emphasis on quality-improvement teams and commitment-building programs is creating a renaissance for financial incentive of pay-for-performance plans. Today financial incentives constitute less than 5% of the U.S. worker's compensation.

Organizations adopt alternative reward systems to increase domestic and international competition. The competitive reasons for the growing emphasis on performance-based compensation are companies cutting costs, restructuring, and boosting performance.

To ensure the reward system is effective and motivates the desired behaviors, it is essential to consider carefully the rewards and strategies utilized and ensure the rewards are linked to or based on performance.

To be effective, any performance measurement system must be tied to compensation or some sort of reward. Rewarding performance should be an ongoing managerial activity, not just an annual pay-linked ritual.

Rewards–Meaning

Reward Management is concerned with the formulation and implementation of strategies and policies that aim to reward people fairly, equitably and consistently in accordance with their value to the organization.

Definition

According to Armstrong and Murlis (2004), Reward Management is concerned to reward people fairly, equitably and consistently in accordance with their value to the organization". Certain basic criteria are essential for rewards to be effective.

These include:

- Reward should be quick.
- Reward should be significant.
- The goals and rewards must be; known, understandable, and attainable.
- Reward must be distinctly and directly related to performance.
- Reward should be irrevocable.
- Reward should be compatible with job measurement.

If the reward plan is seen to be unfair and unrealistic, for example promotion on the basis of seniority or favoritism, it may have a definitely negative effect as a motivator.

For rewards to be effective, they have to be generous and significant as noted above, hence they must be structured to attain a proper balance of motivating people to purpose and at optimum effort.

4.15. TYPES OF REWARDS

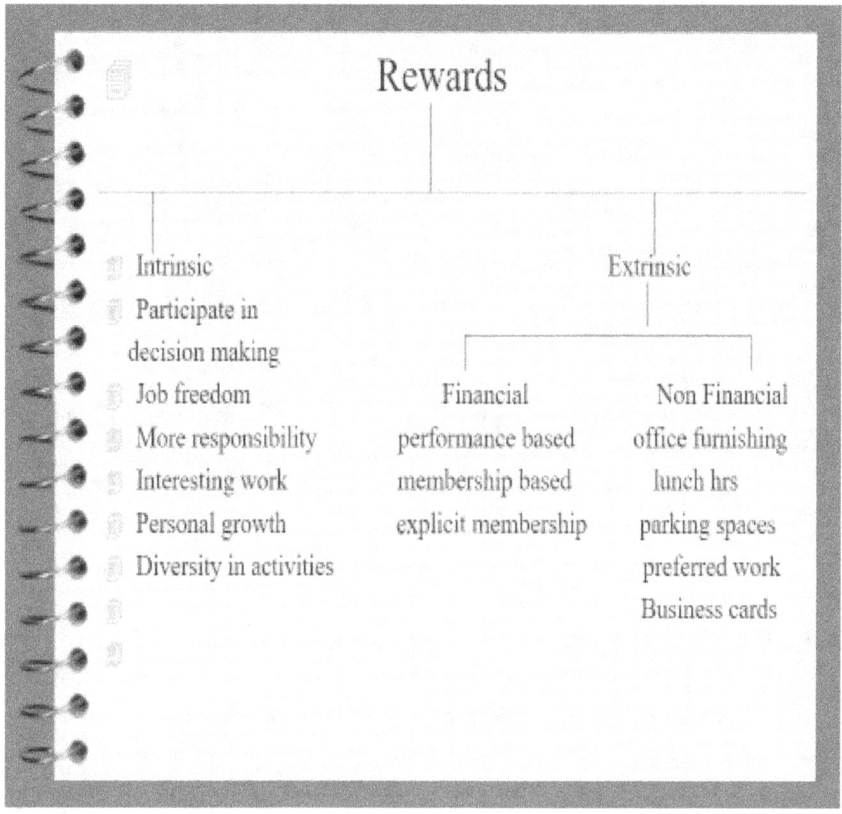

Rewards serve many purposes in organisations. They serve to build a better employment deal, hold on to good employees and to reduce turnover. The principal goal is to increase people's w productivity.

There are two kinds of rewards

I. **EXTRINSIC REWARDS:** concrete rewards that employee receive.

- **Bonuses:** Usually annually, Bonuses motivates the employee to put in all endeavours and efforts during the year to achieve more than a satisfactory appraisal that increases the chance of earning several salaries as lump sum. The scheme of bonuses varies within organizations; some organizations ensure fixed bonuses which eliminate the element of asymmetric information, conversely, other organizations deal with bonuses in terms of performance which is subjective and may develop some sort of bias which may discourage employees and create setback. Therefore, managers must be extra cautious and unbiased.

- **Salary raise:** Is achieved after hard work and effort of employees, attaining and acquiring new skills or academic certificates and as appreciation for employees duty (yearly increments) in an organization. This type of reward is beneficial for the reason that it motivates employees in developing their skills and competence which is also an investment for the organization due to increased productivity and performance. This type of reward offers long-term satisfaction to employees. Nevertheless, managers must also be fair and equal with employees serving the organization and eliminate the possibility of adverse selection where some employees can be treated superior or inferior to others.

- **Gifts:** Are considered short-term. Mainly presented as a token of appreciation for an achievement or obtaining an organizations desired goal. Any employee would appreciate a tangible matter that boosts their self-esteem for the reason of recognition and appreciation from the management. This type of reward basically provides a clear vision of the employee's correct path increasing their efforts to achieve higher returns and attainments.

- **Promotion:** Quite similar to the former type of reward. Promotions tend to effect the long-term satisfaction of employees. This can be done by elevating the employee to a higher stage and offering a title with increased accountability and responsibility due to employee efforts, behaviour and period serving a specific organization. This type of reward is vital for the main reason of redundancy and routine. The employee is motivated in this type of reward to contribute all his efforts in order to gain managements trust and acquire their delegation and responsibility.

II.   INTRINSIC REWARDS

This reward tends to give personal satisfaction to individual Information / feedback: Also a significant type of reward that successful and effective managers never neglect. This type of rewards offers guidance to employees whether positive (remain on track) or negative (guidance to the correct path). This also creates a bond and adds value to the relationship of managers and employees.

- **Recognition:** Is recognize appreciation. This type of reward may take the presence of being formal for example meeting or informal such as esteem pat and on happiness which will result into additional contributing efforts.

- **Trust/empowerment:** In any society or organization, trust is a vital aspect between living individuals in order to add value to any relationship. This form of reliance is essential in order to complete tasks successfully. Also, takes place in empowerment when managers delegate tasks to employees. This adds importance to an employee where his decisions and actions are reflected. Therefore, this reward may benefit organizations for the idea of two minds better than one.

Intrinsic rewards makes the employee feel better in the organization, while Extrinsic rewards focus on the performance and activities of the employee in order to attain a certain outcome.

The principal difficulty is to find a balance between employees' performance (extrinsic) and happiness (intrinsic).One will choose the reward scope in harmony with the work that has been achieved.

1. Individual
   - Base pay, incentives, benefits
   - Rewards attendance, performance, competence
2. Team: Team bonus, rewards group cooperation

Guiding Principles

A. Rewards should be given for significant outstanding performance that advances unit goals, and should be tied to a specific accomplishment.
B. Rewards are most effective when they are meaningful to the individual.
C. Care should be taken in communication and distribution of rewards so that they are not viewed as entitlements.
D. Rewards may be designed to reflect the unique nature of the unit's work culture and organizational structure.
E. Rewards should not be substituted for a competitive salary plan. For example, rewards should not be used as a long-term alternative to permanent salary adjustments when these adjustments are appropriate for consistently high performance, significant changes in responsibility, increased value of a position, or internal pay equity.
F. Rewards are not adjustments to base salary, supplemental compensation, or variable pay programs (such as commission).
G. Rewards should not be used as a substitute for supplies, support services, or training.

Reward systems: The financial rewards are basically of three types:

- profit sharing
- job evaluation; and
- Merit rating.

Profit sharing could be on a macro basis or on a micro basis. The former relates to the entire company as a whole and the latter to a particular section or group dealing with a particular activity and/or product. On a macro level, it would be difficult to identify and reward outstanding performance. This is possible on a micro level by treating the particular activity as a cost and profit center by itself. This is easier said than done, since overheads and other common services have to be charged and this cannot be done completely objectively. The cost allocation in such cases is somewhat arbitrary and the profit will therefore not be a true reflection of the performance of that particular group or activity.

In case of job evaluation, the various component factors have to be isolated and evaluated for purposes of inter-job comparison. Each factor is assigned a rating on the basis of a scale agreed beforehand by the union and the management joint committee. The total rating for each job then forms the basis of wage structure. However, there must be a base level, representing, in effect, the 'minimum wage', depending on the nature of work and the geographical area. In some cases and in some countries these are stipulated by law. A typical, though somewhat broad, list of job factors is as follows:

- Working environment
- Physical characteristics
- Mental characteristics
- Extent of responsibility
- Training and experience.

In case of managers, the factors are:

- Responsibility
- Expertise
- Human relations.
- Merit rating

Merit rating has been used as an indicator of performance.

Each employee is rated, typically as excellent, good, average or poor, in respect of the following abilities:

- Communication
- Human relations, including leadership and motivation

- Intelligence
- Judgment
- Knowledge.

The rating, unfortunately, tends to be carried out purely mechanically and it carries a heavy bias of the rafter who may be too lenient, may not be objective and may also have favorites or otherwise in the group being rated.

4.16. MENTORING

MENTORING

Mentoring is widely recognized today as an extremely beneficial career development tool. Studies have shown that having a mentor is a top factor affecting an employee's success, career satisfaction and whether they stay with an organization. A mentor is an individual, usually older, always more experienced, who helps and guides another individual's development.

Definitions of Mentoring

1. **According to Collins** "Mentoring is a one to one relationship between experienced and non-experienced person until latter reaches Maturity".
2. **According To Reidy – croft** " Mentoring refers to the Information and advice provided by an older experienced individual to a younger and less experienced individual to help in latters growth & development".
3. **The Merriam-Webster Dictionary** defines a mentor as "a trusted counsellor or guide."

What does a mentor do?

The following are among the mentor's functions:

- Teaches the mentoree about a specific issue
- Coaches the mentoree on a particular skill
- Facilitates the mentoree's growth by sharing resources and networks
- Challenges the mentoree to move beyond his or her comfort zone
- Creates a safe learning environment for taking risks
- Focuses on the mentoree's total development

Mentoring is a tool that organizations can use to nurture and grow their people. It can be an informal practice or a formal program. Protégés observe, question, and explore. Mentors demonstrate, explain and model. Regular communication is important in order to effectively maintain the mentor-protégé relationship. Each mentor will be asked to record a short summary of their experience with the young protégé, probably on a quarterly basis. The Mentor Coordinator will also call the mentor periodically, and the mentor will be encouraged to contact the Coordinator if any questions regarding the relationship arise. The closer the communication, the more likely the program will be successful.

The following assumptions form the foundation for a solid mentoring program. Deliberate learning is the cornerstone. The mentor's job is to promote intentional learning, which includes capacity building through methods such as instructing, coaching, providing experiences, modelling and advising.

Both failure and success are powerful teachers. Mentors, as leaders of a learning experience, certainly need to share their "how to do it so it comes out right" stories. They also need to share their experiences of failure, i.e., "how I did it wrong". Both types of stories are powerful lessons that provide valuable opportunities for analyzing individual and organizational realities.

Leader need to tell their stories. Personal scenarios, anecdotes and case examples, because they offer valuable, often unforgettable insight, must be shared. Mentors who can talk about themselves and their experiences establish a rapport that makes them "learning leaders."

Development matures over time. Mentoring--when it works--taps into continuous learning that is not an event, or even a string of discrete events. Rather, it is the synthesis of ongoing event, experiences, observation, studies, and thoughtful analyses.

Mentoring is a joint venture. Successful mentoring means sharing responsibility for learning. Regardless of the facilities, the subject matter, the timing, and all other variables. Successful mentoring begins with setting a contract for learning around which the mentor, the protégé, and their respective line managers are aligned.

Mentorship refers to a personal developmental relationship in which a more experienced or more knowledgeable person helps a less experienced or less knowledgeable person. The receiver of mentorship was traditionally referred to as a protégé or apprentice but with the institutionalization of mentoring the more neutral word "mentee" was invented and is widely used today.

CHARACTERISTICS OF MENTOR

All successful business people do not necessarily make effective mentors; certain individuals are more effective in the role of developing others. Whether or not an individual is suited to the role of mentor may depend on his or her own stage of development and experience. For example, a fairly successful individual may have had a specific, or limited, background and may not have enough general experience to offer. Prior to entering into a mentoring relationship, the protégée should assume the responsibility of assessing the mentor's potential effectiveness.

ROLES OF MENTOR

- Sponsor
- Teacher
- Devil's advocate
- Advocate
- Coach
- Advisor
- Counselor
- Broker

Phases of a Mentoring Relationship

The mentoring relationship typically has four distinct phases:

Orientation-Building the Base

During the first three to six months, both the mentor and protégé are getting to know each other, and building trust. At this time, both the protégé and the mentor are developing expectations of each other. The interaction which occurs at this stage will lay the foundation for a strong and beneficial relationship.

The Middle Period

The middle phase is typically the most rewarding time for both mentor and protégé. The mutual trust which has developed between the two can give the protégé the confidence to challenge the ideas of the mentor, just as the protégé's ideas will be challenged by the mentor.

Dissolving the Relationship

Typically, the relationship begins to draw apart after a year or two. It is important, at this stage, which the mentor step back from the formal relationship to discuss together with the protégé, how they wish to continue their relationship.

Redefining the Relationship

The mentor-protégé relationship enters a new phase, where both parties can regard one another as equals. They continue to have some form of interaction, although it is now on a more casual basis.

Qualities of a Good Coach

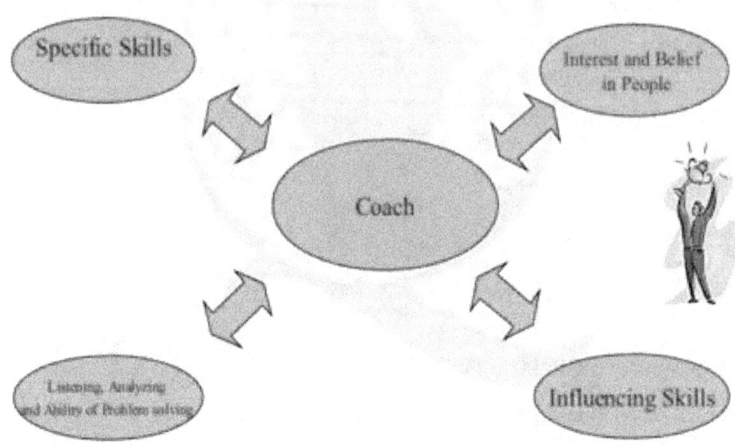

    Coaching and Mentoring

The Qualities which are Essential in an Effective Mentor Include

A Desire to Help

Individuals who are interested in and willing to help others.

Have had Positive Experiences

Individuals who have had positive formal or informal experiences with a mentor tend to be good mentors themselves.

Good Reputation for Developing Others

Experienced people who have a good reputation for helping others develop their skills.

Time &Energy

People who have the time and mental energy to devote to the relationship.

Up-to-date Knowledge

Individuals who have maintained current, up-to-date technological knowledge and/or skills.

Learning Attitude

Individuals who are still willing and able to learn and who see the potential benefits of a mentoring relationship.

Demonstrated Effective Managerial (Mentoring) Skills

Individuals who have demonstrated effective coaching, counselling, facilitating and networking skills.

CHARACTERISTICS OF A PROTÉGÉ

- Committed to expanding their capabilities
- Open and receptive to new ways of learning and trying new ideas
- Able to accept feedback and act upon it
- Willingness to apply learning back on the job
- Focused on achieving desired business results
- Able to communicate and work cooperatively with others
- Knows when to ask for help
- Have a sense of personal responsibility and commitment
- Willing to meet on a regular basis.

BENEFITS FOR PROTÉGÉS

- A nonthreatening learning opportunity
- Improved self-confidence
- Developing business expertise & technical knowledge
- Challenge
- Support and reassurance
- Networking/partnership opportunities
- Coaching; and
- Listening and reassurance.

Benefits for the Mentor

- Increased motivation
- Challenge
- New insights and perspectives
- An opportunity for self-development
- Increased self-esteem & pleasure.

4.17. MENTOR- PROTÉGÉ RELATIONSHIP

Developing Mentor-protégé Relationship

The relationship between an experienced employer and a junior employee in which the experienced person helps the junior person with effective socialization by sharing information gained through experience with the organization.

Requirements for Effective Mentor-protégé Relationship

The status & characteristics of the mentor: Mentors should be seniors in status, experience, age, skills, knowledge.

1. Protégé: Junior employees should have the zeal to learn from their senior employees regarding their career, social and psychological aspect.
2. The relationship: It is based on mutual dependence & mutual trust.
3. The activities: Developing the potentials of the protégé. Improving protégés performance interlinking formal learning & practices Guide, support, providing feedback.
4. Developing higher skills: It should encourage their juniors towards high task performance by reducing weakness & strength of the protégés.
5. Response of the protégé: Protégés should learn carefully regarding career opportunities, personal goals.

Career development is an organized approach used to match employee goals with the business needs of the agency in support of workforce development initiatives. The purpose of career development is to:

- Enhance each employee's current job performance.
- Enable individuals to take advantage of future job opportunities to fulfil agencies 'goals for a dynamic and effective workforce.

UNIT 5

PERFORMANCE EVALUATION AND CONTROL PROCESS

Objective of the Unit 5

- Performance Appraisal – Definitions & its Process
- Methods – Traditional & Modern methods
- Feedback system
- Job changes
- Promotion & its types
- Transfers & its types
- Employee separation
- Employee empowerment
- Employee Grievances and its redderssal machinery
- Participative management
- Collective Bargaining & its characteristics

5.1. PERFORMANCE APPRAISAL

People differ in their abilities and their aptitudes. There is always some difference between the quality and quantity of the same work on the same job being done by two different people. Performance appraisals of Employees are necessary to understand each employee's abilities, competencies and relative merit and worth for the organization. Performance appraisal rates the employees in terms of their performance.

Performance

The first step is to know "performance". The literary meaning of performance is "an act of staging or presenting a play, concert or other form of entertainment." Also, performance goes synonymous with "accomplishment" and "Fulfillment".

As we take the word performance for Business administration, we can define performance as "the accomplishment of a given task with the set standards, precision, quality and completeness".

Popular industrial psychologist Campbell defines Performance as "behaviour of an individual towards the given task".

Job and Performance

Even though Job and Performance are used in many ways, as two different actions or sometimes both together, like "job is performed", "job performance has to be evaluated", it can be considered that when an employee understands and accomplish a given job, he performs, a sort of good job. He improves, involves, fulfills and gets satisfaction when he performs the job, than just doing the job. When we talk about the job of a singer, that is singing, we say "the singer performs". The emphasis being the job artistically done, accomplished with heart and soul involved in the job, may be because he is passionate towards the singing. Hence, the employee in an organisation can also perform the same way, like a singer performs, with involvement and quality improving by every day.

Performance Management

Srinivas Kandula defines performance management as "process of designing and executing motivational strategies, interventions and drivers with an objective to transform the raw potential of human resource into performance".

"Performance Management is a systematic process by an Organisation to improve and evaluate the performance of its employees as individuals as well as groups."

According to Armstrong and Baron (1998), Performance Management is both a strategic and an integrated approach to delivering successful results in organizations by improving the performance and developing the capabilities of teams and individuals.

The term performance management gained its popularity in early 1980's when total quality management programs received utmost importance for achievement of superior standards and quality performance

In broader view, an organisational goal can only be achieved with the people in the organisation aligning their goals to them. The individual's goal often relates to the improvement of skills and knowledge he possess. If the individuals knowledge and skills can be improved through motivation or training or any other methods, the organisational performance increases and easier to attain the goal. The tough task is to make the employee understand the needs of his own self. A successful performance management is:

- Where the employee's interests are understood by the employer and renders his helping hand to develop employee's career as well as his performance and
- The employee understanding the requirements of the organisation, cooperating and accepting the helping hand of employer to increase his performance levels and thus also his self.

Performance management involves much more than just assigning ratings. It is a continuous cycle that involves:

- **Planning** work in advance so that expectations and goals can be set;
- **Monitoring** progress and performance continually;
- **Developing** the employee's ability to perform through training and work assignments;
- **Rating** periodically to summarize performance and,
- **Rewarding** good performance.

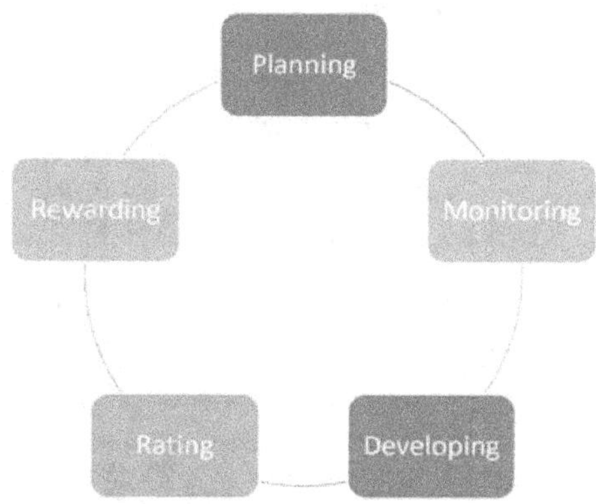

SCOPE OF PERFORMANCE MANAGEMENT

Employees are the most significant resource of an organisation. Performance management is the mirror that shows the commitment of the human capital to the organisation and to their assigned task. This system not only show case the individual performance of the organisation, but it is also a tool to measure the developing steps of the organisation as a whole towards its missions.

The Scope of the Performance Management Includes the Following

- Providing employees a better understanding of their role and responsibilities
- Increase the confidence of the employees through recognizing their strengths
- Identifying training needs to overcome the weak areas
- Improve the relationships in the working areas
- Improve communication between superior and subordinates
- Improve teams and team spirit
- Improve commitment

- Succession planning through grooming subordinates to future managers Providing space for personal reflections
- Providing a platform for personal development
- Providing assistance to achieve personal career goals
- Providing a better work environment and work place
- Providing counseling to make work life balance
- Improving the overall organisational work culture
- Creating qualitative work environment

MEANING OF PERFORMANCE APPRAISAL

Performance Appraisal (PA) refers to all those procedures that are used to evaluate the personality, performance, and potential, of its individual & group members.

Performance Appraisal is a method of evaluating the behavior of employees in the work spot including both quantitative & qualitative aspects of job performance

Performance appraisals are widely used in the society. The history of performance appraisal can be dated back to the 20th century and then to the second world war when the merit rating was used for the first time. An employer evaluating their employees is a very old concept. Performance appraisals are an indispensable part of performance measurement.

Performance appraisal is necessary to measure the performance of the employees and the organization to check the progress towards the desired goals and aims. Performance appraisal takes into account the past performance of the employees and focuses on the improvement of the future performance of the employees.

Performance appraisal helps to rate the performance of the employees and evaluate their contribution towards the organizational goals. If the process of performance appraisals is formal and properly structured, it helps the employees to clearly understand their roles and responsibilities and give direction to the individual's performance. It helps to align the individual performances with the organizational goals and also review their performance.

The first step in the process of performance appraisal is the setting up of the standards which will be used to as the base to compare the actual performance of the employees. This step requires setting the criteria to judge the performance of the employees as successful or unsuccessful and the degrees of their contribution to the organizational goals and objectives. The standards set should be clear, easily understandable and in measurable terms. In case the performance of the employee cannot be measured, great care should be taken to describe the standards.

Who will Appraise?

- Supervisors
- Peers
- Subordinates
- Self-appraisal
- Consultants

5.2.   PROCESS OF PERFORMANCE APPRAISAL

- **Establishing Performance Standards**

The first step in the process of performance appraisal is the setting up of the standards which will be used to as the base to compare the actual performance of the employees. This step requires setting the criteria to judge the performance of the employees as successful or unsuccessful and the degrees of their contribution to the organizational goals and objectives. The standards set should be clear, easily understandable and in measurable terms. In case the performance of the employee cannot be measured, great care should be taken to describe the standards.

- **Communicating the Standards**

Once set, it is the responsibility of the management to communicate the standards to all the employees of the organization.

The employees should be informed and the standards should be clearly explained to them. This will help them to understand their roles and to know what exactly is expected from them. The standards should also be communicated to the appraisers or the evaluators and if required, the standards can also be modified at this stage itself according to the relevant feedback from the employees or the evaluators.

- **Measuring the Actual Performance**

The most difficult part of the Performance appraisal process is measuring the actual performance of the employees that is the work done by the employees during the specified period of time. It is a continuous process which involves monitoring the performance throughout the year. This stage requires the careful selection of the appropriate techniques of measurement, taking care that personal bias does not affect the outcome of the process and providing assistance rather than interfering in an employees work.

- **Comparing the Actual with the Desired Performance**

The actual performance is compared with the desired or the standard performance. The comparison tells the deviations in the performance of the employees from the standards set. The result can show the actual performance being more than the desired performance or, the actual performance being less than the desired performance depicting a negative deviation in the organizational performance. It includes recalling, evaluating and analysis of data related to the employees' performance.

- **Discussing Results**

The result of the appraisal is communicated and discussed with the employees on one-to-one basis. The focus of this discussion is on communication and listening. The results, the problems and the possible solutions are discussed with the aim of problem solving and reaching consensus. The feedback should be given with a positive attitude as this can have an effect on the employees' future performance. The purpose of the meeting should be to solve the problems faced and motivate the employees to perform better.

- **Decision Making**

The last step of the process is to take decisions which can be taken either to improve the performance of the employees, take the required corrective actions, or the related HR decisions like rewards, promotions, demotions, transfers etc. Performance Appraisal is being practiced in 90% of the organizations worldwide. Self-appraisal and potential appraisal also form a part of the performance appraisal processes.

Purpose of Performance Appraisal

- To review the performance of the employees over a given period of time.
- To judge the gap between the actual and the desired performance.
- To help the management in exercising organizational control. To diagnose the training and development needs of the future.
- Provide information to assist in the HR decisions like promotions, transfers etc.
- Provide clarity of the expectations and responsibilities of the functions to be performed by the employees.
- To judge the effectiveness of the other human resource functions of the organization such as recruitment, selection, training and development.
- To reduce the grievances of the employees. Helps to strengthen the relationship and communication between superior – subordinates and management – employees.

CHALLENGES OF PERFORMANCE APPRAISAL

An organization comes across various problems and challenges Of Performance Appraisal in order to make a performance appraisal system effective and successful. The main Performance Appraisal challenges involved in the performance appraisal process are:

- **Determining the evaluation criteria:** Identification of the appraisal criteria is one of the biggest problems faced by the top management. The performance data to be considered for evaluation should be carefully selected. For the purpose of evaluation, the criteria selected should be in quantifiable or measurable terms

- **Create a rating instrument:** The purpose of the Performance appraisal process is to judge the performance of the employees rather than the employee. The focus of the system should be on the development of the employees of the organization.

- **Lack of competence:** Top management should choose the raters or the evaluators carefully. They should have the required expertise and the knowledge to decide the criteria accurately. They should have the experience and the necessary training to carry out the appraisal process objectively.

- **Errors in rating and evaluation:** Many errors based on the personal bias like stereotyping, halo effect (i.e. one trait influencing the evaluator's rating for all other traits) etc. may creep in the appraisal process. Therefore the rater should exercise objectivity and fairness in evaluating and rating the performance of the employees.

- **Resistance:** The appraisal process may face resistance from the employees and the trade unions for the fear of negative ratings. Therefore, the employees should be communicated and clearly explained the purpose as well the process of appraisal. The standards should be clearly communicated and every employee should be made aware that what exactly is expected from him/her.

5.3. METHODS OF PERFORMANCE APPRAISAL

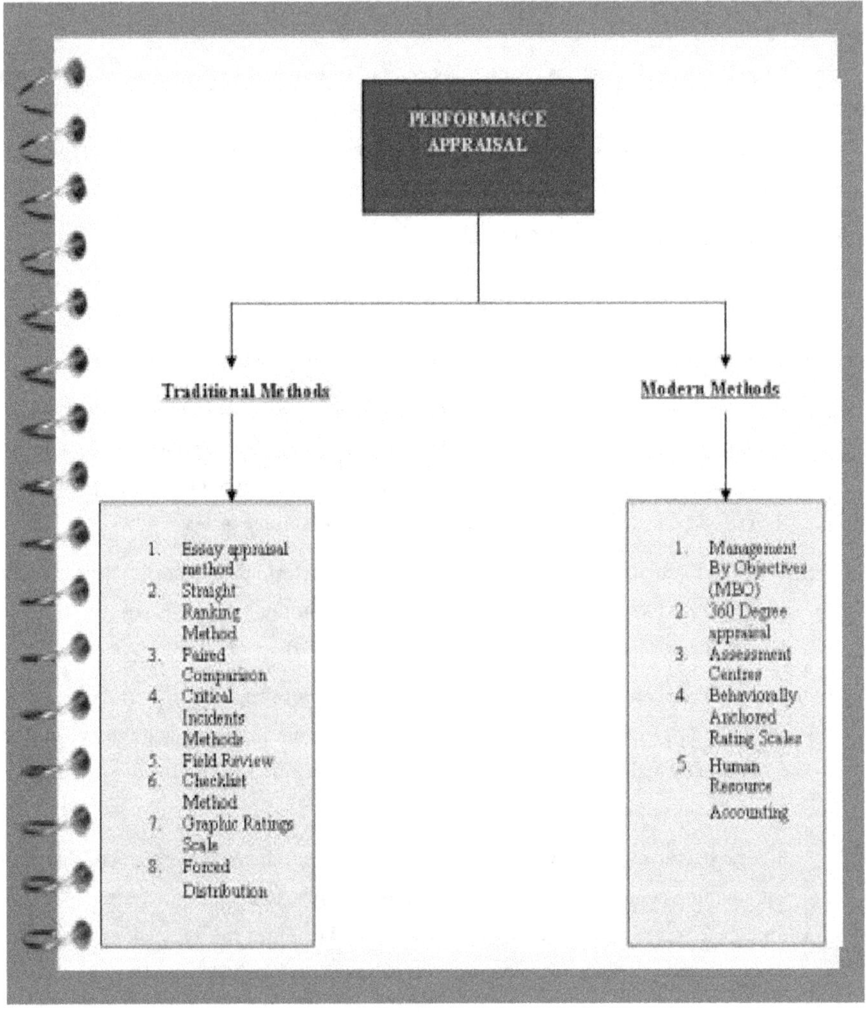

TRADITIONAL METHODS OF PERFORMANCE APPRAISAL

1. Essay Appraisal Method

This traditional form of appraisal, also known as "Free Form method" involves a description of the performance of an employee by his superior. The description is an evaluation of the performance of any individual based on the facts and often includes examples and evidences to support the information. A major drawback of the method is the inseparability of the bias of the evaluator.

2. Straight Ranking Method

This is one of the oldest and simplest techniques of performance appraisal. In this method, the appraiser ranks the employees from the best to the poorest on the basis of their overall performance. It is quite useful for a comparative evaluation.

3. Paired Comparison

A better technique of comparison than the straight ranking method, this method compares each employee with all others in the group, one at a time. After all the comparisons on the basis of the overall comparisons, the employees are given the final rankings.

4. Critical Incidents Methods

In this method of Performance appraisal, the evaluator rates the employee on the basis of critical events and how the employee behaved during those incidents. It includes both negative and positive points. The drawback of this method is that the supervisor has to note down the critical incidents and the employee behaviour as and when they occur.

5. Field Review

In this method, a senior member of the HR department or a training officer discusses and interviews the supervisors to evaluate and rate their respective subordinates. A major drawback of this method is that it is a very time consuming method. But this method helps to reduce the superiors' personal bias.

6. Checklist Method

The rate is given a checklist of the descriptions of the behaviour of the employees on job. The checklist contains a list of statements on the basis of which the rater describes the on the job performance of the employees.

7. Graphic Rating Scale

In this method, an employee's quality and quantity of work is assessed in a graphic scale indicating different degrees of a particular trait. The factors taken into consideration include both the personal characteristics and characteristics related to the on the job performance of the employees. For example a trait like Job Knowledge may be judged on the range of average, above average, outstanding or unsatisfactory.

8. Forced Choice Distribution

To eliminate the element of bias from the rater's ratings, the evaluator is asked to distribute the employees in some fixed categories of ratings like on a normal distribution curve. The rater chooses the appropriate fit for the categories on his own discretion.

9. Essay Method

A trait approach to performance appraisal that requires the rater to compose a statement describing employee behavior.

- Write a Behavioral Statement
- Strengths versus Weaknesses
- Describe Selected Traits
- Evaluate Performance

    Advantages ↔ Disadvantages

MODERN METHODS OF PERFORMANCE APPRAISAL

ASSESSMENT CENTERS

An assessment center typically involves the use of methods like social/informal events, tests and exercises, assignments being given to a group of employees to assess their competencies to take higher responsibilities in the future. Generally, employees are given an assignment similar to the job they would be expected to perform if promoted. The trained evaluators observe and evaluate employees as they perform the assigned jobs and are evaluated on job related characteristics.

The major competencies that are judged in assessment centers are interpersonal skills, intellectual capability, planning and organizing capabilities, motivation, career orientation etc. assessment centers are also an effective way to determine the training and development needs of the targeted employees.

BEHAVIORALLY ANCHORED RATING SCALES

Behaviorally Anchored Rating Scales (BARS) is a relatively new technique which combines the graphic rating scale and critical incidents method. It consists of predetermined critical areas of job performance or sets of behavioral statements describing important job performance qualities as good or bad (for eg. the qualities like inter personal relationships, adaptability and reliability, job knowledge etc). These statements are developed from critical incidents.

In this method, an employee's actual job behaviour is judged against the desired behaviour by recording and comparing the behaviour with BARS. Developing and practicing BARS requires expert knowledge.

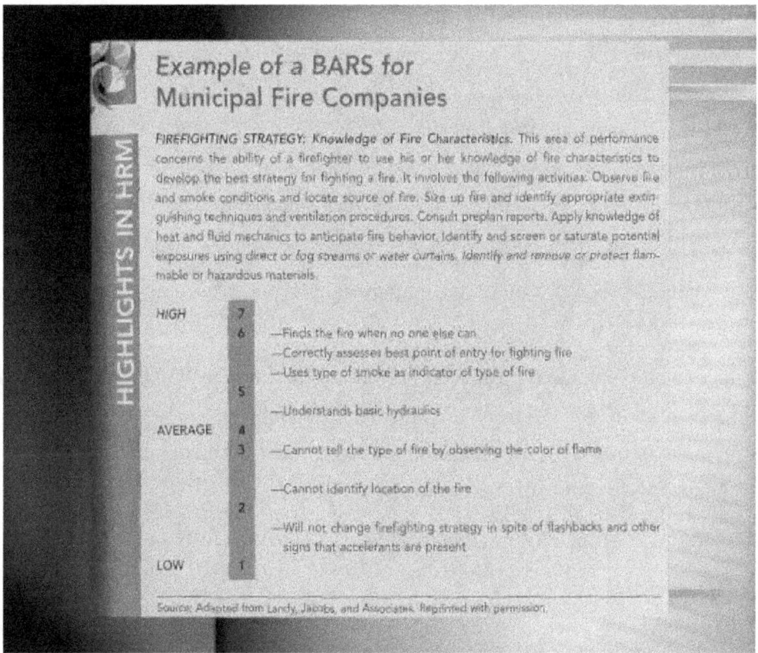

HUMAN RESOURCE ACCOUNTING METHOD

Human resources are valuable assets for every organization. Human resource accounting method tries to find the relative worth of these assets in the terms of money. In this method the Performance appraisal of the employees is judged in terms of cost and contribution of the employees. The cost of employees include all the expenses incurred on them like their compensation, recruitment and selection costs, induction and training costs etc whereas their contribution includes the total value added (in monetary terms). The difference between the cost and the contribution will be the performance of the employees. Ideally, the contribution of the employees should be greater than the cost incurred on them.

360 DEGREE PERFORMANCE APPRAISALS

Most organizations that focus on employee development use the 360-degree tool to assess performance and potential of staff and enable the employees to map their career path based on the feedback. Organizations take 360-degree feedback about an employee before taking a major decision about the professional's career.

The results from 360-degree feedback are often used by the person receiving the feedback to plan training and development. Results are also used by some organizations in making administrative decisions, such as pay or promotion. When this is the case, the 360 assessment is for evaluation purposes, and is sometimes called a "360-degree review."360 degree feedback is the most comprehensive appraisal where the feedback about the employees' performance comes from all the sources that come in contact with the employee on his job. This method is being used in the (MARUTHI SUZUKI Motors and HCL).

360 degree feedback, also known as 'multi-rater feedback', is the most comprehensive appraisal where the feedback about the employees' performance comes from all the sources that come in contact with the employee on his job.

360 degree respondents for an employee can be his/her peers, managers (i.e. superior), subordinates, team members, customers, suppliers/ vendors - anyone who comes into contact with the employee and can provide valuable insights and information or feedback regarding the "on-the-job" performance of the employee.

360 DEGREE APPRAISAL HAS FOUR INTEGRAL COMPONENTS

    i.   Self appraisal
    ii.   Superior's appraisal
    iii. Subordinate's appraisal
    iv.   Peer appraisal.

SELF APPRAISAL gives a chance to the employee to look at his/her strengths and weaknesses, his achievements, and judge his own performance. Superior's appraisal forms the traditional part of the 360 degree performance appraisal where the employees' responsibilities and actual performance is rated by the superior.

SUBORDINATES APPRAISAL gives a chance to judge the employee on the parameters like communication and motivating abilities, superior's ability to delegate the work, leadership qualities etc. Also known as internal customers, the correct feedback given by peers can help to find employees' abilities to work in a team, co-operation and sensitivity towards others.

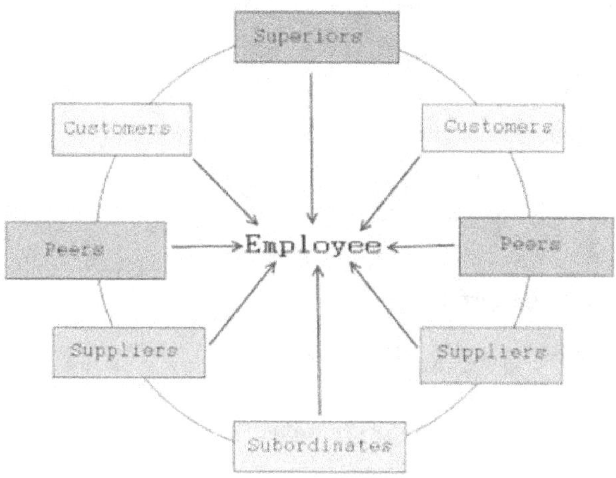

Subordinates appraisal gives a chance to judge the employee on the parameters like communication and motivating abilities, superior's ability to delegate the work, leadership qualities etc. Also known as internal customers, the correct feedback given by peers can help to find employees' abilities to work in a team, co-operation and sensitivity towards others.

Self-Assessment is an indispensable part of 360 degree appraisals and therefore 360 degree Performance appraisal have high employee involvement and also have the strongest impact on behavior and performance. It provides a "360-degree review" of the employees' performance and is considered to be one of the most credible performance appraisal methods.

360 degree performance appraisal is also a powerful developmental tool because when conducted at regular intervals (say yearly) it helps to keep a track of the changes others' perceptions about the employees.

A 360 degree appraisal is generally found more suitable for the managers as it helps to assess their leadership and managing styles. This technique is being effectively used across the globe for performance appraisals. Some of the organizations following it are Wipro, Infosys, and Reliance Industries etc.

MANAGEMENT BY OBJECTIVES

The concept of 'Management by Objectives' (MBO) was first given by Peter Drucker in 1954. It can be defined as a process whereby the employees and the superiors come together to identify common goals, the employees set their goals to be achieved, the standards to be taken as the criteria for measurement of their performance and contribution and deciding the course of action to be followed.

The essence of MBO is participative goal setting, choosing course of actions and decision making. An important part of the MBO is the measurement and the comparison of the employee's actual performance with the standards set. Ideally, when employees themselves have been involved with the goal setting and the choosing the course of action to be followed by them, they are more likely to fulfill their responsibilities.

BALANCE SCORECARD METHOD

The balanced scorecard provides a list of measures that balance the organizations internal and process measures with results, achievements and financial measures. The two basic features of the balanced scorecard are: A balanced set of measures based on. The four perspectives of balanced scorecard. Linking the measures to Employee Performance.

The four Perspectives recommended by Kaplan and Norton for the managers to collect information are:

- **The financial measures** – The financial measures include the results like profits, increase in the market share, return on investments and other economic measures as a result of the actions taken.

- **The customers' measures** - These measures help to get on customer satisfaction, the customer's perspective about the organisation, customer loyalty, acquiring new customers. The data can be collected from the frequency and number of customer complaints, the time taken to deliver the products and services, improvement in quality etc.

- **The internal business measures** – These are the measures related to the organization's internal processes which help to achieve the customer satisfaction. It includes the infrastructure, the long term and short term goals and objectives, organisational processes and procedures, systems and the human resources.

- **The innovation and learning perspective** - The innovation and learning measures cover the organization's ability to learn, innovate and improve. They can be judged by employee skills matrix, key competencies, value added and the revenue per employee.

TEAM PERFORMANCE APPRAISAL

According to a wall street journal headline, "Teams have become commonplace in U.S. Companies". Most of the performance appraisal techniques are formulated with individuals in mind i.e. to measure and rate the performance of the individual employee. Therefore, with the number of teams increasing in the organisations, it becomes difficult to measure and appraise the performance of the team.

The question is how to separate the performance of the team from the performance of the employees. A solution to this problem that is being adopted by the companies is to measure both the individual and the team performance. Sometimes, team based objectives are also included in the individual performance plans.

Rank and Yank Strategy

Also known as the "Up or out policy", the rank and yank strategy refers to the performance appraisal model in which best-to-worst ranking methods are used to identify and separate the poor performers from the good performers. Then the action plans and the improvement opportunities of the poor performers are discussed and they are given to improve their performance in a given time period, after which the appropriate HR decisions are taken. Some of the organisations following this strategy are Ford, Microsoft and Sun Microsystems.

APPRAISAL INTERVIEW

Appraisal Interview, also called as Feedback interview is a discussion between the supervisor and the employee concerning the employees past performance and how that performance can be improved in the future.

The reasons for this interview are to encourage to improve performance. To tell what is expected from them and helps to plan future performance improvement

Types of Appraisal Interview

1. Tell and Sell approach
2. Tell and Listen approach
3. Problem Solving Interview

Factors that distorts Appraisal

- **Leniency/ Strictness error**: Performance-rating error in which the appraiser tends to give employees either unusually high or unusually low ratings.

- **Central tendency error** : Performance-rating error in which all employees are rated about average
- **Regency error :** Performance-rating error in which the appraisal is based largely on the employee's most recent behavior rather than on behavior throughout the appraisal period
- **Halo error:** Encourage Frequent Evaluation and job rating is excellent on all factors.

SELF-APPRAISAL FORM

Self-appraisal is the self-evaluation where the employee himself gives the feedback or his views and points regarding his performance.

The employee himself critically analyses the performance, his strengths, weaknesses, accomplishments, problems faced, the training and development needs (if any) etc.

The self-appraisal form generally starts with the employee details like:

- The name of the employee
- Designation
- Date of joining
- Date of last appraisal
- Department
- Reporting officer

The next section is, commonly, designed to gather the information from the employee regarding his on-the-job performance and his responsibilities:

The Current Responsibilities Held by the Employee

- Accomplishments
- Goals for the next appraisal period
- Areas for improvement
- Training requirements felt for the present job
- Responsibilities the employee would like to add to his current responsibilities
- Problems faced
- Solutions tried
- Measures taken for personal and professional development
- Best and worst aspects of the job
- Is the superior supportive?

The form also includes a section where the employee rates himself on various behavioral parameters like

- Communication skills
- Inter-personal skills
- Problem-solving
- Team work
- Adaptability/Flexibility
- Initiative
- Decision Making
- Leadership
- Maturity

The self-appraisal form also includes a section where the employee can quote examples and incidents to support his ratings and answers. The self-appraisal form generally ends with a subjective section asking for suggestions and the choice of discussing any other topic that the employee feels the need to raise and discuss.

ADVANTAGES OF 360 DEGREE APPRAISALS

- Offer a more comprehensive view towards the performance of employees.
- Improve credibility of performance appraisal.
- Such colleague's feedback will help strengthen self-development.
- Increases responsibilities of employees to their customers.
- The mix of ideas can give a more accurate assessment.
- Opinions gathered from lots of staff are sure to be more persuasive.
- Not only manager should make assessments on its staff performance but other colleagues should do, too.
- People who undervalue themselves are often motivated by feedback from others.
- If more staff takes part in the process of performance appraisal, the organizational culture of the company will become more honest.

DISADVANTAGES OF 360 DEGREE APPRAISAL

- Taking a lot of time, and being complex in administration
- Extension of exchange feedback can cause troubles and tensions to several staff.

Limitations of Performance Appraisal: The main problems involved in performance appraisal are as follows:

Errors in Rating: Performance appraisal may not be valid indicator of performance and potential of employees due to the following types of errors:

- **Halo Effect:** It is the tendency to rate an employee consistently high or low on the basis of overall impression. One trait of the employee influences the rated appraisal on all other traits. For example, an employee may be rated high on performance just because he sits on the job late in the evening. Similarly, a person who does not shave regularly may be considered lazy at work and may be underrated. This error may be minimised by rating all the employees on one trait before taking up another trait.

- **Stereotyping:** This implies forming a mental picture of a person on the basis of his age, sex, caste or religion. It results in an over-simplified view and blurs the assessment of job performance.

- **Central Tendency:** It means assigning average ratings to all the employees in order to avoid commitment or involvement. This is adopted because the rater has not to justify or clarify the average ratings. As a result, the ratings are clustered around the midpoint.

- **Constant Error:** Some evaluators tend to be lenient while others are strict in assessing performance. In the first case, performance is overrated (leniency error) while in the second type it is underrated (strictness error). This tendency may be avoided by holding meetings so that the rates understand what is required of them.

- **Personal Bias:** Performance appraisal may become invalid because the rater dislikes an employee. Such bias or prejudice may arise on the basis of regional or religious beliefs and habits or interpersonal conflicts. Bias may also be the result of time. Recent experience or first impression of the rate may affect the evaluation.

- **Spill over Effect:** This arises when past performance affects assessment of present performance. For instance, recent behaviour or performance of an employee may be used to judge him. This is called regency.

- **Lack of Reliability:** Reliability implies stability and consistency in the measurement. Lack of consistency over time and among different rates may reduce the reliability of performance appraisal. Inconsistent use of measuring standards and lack of training in appraisal techniques may also reduce reliability. Different qualities may not be given proper weight age. Factors like initiative are highly subjective and cannot be quantified.

- **Incompetence:** Rates may fail to evaluate performance accurately due to lack of knowledge and experience. Post appraisal interview is often handled ineffectively

5.4.   JOB CHANGES

Reasons for Job Change

There are many deeply personal reasons to change employment situation. However, from a purely strategic point of view, there are four good reasons to change jobs.

- Changing jobs gives a broader base of experience.
- A more varied background creates a greater demand for the skills. Depth of experience means the employee is more valuable to a larger number of employers.
- A job change results in an accelerated promotion cycle. Many people view a job change as a way of promoting themselves to a better position.
- More responsibility leads to greater earning power.
- Dissatisfaction with a current employer, either in terms of recognition, prospects or pay.
- Midlife career changes might be the result of a sort of career midlife crisis. This can particularly be so for someone who has always done the same job, and suddenly realize their years are slipping away and they have really done very little with their working years.
- Boredom is a common cause of wanting a career change.
- Lack of fulfilment in the current career or employment.

You can easily say that you are looking for a change in role and wanted more growth, or even that your position was getting stagnant. This might be an acceptable reason for quitting your job, but this by no means gives you leeway to criticize your job.

- **Your career path:** One reason is basic dissatisfaction with your career. Remember that it is not about the particular company or the department, but your career on the whole. This reason would hold true if you have a rich career profile and are currently applying for a job in a new profession.
- **Looking for challenges:** One of the most common and simple reasons is that your job was at a standstill and you wished to seek newer avenues and greater challenges.
- **Restructuring:** Another common reason nowadays is company restructuring. When a company restructures, it can lay off several people, and in a timeframe. Therefore, even if you have not been directly told to go, nobody would blame you if you are

looking for avenues because your colleagues or some other department has been told to go.

- **Relocation:** More often than not, relocation is another reason that is blindly accepted by a company as a reason for looking for another job.While these are just some of the traditional reasons for a job change, there are some reasons that are more or less accepted today.

- **Enhanced Education:** Another reason that can be provided is enhancement of abilities and education. If you have recently acquired a degree and have decided to utilize your education to enhance your professional profile, this would be a good reason to give for this question.

- **Workplace distance:** Sometimes, even reasons related to daily commutation, like spending too much time commuting from your place of work to your place of residence, as well as less time spent with family can be considered to be the reason/one of the reasons for leaving a job.

5.5. PROMOTION

A promotion is the advancement of an employee's rank or position in an organizational hierarchy system. Promotion may be an employee's reward for good performance i.e. positive appraisal.

Promotion is defined as giving higher position to the employee, which carries high status more responsibilities and higher status. Promotion means advancement of employee in terms of pay and status also improvement in working conditions. Before a company promotes an employee to a particular position it ensures that the person is able to handle the added responsibilities by screening the employee with interviews and tests and giving them training or on-the-job experience. A promotion can involve advancement in terms of designation, salary and benefits, and in some organizations the type of job activities may change a great deal. The opposite of a promotion is a demotion.

DEFINITIONS OF PROMOTION

According to Scott and Spreigal: "A promotion is the transfer an employee to a job that pays more money or that enjoys some preferred status.

According Edwin.B. Flippo: "A promotion involves a change from one to another that is better in terms of status and responsibility

Purpose of Promotion

- To put the employee in a position where he will be of greater value to the company. This will imply, utilizing the employee skills and knowledge at the appropriate level in the organization hierarchy resulting in organizational effectiveness and satisfaction.
- To develop competitive spirit and zeal in the employees to acquire the skill and knowledge etc. required by higher level jobs.
- To develop internal source of employees ready to take jobs at higher levels in the organization.
- To promote employee self-development and make them await their turn of promotions. It reduce labour turnover.
- To build loyalty among employees and to boost their morale.
- To reward committed, loyal and deserving employees.
- To create atmosphere among employees with their present working conditions and encourage them to succeed in the company

Promotion Policy

1. The promotion policy should be in writing and must be understood by all employees to avoid any suspicion regarding line of promotion in the minds of employees.
2. Promotion programs should be closely allied to training programs; which enables the employees to improve themselves for promotion.

TYPES OF PROMOTIONS

1. **Horizontal promotion:** When an employee is shifted in the same category, it is called 'horizontal promotion'. Eg. A junior clerk promoted to senior clerk is an example.
2. **Vertical Promotion:** This is the kind of promotion when an employee is promoted from a lower category to lower category involving increase in salary, status, authority and responsibility.
3. **Dry Promotion:** When promotion is made without increase in salary, it is called 'dry promotion'. Eg. A lower level manager is promoted to senior level manager without increase in salary or pay.

Advantages of Promotion

Present employees if promoted can handle the process products and problems easily as they are already connected to organization but new incumbent may take some to adjust him or may not adjust himself at all.

The cost of training the insiders for the higher position is nearly nil hence no extra training cost. Employees will give their best as they know that reward of giving good performance is sure. High morale of the employees is achieved.

Promotions are used to fill the positions which are more important to fill rather than the present position of employee. It can be filled by external recruitment but employees having eligibility and experience must be appointed for their motivation. Also it will decrease labour turn over as external recruitment costs more. Also increase in salary and status will increase job satisfaction. When scale of pay is increased without changing job it is called up-gradation and promotion involves changes in job as well as high salary.

When higher position is given without change in salary it is known as Dry Promotion.

All these, Promotion Up-Gradation and Dry Promotion are used by management to increase morale of employee and as giving reward also.

Following are the principles of promotion, which are followed as alternatives or in combination.

1. Principle of Seniority
2. Merit Principle
3. Seniority-cum-Merit Principle

Seniority Principle

Seniority means length of service in a particular post or scale or grade. It is a very simple principle. The length of service or seniority is the sole basis in making promotions. According to it, one who has longer length of service must get the promotion. The senior most person is eligible for promotion first. A seniority list can be prepared and order of precedence can be decided according to experience and age. The principle of seniority is very simple to apply. It is most objective. It leaves no scope for favouritism or nepotism. It gives respect to age and experience. It is in accordance with the established practices in society. A younger person does not become a boss of the older and more experienced persons. It is more democratic because it gives a chance of promotion to everybody irrespective of merit. Everybody cannot become meritorious but everybody is bound to become senior with the passage of time. It is safe for every employee and, therefore, seniority principle is readily accepted by the staff as against the merit principle.

But principle of seniority has many drawbacks. Those who are senior are not necessarily fit for promotion. Mere length of service is not a criterion of fitness. Experience is gained by a person in the first few years of service, but afterwards his experience does not increase indefinitely with the length of service. It is said that ten years' experience is nothing but one year's experience repeated ten times. Seniority and experience are, therefore, not a rational criteria. All persons in a grade are not fit for promotion. Promotions are few and, therefore, all persons cannot get promotions. Seniority does not necessarily coincide with age.

Principle of Merit: Principle of merit is contrary to the principle of seniority. This principle implies that the most meritorious, best qualified and most competent person must be selected for promotion to the higher post. In the civil service higher position means more powers and responsibilities and it requires more competent and hard .working persons. Therefore, those who have merit and qualifications must be promoted to higher positions. Merit, therefore, must be the sole criterion for promotion.

The principle of merit is accepted becau3e able and competent persons only deserve promotions and incompetent persons should be left behind. At higher required. The merit principle selects the most suitable person for promotion. Energy, initiative and hard work are rewarded by merit principle. n is increases efficiency and competitive spirit in the administration. It motivates the employees at the lower levels to work hard and take interest in their work.

Practical Combination of Seniority and Merit Principles

We have seen that both the principles of seniority and of merit have some advantages as well as drawbacks. In practice, therefore, a third method is adopted where the seniority and merit principles are combined for making promotions.

For example, a minimum lengthy years of service (seniority) is fixed and then the fittest and meritorious person amongst those who possess that minimum experience, is selected for promotion. This means the 'fittest amongst the seniors' is selected for promotions. Another way of combining these two principles is that he minimum qualification and competence is tested and then all other things being equal the senior most of them is preferred for promotion. This means the "senior most amongst the meritorious" persons is selected.

It is observed that in most of the countries including India, the general pattern of promotion is based on the following lines:

a. Promotions to the higher posts are made on the basis of merit principle only.

b. Promotion to middle level posts are made on the basis of seniority-cum-merit principle

c. Promotions to lower level posts, are made on the basis of seniority principle.

Methods of Testing Merit for Promotion

Normally the following three methods are employed for testing the merit for promotion:

1. Written and Oral Examination
2. Efficiency Rating
3. Personal Judgment of the Head of the Organisation.

Demotion

Demotion is just opposite to promotion. In demotion, the employee is shifted to a job lower in status, grade and responsibilities. "Demotion refers to the lowering down of status, salary and responsibility of the employee." It is a type of punishment for serious mistakes or irregularities on the part of the employee. It is a lesser punishment as compared to dismissal.

According Dale Yoder," Demotion is the shift to a position in which responsibilities are decreased. Promotion is, in a sense, an increase in rank and demotion is decrease in rank."

CAUSES OF DEMOTION

- Inadequacy on the part of the employees in terms of job performance, attitude and capability. It happens when an employee finds it difficult to meet job requirement standards, following his promotion.
- Demotion may be used as disciplinary tools against errant employees.
- Due to adverse business conditions
- If there is a mistake in staffing i.e. a person is promoted wrongly.
- Change in technology, method and practices
- Due to ill health or personal reasons

Demotion Policy

Demotion is very harmful for the employees' morale. It is an extremely pain for action, impairing relationships between people permanently. While, effecting demotions, a manager should be extremely careful not to place himself on wrong side of the fence. It is therefore, very necessary to formulate a demotion policy so that there may be no grievance on the part of the trade unions.

Yoder, Heneman and Stone have suggested a fivefold policy in this regard

- A clear list of rules along with punishable offences be made available to all the employees.
- Any violation be investigated thoroughly b a competent authority.

- In case of violations, it is better to state the reasons for taking such a punitive step clearly and elaborately.
- Once violations are proved, there should be a consistent and equitable application of the penalty.
- There should be enough room for the review.

5.6. TRANSFER

Transfer refers to the shifting of employees form one job to another within the same organization where salary, responsibilities and category of the new job and the previous job are almost same. Transfer of an employee can be done in other department of the same plant or office or to the same department of plant or office located in other region/city.

Definition

1. "Transfer is change in job where the new job is substantially the equal to the old in terms of pay status and responsibilities" - **Edwin B.Flippo.**
2. **According to Dale Yoder** "A transfer involves the shifting of an employee from one job to another without special reference to change in responsibilities or compensation". Usually transfer takes place between jobs paying approximately the same salaries. A slight change in responsibilities, duties and pay increase may also take place occasionally.
3. **According to J. Lundy** "A transfer involves a change of job without any significant increase in responsibility or income and a promotion involves a change in which a significant increase in responsibility or income occurs".

REASON/OBJECTIVES FOR TRANSFER

Transfer can be done on the request of employee due to personal reason like family problem or health problem. Due to HR policy which states that one employee can work in department or place for specific time period. Transfers are common in the organizations where the work load varies timely.

If an employee is not able to do the work or job assigned effectively he can be transferred to the other job where he can use his skills properly according to his interest and abilities. Departmental vacancies can be filled with transfer of employees from overstaffed department. Employees can be transferred to the position or department with the higher priority workload.

The Following Factors are Mainly Responsible for Transfer

(a) The demand of manpower in a department may increase or decrease resulting into surpluses or shortage of personnel. If a machine breaks down, its employees will have to be transferred to some other machines in the same department or may be in some other department.

(b) A transfer may be at the request of an employee. It may be on the health grounds, family circumstances, lack of interest in the job etc. A faulty selection procedure may be responsible for such transfers.

(c) Employees may be transferred for imparting training to them.

(d) In certain departments, transfers are made as a policy matter after an employee stays on the job for certain number of years in one area.

(e) Transfers may also be made for increasing efficiency of the employee. A transfer is an important source of internal recruitment.

TYPES OF TRANSFERS

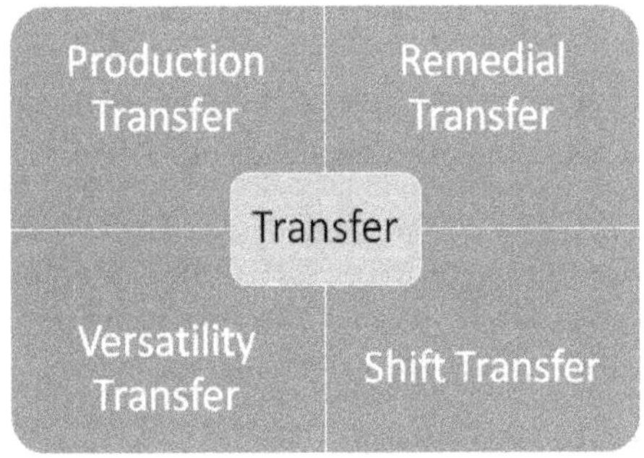

1. **Production Transfer:** When the transfers are being made for filling the position in such departments having lack of staff, from the departments having surplus manpower it is called production transfer. It prevents the layoffs form the organization. Also it is good to adjust existing staff rather than to hire the new one.

2. **Remedial Transfer**: Remedial transfer refers to rectification of wrong selection or placement of employees. If the employee can adjust himself in the given job he can be transferred to the job where he can use his skills and abilities accordingly.

3. **Versatility Transfer:** Such transfers are done to increase the versatility in the employees so that he can work different kind of jobs. This is done by transferring employee to different jobs closely related in same department or process line. This is

used as a training device. It helps employee to develop him and he is equipped for the high responsibility jobs as he is having knowledge of the whole process.

4. **Shift Transfer:** In many multi-shifts jobs such as call centers employees are transferred from one shift to another due to their personal reasons like health problem or evening college for higher studies or any family problems.

5. **Replacement Transfers:** An employee with a long service may be transferred in some other department to replace a person with a shorter service.

6. **Miscellaneous Transfers:** Transfers may also be classified as temporary or permanent transfers. If a transfer is from one department to another, it is known as departmental transfer. If a transfer is made within the department, such a transfer is known as sectional transfer. An employee may be transferred from one plant to another plant. Such a transfer is known as inter-plant transfer.

5.7. EMPLOYEE SEPARATION

Employee Separation is the process of ensuring that an employee who quits the company is exited in a structured and orderly manner. The process of employee separation is taken quite seriously by many firms and there is a dedicated department to handle employee exits from the company. In this article we discuss the process of employee separation and the differences between voluntary and involuntary exits.

An employee separation occurs when an employee ceases to be a member of an organization. Generally, an employee separation describes any event that separates the employer and the employee.

Turnover Rate

The rate of employee separation in an organization, the turnover rate, is a measure of a rate at which employees leave the organization.

Costs & Benefits of Employee Separations

Costs depends on need for replacement

- Recruitment Costs
- Selection Costs
- Training Costs
- Separation Costs
- Severance pay
- Exit interview
- Outplacement Assistance

Benefits

- Reduced Labour Costs
- Replacement of Poor Performers
- Increased Innovation
- Greater Diversity

TYPES OF EMPLOYEE SEPARATION

VOLUNTARY AND INVOLUNTARY SEPARATION

Voluntary Separation

Employee separation can be voluntary as well as involuntary. The former is when the employee quits the company on his or her own accord. This is the most common form of employee separation though in these recessionary times, involuntary separation or the act of asking the employee to leave by management is quite common. This form of employee separation where an employee is asked to quit is called involuntary separation. The difference in these two forms of separation is that for voluntary exits, the employee stands to get most of the benefits and perks due to him or her whereas when an employee is asked to leave, he or she might get a separation package or in instances where disciplinary or performance related exits take place, the employee might not get anything at all.

- Discharges
- Layoffs
- Downsizing
- Rightsizing

Components of the Employee Separation Process

The employee separation process starts from the time the employee gives notice to his or her employer about the intention to quit. This is usually called "putting in one's papers" because in earlier times, an employee was required to submit a formal resignation letter, though in recent times, this is being done by email. Once the employee gives notice, all the financial transactions and records of the employee are "frozen" by the HR department and the employee's manager is tasked with the process of ensuring proper handover and closure of work tasks allotted to the employee. Usually, the notice period ranges from a month to two to three months depending on the level at which the employee is working. Further, there has to be a well-defined handover plan drawn up by the employee's manager that covers all aspects of closing out on the work that the employee is performing.

Participants in the Employee Separation Process

Typically, the employee separation process proceeds along two parallel tracks. One involves the employee and the manager and is concerned with the handover of work and other tasks. The other track is by the separations team and deals with the employee benefits accruing as a result of separation as well as other benefits like PF (Provident Fund), Gratuity (If applicable) etc. The HR manager is needed at all steps of this process and in the final exit interview that is conducted to assess the reasons for the employee leaving the company and taking the employee's views on work and the company in general as well as any "de-motivating" factors that might have caused the employee to resign.

Resignation

An employee may terminate services with the State by submitting a resignation to the appointing authority. Normally, it is expected that an employee will give at least two weeks' notice prior to the last day of work. Unused vacation leave not to exceed 240 hours plus unused bonus leave is paid in a lump sum. Payment shall not be made for unused sick leave. It shall be reinstated if the employee returns within five years or it may be applied toward retirement if eligible to retire within five years.

Voluntary Resignation without Notice

An employee who is absent from work and does not contact the employer for three consecutive scheduled workdays may be separated from employment as a voluntary resignation. A factor to be considered when determining whether the employee should be deemed to have voluntarily resigned is the employee's culpability in failing to contact his or her employer.

Layoff

Layoff implies denial of employment to the employees for the reasons beyond the control of employer. Layoff may be temporary. It may also occur for indefinite time.

Separation Due to Unavailability

An employee may be separated on the basis of unavailability when the employee becomes or remains unavailable for work after all applicable leave credits have been exhausted and agency management does not grant a leave without pay, or does not extend a leave without pay period, for reasons deemed sufficient by the agency. Such reasons include, but are not limited to, lack of suitable temporary assistance, criticality of the position, budgetary constraints, etc. Such a separation is an involuntary separation and not a disciplinary dismissal as described in G.S. 126-35, and may be grieved or appealed.

Reduction in Force

An employee may be reduced in force for reasons of shortage of funds or work, abolishment of a position, or other material changes in duties or organization. Employees may elect, subject to approval by management, to exhaust vacation leave after their last day of work and be paid in a lump sum for the balance not to exceed 240 hours (plus bonus leave). If an employee had over 240 hours of vacation leave at the time of reduction in force, the excess leave shall be reinstated when reemployed within one year.

Employees separated due to reduction-in-force shall be informed that their sick leave shall be reinstated if employed in any agency within five years.

Dismissal

Dismissal is involuntary separation for cause in accordance with the provisions of the policy on Disciplinary Action, Suspension, and Dismissal.

Appointment Ended

An "Appointment Ended" separation occurs when an employee is terminated for reasons other than just cause from one of the following positions:

- Exempt positions appointed by the Governor
- Policy/making positions

Conclusion

In recent years, with the high levels of attrition in the service sector, it has become imperative for firms to have a structured separation plan for orderly exits of employees. Of course, the concept of "pink slips" or involuntary exits are another matter altogether and involve some bitterness that results because of the employee losing his or her job. In conclusion, it is our view that employee separations must be handled in a professional and mature manner and though attrition is a fact

5.8.   EMPLOYEE EMPOWERMENT

Employee Empowerment is creating a working environment where an employee is allowed to make his own decisions in specific work-related situations. The decisions can be big or small, and the size and effect of the decision is up to the employer. The logic behind employee empowerment is to increase the employee's responsibility, to build employee morale and to improve the quality of your employee's work life. Ideally, when an employee feels vested in an organization, he will be more productive, loyal and more confident.

Empowerment can be defined as 'harnessing ordinary people to do extra ordinary performance'. Employee Empowerment is Employee Involvement that matters. It could also be defined as controlled transfer of authority to make decisions and take actions.

- A primary goal of employee empowerment is to give workers a greater voice in decisions about work-related matters.
- Their decision-making authority can range from offering suggestions to exercising veto power over management decisions.
- possible areas include: how jobs are to be performed, working conditions, company policies, work hours, peer review, and how supervisors are evaluated

The Ways of Empowerment

- The employee should be properly   trained, couched and guided to enable them to master the skills required for their job
- The confidence of employees should be raised through persuasion and social reinforcement techniques like appreciation, encouragement and positive feedback.
- The Manager should draw the attention of employees to those who have attained remarkable success in the job so that they can observe the working style of their more successful colleagues and emulate them. Thus they have good role models in their colleagues.
- The Manager should provide the employees with clear definition of their roles, and extend assistance when required so that their stress and anxiety can be reduced.

Benefits of Empowering

Allocation of authority here is "trust based relationship". It enables a person to develop personally & professionally.

- First, empowerment can strengthen motivation by providing employees with the opportunity to attain intrinsic rewards from their work, such as a greater sense of accomplishment and a feeling of importance.
- The second means by which employee empowerment can increase productivity is through better decisions. Especially when decisions require task-specific knowledge, those on the front line can often better identify problems.
- Empowerment Encourages employees to share responsibility and use their initiative to take decision and solve problem.
- Adequate authority and resources are given to employees for taking initiatives and decisions.

An Empowered Situation

1-Encourages participation

2-Improve communication

3-Promote creativity and innovation

4-Create positive attitude and a sense of belongings

Toyota Motor Company empowers some of its employees to identify and help remedy problems occurring during product assembly. An automobile coming off Toyota's assembly line with a paint defect is seen as an opportunity to delve into the root cause of the defect, as opposed to merely fixing the defect and passing it on to distributors for resale.

Guidelines for Effective Empowerment

- Select the right managers.
- Choose the right employees.
- Provide training.
- Offer guidance.
- Hold everyone accountable.
- Build trust.
- Focus on relationships.
- Stress organizational values.
- Transform mistakes into opportunities.
- Reward and recognize.
- Share authority instead of giving it up.
- Encourage dissent.
- Give it time.
- Accept increased turnover.
- Share information.
- Realize that empowerment has its limitations.
- Watch for mixed messages.
- Face your own ambivalence
- Involve employees in decision-making.
- Be prepared for increased variation.

One easy way to begin employee empowerment in the workplace is to install a suggestion box, where workers can make suggestions without fear of punishment or retribution. However, simply placing a suggestion box somewhere is only the first step. Managers must then be willing to read and consider suggestions. They might provide a forum where questions or suggestions receive a response, like a weekly or monthly newsletter. In addition, managers can hold a once monthly meeting open to employees where all suggestions are addressed.

At least some suggestions have to be approved in order for employees to feel that they are having some impact on their company. Failure to approve or implement any suggestions reinforces that all the power belongs to the managers and not the workers. Employee empowerment of any form can only work when managers are willing to be open to new ideas and strategies. If no such willingness exists, employee empowerment is likely to be non-existent.

5.9. CONTROLLING

Controlling generally means comparing the results with standards or benchmarks or regulating something. We understand that controllers develop in accompany the

- Management process of defining goals,
- The planning and controlling of business processes
- And thus share responsibility for achieving entrepreneurial goals.

What is Control?

Controlling is the process of monitoring activities to ensure that they are being accomplished as planned and of correcting any significant deviations.

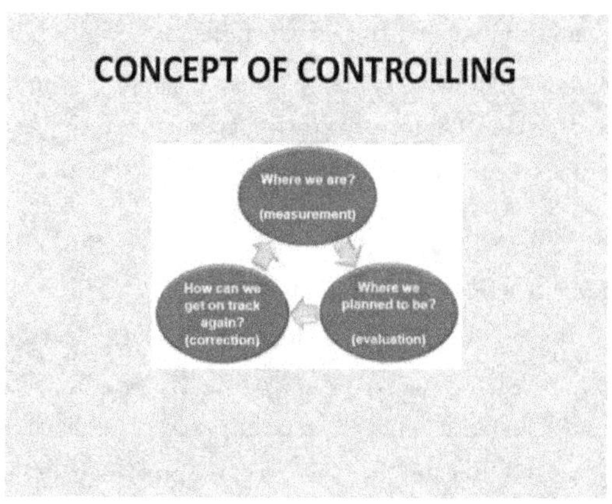

DEFINITIONS

1. Control of an undertaking consists of seeing that everything is being carried out in accordance with the plan which has been adopted, the orders which have been given, and the principles which have been laid down. Its object is to point out mistakes in order that they may be rectified and prevented from recurring **- Henry Fayol**

2. **According to EFL Brech**: Control is checking current performance against pre-determined standards contained in the plans, with a view to ensure adequate progress and satisfactory performance.

3. **According to Harold Koontz**: Controlling is the measurement and correction of performance in order to make sure that enterprise objectives and the plans devised to attain them are accomplished.

Purpose of Controlling

The six major purposes of controls are as follows:

- Controls make plans effective. Managers need to measure progress, offer feedback, and direct their teams if they want to succeed.

- Controls make sure that organizational activities are consistent. Policies and procedures help ensure that efforts are integrated.

- Controls make organizations effective. Organizations need controls in place if they want to achieve and accomplish their objectives.

- Controls make organizations efficient. Efficiency probably depends more on controls than any other management function.

- Controls provide feedback on project status. Not only do they measure progress, but controls also provide feedback to participants as well. Feedback influences behavior and is an essential ingredient in the control process.

- Controls aid in decision making. The ultimate purpose of controls is to help managers make better decisions. Controls make managers aware of problems and give them information that is necessary for decision making.

The Importance of Controlling

1. **Accomplishing Organisational Goals:** The controlling process is implemented to take care of the plans. With the help of controlling, deviations are immediately detected and corrective action is taken. Therefore, the difference between the expected results and the actual results is reduced to the minimum. In this way, controlling is helpful in achieving the goals of the organisation.

2. **Judging Accuracy of Standards:** While performing the function of controlling, a manager compares the actual work performance with the standards. He tries to find out whether the laid down standards are not more or less than the general standards. In case of need, they are redefined.

3. **Making Efficient Use of Resources:** Controlling makes it possible to use human and physical resources efficiently. Under controlling, it is ensured that no employee deliberately delays his work performance. In the same way, wastage in all the physical resources is checked.

4. **Improving Employee Motivation:** Through the medium of controlling, an effort is made to motivate the employees. The implementation of controlling makes all the employees to work with complete dedication because they know that their work performance will be evaluated and if the progress report is satisfactory, they will have their identity established in the organisation.

5. **Ensuring Order and Discipline:** Controlling ensures order and discipline. With its implementation, all the undesirable activities like theft, corruption, delay in work and uncooperative attitude are checked.

6. **Facilitating Coordination in Action:** Coordination among all the departments of the organisation is necessary in order to achieve the organisational objectives successfully. All the departments of the organisation are interdependent. For example, the supply of orders by the sales department depends on the production of goods by the production department.

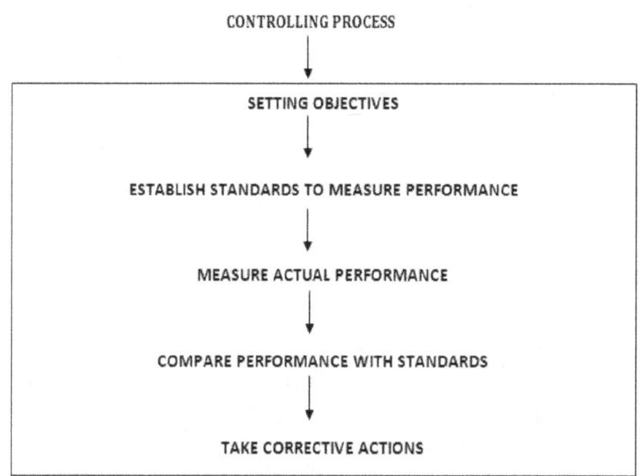

1. **Setting Objectives:** Performance objectives are defined and standards for measuring are set. There are two types of standard input standard and output standard. Input standard measures work efforts that go into performance task. Output standard measures performance results in terms of quantity, quality, time or cost.

2. **Establish standards to measure performance.** Within an organization's overall strategic plan, managers define goals for organizational departments in specific, operational terms that include standards of performance to compare with organizational activities.

3. **Measure actual performance.** Most organizations prepare formal reports of performance measurements that manager's review regularly. These measurements should be related to the standards set in the first step of the control process. For example, if sales growth is a target, the organization should have a means of gathering and reporting sales data.

4. **Compare performance with the standards.** This step compares actual activities to performance standards. When managers read computer reports or walk through their plants, they identify whether actual performance meets, exceeds, or falls short of standards. Typically, performance reports simplify such comparison by placing the performance standards for the reporting period alongside the actual performance for the same period and by computing the variance—that is, the difference between each actual amount and the associated standard.

5. **Take corrective actions.** When performance deviates from standards, managers must determine what changes, if any, are necessary and how to apply them. In the productivity and quality-centered environment, workers and managers are often empowered to evaluate their own work. After the evaluator determines the cause or causes of deviation, he or she can take the fourth step—corrective action. The most effective course may be prescribed by policies or may be best left up to employees' judgment and initiative.

These steps must be repeated periodically until the organizational goal is achieved.

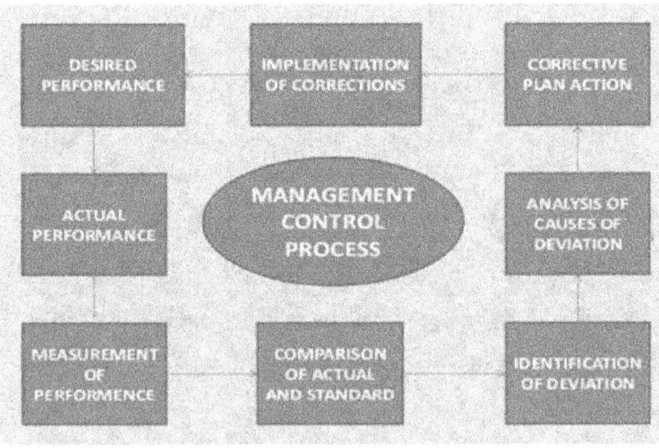

TYPES OF ORGANIZATIONAL CONTROLS

Control can focus on events before, during, or after a process. For example, a local automobile dealer can focus on activities before, during, or after sales of new cars. Careful inspection of new cars and cautious selection of sales employees are ways to ensure high quality or profitable sales even before those sales take place. Monitoring how salespeople act with customers is a control during the sales task. Counting the number of new cars sold during the month and telephoning buyers about their satisfaction with sales transactions are controls after sales have occurred. These types of controls are formally called feed forward, concurrent, and feedback, respectively.

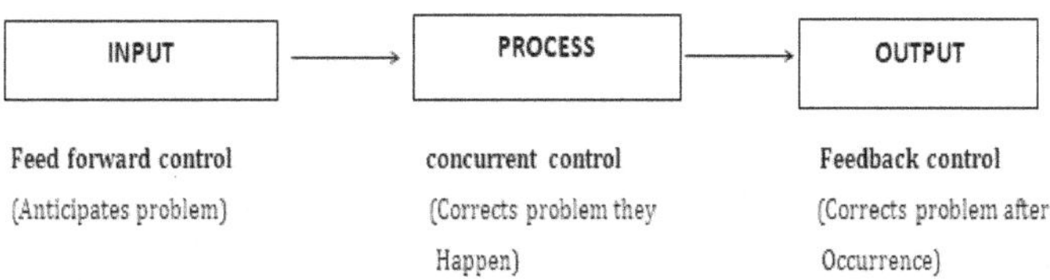

Feed forward Controls sometimes called preliminary or preventive controls, attempt to identify and prevent deviations in the standards before they occur. Feed forward controls focus on human, material, and financial resources within the organization. These controls are evident in the selection and hiring of new employees. For example, organizations attempt to improve the likelihood that employees will perform up to standards by identifying the necessary job skills and by using tests and other screening devices to hire people with those skills.

Concurrent Controls monitor ongoing employee activity to ensure consistency with quality standards. These controls rely on performance standards, rules, and regulations for guiding employee tasks and behaviors. Their purpose is to ensure that work activities produce the desired results. As an example, many manufacturing operations include devices that measure whether the items being produced meet quality standards. Employees monitor the measurements; if they see that standards are not being met in some area, they make a correction themselves or let a manager know that a problem is occurring.

Feedback Controls involve reviewing information to determine whether performance meets established standards. For example, suppose that an organization establishes a goal of increasing its profit by 12 percent next year. To ensure that this goal is reached, the organization must monitor its profit on a monthly basis. After three months, if profit has increased by 3 percent, management might assume that plans are going according to schedule.

EFFECTIVE ORGANISATIONAL CONTROL SYSTEM

The management of any organization must develop a control system tailored to its organization's goals and resources. Effective control systems share several common characteristics. **These characteristics are as follows:**

- A focus on critical points. For example, controls are applied where failure cannot be tolerated or where costs cannot exceed a certain amount. The critical points include all the areas of an organization's operations that directly affect the success of its key operations.
- Integration into established processes. Controls must function harmoniously within these processes and should not bottleneck operations.
- Acceptance by employees. Employee involvement in the design of controls can increase acceptance.
- Availability of information when needed. Deadlines, time needed to complete the project, costs associated with the project, and priority needs are apparent in these criteria. Costs are frequently attributed to time shortcomings or failures.
- Economic feasibility. Effective control systems answer questions such as, "How much does it cost?" "What will it save?" or "What are the returns on the investment?" In short, comparison of the costs to the benefits ensures that the benefits of controls outweigh the costs.
- Accuracy. Effective control systems provide factual information that's useful, reliable, valid, and consistent.
- Comprehensibility. Controls must be simple and easy to understand.

VARIOUS ORGANISATIONAL PERFORMANCE CONTROL SYSTEMS

- Strategy and objectives
- Policies and procedures
- Selection and training
- Performance appraisal
- Job design and work structure
- Performance modelling, norms and organizational culture
- Compensation and benefits to attract talented people and retain them, motivate people to exert maximum effort in their work and recognize the value of their performance contribution.
- Employee discipline (Hot stove rule)

- Information and financial – Activity based costing, Economic value added and understanding the implications of key financial measures (ratios) organizational performance.

- Operations and management control – economic order quantity, just in time, scheduling, project management (PERT & CPM) and statistical quality control.

- Benchmark - a standard of excellence against which to measure and compare. It is a control tool used to identify the performance gaps and area for improvement.

5.10. EMPLOYEE GRIEVANCES

Grievances are raised due to low pay scale than the market rate of pay for the same level. This often brings complaints in written form. Grievances are employee's perception of unfair treatment on the job. It is the feeling of dissatisfaction among the employees in working condition in the organization. The causes of grievances can be management practices, labor union practices, working condition, organization culture, personality traits and interpretation differences

Definitions

According to the Keith Davis," Grievances is any real or image feeling of personal injustice that an employee has abounded the employment personal relationship."

According to the Wendell French," Grievances is a formal complaint filed by an employee following and established grievances procedure."

According to Michael Jucius," A grievance can be any discontent or dissatisfaction, whether expressed or not, whether valid or not, and arising out of anything connected with the company that an employee thinks, believes, or even feels as unfair, unjust, or inequitable."

OBJECTIVES OF MANAGING EMPLOYEE GRIEVANCES

- The Purpose of the Grievance Procedure
- How to Prevent a Grievance
- Grievance Timelines
- Benefits of Early Settlement
- Steps in the Grievance Process
- Preparing for a Grievance
- Conducting the Grievance Meeting
- Preparing the Grievance Response

Grievances are formal complaints presented to management due to the dissatisfied feelings arises during of action. Grievances are simple and complex of both types. Management has to take grievances positively and try to solve them promptly. Effective grievances help to redress the grievance to the mutual satisfaction of both the employees and the managers. It also helps the management to frame policies and procedures acceptable to the employees. It becomes an effective medium for the employees to express feelings, discontent and dissatisfaction openly and formally. Employees' aspect of getting compensation equal to the value of grievances. Management tries to minimize their values. Management should settle grievances promptly otherwise, they take unsolved form, so, it needs scientific way of setting disputes.

Features of Grievance

- A grievance refers to any form of discontent or dissatisfaction with any aspect of the organization.

- The dissatisfaction must arise out of employment and not due to personal or family problems.

- The discontent can arise out of real or imaginary reasons. When employees feel that injustice has been done to them, they have a grievance. The reason for such a feeling may be valid or invalid, legitimate or irrational, justifiable or ridiculous.

- The discontent may be voiced or unvoiced, but it must find expression in some form. However, discontent per se is not a grievance. Initially, the employee may complain orally or in writing. If this is not looked into promptly, the employee feels a sense of lack of justice. Now, the discontent grows and takes the shape of a grievance.

- Broadly speaking, thus, a grievance is traceable to be perceived as non-fulfilment of one's expectations from the organization.

GRIEVANCE IN INDUSTRY

Grievance means any type of dissatisfaction or discontentment's arising out of factors related to an employee's job which he thinks are unfair. A grievance arises when an employee feels that something has happened or is happening to him which he thinks is unfair, unjust or inequitable.

In an organization, a grievance may arise due to several factors such as: Violation of management's responsibility such as poor working conditions. Violation of company's rules and regulations, Violation of labor laws, Violation of natural rules of justice such as unfair treatment in promotion, etc.

Various sources of grievance may be categorized under three heads: (i) Management policies, (ii) Working Conditions, and (Iii) Personal Factors

GRIEVANCE RESULTING FROM MANAGEMENT POLICIES INCLUDE

1. Wage rates
2. Leave policy
3. Overtime
4. Lack of career planning
5. Role conflicts
6. Lack of regard for collective agreement
7. Disparity between skill of worker and job responsibility
8. Grievance resulting from working conditions include:
9. Poor safety and bad physical conditions
10. Unavailability of tools and proper machinery
11. Negative approach to discipline
12. Unrealistic targets
13. Grievance resulting from inter-personal factors include
14. Poor relationships with team members
15. Autocratic leadership style of superiors
16. Poor relations with seniors
17. Conflicts with peers and colleagues.

It is necessary to distinguish a complaint from grievance. A complaint is an indication of employee dissatisfaction that has not been submitted in written. On the other hand, a grievance is a complaint that has been put in writing and made formal.

Grievances are symptoms of conflicts in industry. Therefore, management should be concerned with both complaints and grievances, because both may be important indicators of potential problems within the workforce. Without a grievance procedure, management may be unable to respond to employee concerns since managers are unaware of them. Therefore, a formal grievance procedure is a valuable communication tool for the organization.

CAUSES OF GRIEVANCES

Grievances are the symbol of dissatisfaction of employees. There are different causes of dissatisfaction on the job like improper working condition, irrational management policies and violation of organizational rules, regulation and practices that result in grievances.

They are Caused Due to the Misleading of Following Factors

Remuneration

Remuneration is a major reason of grievances. It comprises salary and wages. Salary differences in the same level and weight of job cause grievances. False method of determining salary, the rate of pay lower than market rate etc are reasons for rising grievances. Management should positive regarding such reason for grievances.

Organizational culture: Key reason of grievances is organizational culture. Trends, norms, values, attitudes are included in culture. Organizational culture should be acceptable to all the aspects of organizational. So, organizational culture is to be developed in such a way that they can be adjusted in the organizational environment. If cultural differences cannot match the organizational culture then grievances increase from employees.

The Difference in Understanding

Difference in understanding in between employees and management leads to disputes. There are different terms and condition of workers at the time of appointment. Such terms and conditions may not fulfill. They are remuneration, fringe, benefits, appointment and others. Difference in understanding of those terms and conditions in between labor union or worker and management are causes of grievances. So, management should keep the record of them for recall time and again.

Working Condition

Working condition is environment aspects of job location. It must be comfortable and favorable to employees that support performance efficiency. Unhealthy environment, darkness, noise, inadequacy of resources are reasons for employee's grievances under working condition. It is sports grievances. So, management should be highly careful on this issue.

Fringe Benefits

Basic pay is compulsory to be paid. Organizations should provide others extra pay as an incentive are fringe benefits. They are direct or indirect in nature. Social security, medicine, insurance, gratuity plan, holidays etc. are benefits. Provision of them satisfies employees. Reduction or no increment of such benefits causes grievances. Employees take such benefits as their right when once provided. So, its management must be scientific.

Trade Union

Group of employees who have similar interests and thoughts, so formed for the protection and promotion of their mutual interest are called trade unions. Employees who are associated with union are politically instructed. They present their own views for their own sake. Trade unions inspire their members to build pressure on minor and simple issues. So, unions are the reason for grievances.

Handling Employee's Grievances

Raising grievances in the organization is continuous and simple matter. Grievances lead to progress and development. So, it must be accepted positively. Management should manage them but should not control to remove from each level of organizations. Prompt settlement of grievances as much as possible is a must for the smooth running of an organization.

METHODS OF HANDLING EMPLOYEE GRIEVANCES

Organization must try to satisfy employee through employee development mechanism that minimizes grievances of employees. Timely settlement of grievances is favourable to the organization, but untimely settlement may not be effective and comes under the unsolved issue. So, two methods of handling grievances are developed which are presented under. Grievance procedure is a formal communication between an employee and the management designed for the settlement of a grievance. The grievance procedures differ from organization to organization.

1. Open door policy
2. Step-ladder policy

Open Door Policy

Under this policy, the aggrieved employee is free to meet the top executives of the organization and get his grievances redressed. Such a policy works well only in small organizations. However, in bigger organizations, top management executives are usually busy with other concerned matters of the company. Moreover, it is believed that open door policy is suitable for executives; operational employees may feel shy to go to top management.

Step Ladder Policy

Under this policy, the aggrieved employee has to follow a step by step procedure for getting his grievance redressed. In this procedure, whenever an employee is confronted with a grievance, he presents his problem to his immediate supervisor. If the employee is not satisfied with superior's decision, then he discusses his grievance with the departmental head. The departmental head discusses the problem with joint grievance committees to find a solution. However, if the committee also fails to redress the grievance, then it may be referred to chief executive. If the chief executive also fails to redress the grievance, then such a grievance is referred to voluntary arbitration where the award of arbitrator is binding on both the parties.

HOW WILL YOU UNDERSTAND EMPLOYEE GRIEVANCES?

- Exit interview
- Opinion surveys
- Gripe Boxes
- Open door policy

GRIEVANCE vS DISCIPLINE

Grievances - provides the employer with a process for resolving a complaint they are unable resolve regular communications with their superiors/managers.

Discipline –Gives employer a process for handling an employee who is not meeting the expected standards of performance or behavior.

5.11. GRIEVANCE HANDLING PROCEDURE/MACHINERY FOR REDRESSAL OF GRIEVANCE

Grievance handling process is continuous and helps to reduce employee dissatisfaction in the organization. Managers must address and change the grievances in the initial stage itself. The grievance ought to be tended to and reviewed as well as is by all accounts changed according to the included gatherings. Grievance handling process must be clear and simple that are described below:

- ***Defining and Describing the Nature of Grievance***

Defining and describing is the first process of the grievance handling. This step helps to define and describe the nature of grievance as clearly as possible. It helps to identify the grievances.

- ***Collect All the Facts***

Collects all the facts is another step where this process helps to explain how, when, where, why and to whom the grievance occurred. After defining the nature of the grievance, the next step is to gather all the facts that are concerned with the case. This step helps to gather all the information with facts and figure.

- ***Establishing Tentative Solution to the Grievance***

After getting the clear picture of the grievance, the next step involves the establishment of the tentative solution to the grievance.

- ***Check the Validity of Tentative Solution***

Facts are gathered on the basis of the tentative solutions. The executives establish a tentative solution and then observe critically whether his hypothesis is right or wrong. It analyzes and searches for multiple solutions to the grievance.

- ***Applying the Solution***

The executive may hold conference with aggrieved employee and question other employees for applying the solution. It finally selects the best feasible and possible solution and implements the same

- ***Follow up***

Follow up is the last step, the executive may not conclude that the grievance has been until a check is made to determine whether the employee's attitude has been favorably changed. Checking can be done through casual observation while the employees are working.

GRIEVANCE PROCEDURE IN INDIAN INDUSTRY

The 15th session of Indian Labor Conference held in 1957 emphasized the need of an established grievance procedure for the country which would be acceptable to unions as well as to management. In the 16th session of Indian Labor Conference, a model for grievance procedure was drawn up. This model helps in creation of grievance machinery. According to it, workers' representatives are to be elected for a department or their union is to nominate them. Management has to specify the persons in each department who are to be approached first and the departmental heads who are supposed to be approached in the second step. The Model Grievance Procedure specifies the details of all the steps that are to be followed while redressing grievances. The Grievance Committee shall consist of 4 to 6 members.

Employee Grievance Cont..

THESE STEPS ARE

STEP 1: In the first step the grievance is to be submitted to departmental representative, who is a representative of management. He has to give his answer within 48 hours.

STEP 2: If the departmental representative fails to provide a solution, the aggrieved employee can take his grievance to head of the department, who has to give his decision within 3 days.

STEP 3: If the aggrieved employee is not satisfied with the decision of departmental head, he can take the grievance to Grievance Committee. The Grievance Committee makes its recommendations to the manager within 7 days in the form of a report.

The final decision of the management on the report of Grievance Committee must be communicated to the aggrieved employee within three days of the receipt of report. An appeal for revision of final decision can be made by the worker if he is not satisfied with it. The management must communicate its decision to the worker within 7 days.

a.   An arrived employee shall first present his grievance verbally in person to the officer designated by the management for this purpose. The response shall be given by the officer within 48 hours of the presentation of the complaint. If the worker is not satisfied with the decision of the officer or fails to receive the answer within 48 hours he will, either in person or accompanied by is departmental head, present his grievance to the head of the department.

b.   The head of the department shall give his answer within 3 days or if action cannot be taken within this period, the reason for delay should be recorded. If the worker is dissatisfied with the decision of the department all head, he may request that his grievance be forwarded to the Grievance Committee.

c.   The Grievance committee shall make its recommendation to the manager within 7 days if the workers request. If decision cannot be given within this period, reason should be recorded. Unanimous decision of the committee shall be implemented by the management. If there is a difference of opinion among the members of the committee, the matter shall be referred to the manager along with the views of the members and the relevant papers for final decision.

d.   In either case, the final decision of the manger shall be communicated to the employee within three days from the receipt of the Grievance Committee's recommendations.

e.   If the worker is not satisfied even with the final decision of the manager, he may have the right to appeal to the manager for revision. In making this appeal he may take a union official with him to facilitate discussion with the management. The management will communicate the decision within 7 days of workman's revision petition.

f.   If worker is still not satisfied, the mater may be referred to voluntary arbitration.

g.   Where a workers has taken a grievance for readdress under the grievance procedure the formal conciliation machinery shall not interview till all steps in the procedure have exhausted. A grievance shall be presumed to assume the form of a dispute only when the final decision of top management is turned down by the worker.

5.12. PARTICIPATIVE MANAGEMENT

Participative (or participatory) management, otherwise known as employee involvement or participative decision making, encourages the involvement of stakeholders at all levels of an organization in the analysis of problems, development of strategies, and implementation of solutions. Employees are invited to share in the decision-making process of the firm by participating in activities such as setting goals, determining work schedules, and making suggestions. Other forms of participative management include increasing the responsibility of employees (job enrichment); forming self-managed teams, quality circles, or quality-of-work-life committees; and soliciting survey feedback.

Participative management, however, involves more than allowing employees to take part in making decisions. It also involves management treating the ideas and suggestions of employees with consideration and respect. The most extensive form of participative management is direct employee ownership of a company.

PROCESS OF PARTICIPATIVE MANAGEMENT

Four processes influence participation. These processes create employee involvement as they are pushed down to the lowest levels in an organization

Information sharing, which is concerned with keeping employees informed about the economic status of the company.

Training, which involves raising the skill levels of employees and offering development opportunities that allow them to apply new skills to make effective decisions regarding the organization as a whole?

Employee decision making, which can take many forms, from determining work schedules to deciding on budgets or processes.

Rewards, which should be tied to suggestions and ideas as well as performance.

BENEFITS OF PARTICIPATIVE MANAGEMENT

1. Increase Productivity (Effectiveness and efficiency)
2. Better Decisions
3. Employee Morale
4. Improved job satisfaction
5. Greater Commitment
6. Faster Adaptation to Change

7. Greater trust

8. Better Communication

9. Better Teamwork

10. Sense of ownership

11. It motivates employees to increase productivity

12. Sense of self-esteem gets heightened

13. Participation keeps employees informed of upcoming events

14. Creativity and innovation are two important benefits of participative management.

15. By allowing a diverse group of employees to have input into decisions, the organization benefits from the synergy that comes from a wider choice of options.

Requirements of Participative Management

Managers must be willing to relinquish some control to their workers; managers must feel secure in their position in order for participation to be successful. The success of participative management depends on careful planning and slow, phased approach. The employees must be able to trust their managers and feel they are respected.

Successful participation requires managers to approach employee involvement with an open mind. They must be open to new ideas and alternatives in order for participative management to work. It is important to remember that although the manager may not agree with every idea or suggestion an employee makes, how those ideas are received is critical to the success of participative management.

Employees must also be willing to participate and share their ideas. Before expecting employees to make valuable contributions, managers should provide them with the criteria that their input must meet. Another important element for implementing a successful participative management style is the visible integration of employees' suggestions into the final decision or implementation. Employees need to know that they have made a contribution. Offering employees a choice in the final decision is important because it increases their commitment, motivation, and job satisfaction.

5.13. COLLECTIVE BARGAINING PROCESS

Collective bargaining generally includes negotiations between the two parties (employees' representatives and employer's representatives). Collective bargaining consists of negotiations between an employer and a group of employees that determine the conditions of employment. Often employees are represented in the bargaining by a union or other labor organization. The result of collective bargaining procedure is called the collective bargaining agreement (CBA).

Collective agreements may be in the form of procedural agreements or substantive agreements. Procedural agreements deal with the relationship between workers and management and the procedures to be adopted for resolving individual or group disputes.

This will normally include procedures in respect of individual grievances, disputes and discipline. Frequently, procedural agreements are put into the company rule book which provides information on the overall terms and conditions of employment and codes of behavior. A substantive agreement deals with specific issues, such as basic pay, overtime premiums, bonus arrangements, holiday entitlements, hours of work, etc. In many companies, agreements have a fixed time scale and a collective bargaining process will review the procedural agreement when negotiations take place on pay and conditions of employment.

THE COLLECTIVE BARGAINING PROCESS COMPRISES OF FIVE CORE STEPS

- ### Prepare

This phase involves composition of a negotiation team. The negotiation team should consist of representatives of both the parties with adequate knowledge and skills for negotiation. In this phase both the employer's representatives and the union examine their own situation in order to develop the issues that they believe will be most important. The first thing to be done is to determine whether there is actually any reason to negotiate at all. A correct understanding of the main issues to be covered and intimate knowledge of operations, working conditions, production norms and other relevant conditions is required.

- ### Discuss

Here, the parties decide the ground rules that will guide the negotiations. A process well begun is half done and this is no less true in case of collective bargaining. An environment of mutual trust and understanding is also created so that the collective bargaining agreement would be reached.

- ### Propose

This phase involves the initial opening statements and the possible options that exist to resolve them. In a word, this phase could be described as 'brainstorming'. The exchange of messages takes place and opinion of both the parties is sought.

Bargain: negotiations are easy if a problem solving attitude is adopted. This stage comprises the time when 'what ifs' and 'supposals' are set forth and the drafting of agreements take place.

- ***Settlement***

Once the parties are through with the bargaining process, a consensual agreement is reached upon wherein both the parties agree to a common decision regarding the problem or the issue. This stage is described as consisting of effective joint implementation of the agreement through shared visions, strategic planning and negotiated change.

CHARACTERISTICS OF COLLECTIVE BARGAINING

- It is a group process, wherein one group, representing the employers, and the other, representing the employees, sit together to negotiate terms of employment. Negotiations form an important aspect of the process of collective bargaining i.e., there is considerable scope for discussion, compromise or mutual give and take in collective bargaining.
- Collective bargaining is a formalized process by which employers and independent trade unions negotiate terms and conditions of employment and the ways in which certain employment-related issues are to be regulated at national, organizational and workplace levels. Collective bargaining is a complementary process i.e. each party needs something that the other party has; labor can increase productivity and management can pay better for their efforts.
- Collective bargaining tends to improve the relations between workers and the union on the one hand and the employer on the other.

CASE STUDY DISCUSSIONS

Case Study 1

Satish was a Sales Manager for Industrial Products Company in City branch. A week ago, he was promoted and shifted to Head Office as Deputy Manager-Product Management for a division of products which he was not very familiar with. Three days ago, the company VP - Mr. George, convened a meeting of all Product Managers. Satish's new boss (Product Manager Ketan) was not able to attend due to some other preoccupation. Hence, the Marketing Director, Preet - asked Satish to attend the meeting as this would give him an exposure into his new role. At the beginning of the meeting, Preet introduced Satish very briefly to the VP. The meeting started with an address from the VP and soon it got into a series of questions from him to every Product Manager. George, of course, was pretty thorough with every single product of the company and he was known to be pushy and a blunt veteran in the field. Most of the Product Managers were very clear of George's ways of working and had thoroughly prepared for the meeting and were giving to the point answers. George then started with Satish. Satish being new to the product, was quite confused and fared miserably. Preet immediately understood that George had possibly failed to remember that Satish was new to the job. He thought of interrupting George's questioning and giving a discrete reminder that Satish was new. But by that time, George who was pretty upset with the lack of preparation by Satish made a public statement "Gentlemen, you are witnessing here an example of sloppy work and this can't be excused". Now Preet was in two minds - should he interrupt George and tell him that Satish is new in that position OR should he wait till the end of the meeting and tell George privately. Preet chose the second option. Satish was visibly angry at the treatment meted out by George but he also chose to keep mum. George quickly closed the meeting saying that he found in general, lack of planning in the department and asked Preet to stay back in the room for further discussions. Before Preet could give any explanation on Satish, George asked him "Tell me openly, Preet, was I too rough with that boy?" Preet said "Yes, you were. In fact, I was about to remind you that Satish is new to the job". George explained that the fact that Satish was new to the job didn't quite register with him during the meeting. George admitted that he had made a mistake and asked his secretary to get Satish report to the room immediately. A perplexed and uneasy Satish reported to George's room after few minutes. George looking Satish straight into his eyes said "I have done something which I should have never even thought of and I want to apologise to you. It is my mistake that I did not recollect that you were new to the job when I was questioning you". Satish was left speechless. George continued "I would like to state few things clearly to you. Your job is to make sure that people like me and your bosses do not make stupid decisions. We have good confidence in your abilities and that is why we have brought you to the Head Office. For everybody, time is required for learning. I will expect you to know all the nuances of your product in three months' time. Until then you have my complete confidence". George closed the conversation with a big reassuring handshake with Satish.

Questions

1. Was it at all necessary for George to apologise to such a junior employee like Satish?
2. If you were in Satish's place, how would you to respond to George's apology?
3. Was George correct in saying that Satish is there to correct the "stupid mistake" of his Boss and George?
4. Would you employ George in your company?
5. Did Preet make a mistake by not intervening during the meeting and correct George's misconception about Satish?
6. As an HR man, how would you define the character of George - bullying but later regretting? Does his attitude need to be corrected?
7. Would you be happy to have George/Preet as your boss?

Case Study 2

Adam, fresh from school was a newly recruited HR practitioner. During his one month into the job, he was asked to be in-charge of the orientation programme for the entire organisation. Being new, he followed closely to the processes. Recently, Roy joined the organisation and Adam was required to orientate him. On Roy's first day of work, Adam brought him around the organisation for introduction to the rest of the staffs. Unfortunately, Roy's assigned mentor was not around hence, Adam was unable to make an official introduction for Roy to meet up with his mentor. In the afternoon, during the HR briefing, Adam mentioned to Roy that there is a buddy system in place but it is only on an opt-in basis. Roy requested to opt for a buddy. Adam was rather surprised by Roy's request as according to Adam's manager-Jean, no one in the organisation has requested for a buddy. Hence, Adam checked with Jean on the criteria in getting a buddy for Roy and according to her, Adam found out that it needed to be someone preferably from Roy's department. Having clarified on the criteria, Adam was supposed to get a buddy for Roy, unfortunately, this issue was clearly forgotten by Adam due to his busy schedule as he was involved in other HR matters as well and he did not follow up with Roy's request promptly. One week later, Adam met Roy in a lunch gathering and Adam greeted Roy and asked him casually how he is doing and if he has adapted well to his job. Roy, asked Adam blatantly and angrily where is his buddy that he had requested. At that moment, Adam recalled on the existence of this request and unwittingly told Roy that he thought Roy was joking with him on the request for a buddy as he did not want to admit to Roy that he had clearly forgotten about the whole issue. Roy was very angered by Adam's response and told him off that he was very serious in getting a buddy and that its Adam's responsibility to do so. Adam, clearly embarrassed and guilty about his mistake, apologized immediately and promised to get him a buddy. On the very day, a buddy-Sam, was found for Roy. Roy was very unhappy with Adam and confronted Adam and his buddy when he was able to have an official meet up session with his mentor. Adam explained to Roy that the organisation has no current practice in place for meet up sessions to be arranged between mentors and mentees and it's a practice for mentees to take self-initiative to do so in arranging for meetings with their mentors and also that his mentor is currently out of town and will only be back the next day. Adam, himself being a new staff also was at that moment in time speaking on personal experience and also based on what Jean had told him. Sam, who was present agreed and helped to explain to Roy on the practice. Roy kept quiet and Adam unknowingly thought that Roy has understood the organisation practice. Hence, Adam did not continue to check with Roy on this aspect. The following day, Roy had a feedback session with his manager and Adam was called upon to sit in as a part of the orientation programme. Roy brought up the issue on Adam's failure to get him a buddy promptly and that he was not introduced to his mentor at all. He complained about the poor management of the HR mentor and buddy system and that it was not effective at all and that he expressed that he is very unhappy with Adam as he felt that he was not doing his job at all. Adam tried to explain to Roy and his manager about what happened and also reassured Roy that he will take his suggestions of improving on the system and was apologetic about the issue. He told Roy's manager that he will bring Roy to see his mentor after the session as his mentor is back in the office after being on leave for the past week. Roy was still very unhappy with Adam and continued telling Adam off in front of his manager.

Questions

1. On an HR practitioner point of view, what should Adam do to resolve the issue?
2. Roy is very unhappy with Adam and holds it against him even though all has been done and followed up. What should Adam as HR do to resolve this and should Jean, as Adam's manager do something?
3. What role does Roy's manager play in this issue and should he be implicated?

Case Study 3

The manager of A.B.C.Ltd. Realized that the level of moral and Motivation of their employees was very low and there was dissatisfaction among. The employees. Labour productivity was also found to be very low. After investigating the cause's dissatisfaction, the managers decided that if employees were to be motivated, there was a need to establish and maintain good interpersonal relation, over and above good salary, job security, roper working conditions and supervision. So they put in sincere efforts to improve all these factors during one year. Yet, surprisingly, they came to know that in spite of reduction in the degree of dissatisfaction, the level of morale and motivation was low and there was no significant increase in their productivity. Therefore, the managers are worried

Question

What managerial problem is involved in the above case? Suggest Solution and make argument to justify your answer.

Case Study 4

The manager of A.B.C.Ltd. Realized that the level of moral and Motivation of their employees was very low and there was dissatisfaction among the employees. Labour productivity was also found to be very low. After investigating the causes of dissatisfaction, the managers decided that if employees were to be motivated, there was a need to establish and maintain good interpersonal relation, over and above good salary, job security, proper working conditions and supervision. So they put in sincere efforts to improve all these factors during one year. Yet, surprisingly, they came to know that in spite of reduction in the degree of dissatisfaction, the level of morale and motivation was low and there was no significant increase in their productivity. Therefore, the managers are worried.

Question to Discuss

- What managerial problem is involved in the above case? Suggest solution and make argument to justify your answer.

SITUATIONAL CASE STUDY

Situation 1

The Hawkins Supply company is currently faced with an inventory rotation problem. This difficulty stems from the fact that some supplies must be used prior to a stated expiration date. Upon receipt, a new shipment of these perishable items must be stacked beneath the boxes that are currently in inventory. A substantial amount of time is consumed in restacking the items according to their expiration dates.

Question

The company would like to reduce the double and sometimes triple handling of items. How can this goal be achieved? Are there alternative solutions which might also be effective?

Situation 2

The JAW Bottling Company has recently introduced a new beer to the market called HEAVY. It is extra high in calories. It has been developed specifically for those people that enjoy feeling full after only one beer. The materials handling supervisors at JAW Bottling have been receiving complaints from lift truck drivers that cases of the new HEAVY beer are slipping off pallets during intra-plant movement and truck deliveries. Thus far the JAW engineering department has tried to eliminate or reduce case slippage through the use of the following methods: 1. Top case clamp on the fork truck. 2. Strapping cases to pallet. 3. Plastic wrapper around cases. 4. The use of a large size pallet with a retainer strip nailed along the edges.

Question

Using a method other than those described above, can the case slippage problem be solved?

Situation 3

The Sure To Peal Paint Company stores all its metal compressed gas containers in a warehouse. These long cylindrical metal tanks contain various gases used in manufacturing cans of spray paint. The gas tanks are delivered to the warehouse by truck. Two receiving dock workers unload the containers from the delivery trucks and place them on four wheel trucks. Two materials handlers are responsible for pushing the loaded trucks into the warehouse, unloading the tanks and setting them up on end. The two materials handlers spend a major portion of their day moving loads of the gas tanks into the warehouse and placing them into the proper storage locations. In total, there are five different types of gases that in equal proportion make up 98% of all gas handled.

Question

Management would like to identify a better way to handle these gas tanks. How can the handling operation be improved?

Situation 4

The White Manufacturing Company produces a spring-loaded replacement spike for power rakes. Because of the small size of this item, they are packaged in separate small containers that are in turn packed into a larger carton (24 count) for shipping. The packing operation for this unit is on the third floor of a multi-story building. Upon completion of the packing operation the shipping cartons are placed on semi-live skids and taken to the second floor using an elevator.

The same elevator is also used to move other materials to various floors in the plant for processing. On the second floor packages are sorted according to trucking line. After sorting, all packages are placed on a semi-live skid and moved to the first floor via the same elevator. On the first floor, the packages are stored awaiting shipment (pick up by the assigned truck line).

Question

Disregarding labor requirements, how can the movement of packages be improved?

Situation 5

The Acme Tube Company has for the last 10 years used 42" square reusable wooden boxes to ship custom length short tubing. During the past year the unit cost of a shipping box has soared from $14.50 to $40.00 per unit. In addition, box maintenance has gone up from $5 per year to $22 per year. Reusability has turned into a cost trap for Acme. Extra truck runs and outside trucking services are being employed to recover the returnable wooden boxes since on return trips the firm's trucks are needed to pick up raw stock. Another major problem being faced is that warehouse space is getting very scarce but to operate Acme must have an inventory of about $10,000 worth of wooden boxes in the system at all times.

Question

As a material handling engineer, how would you improve this system? Give a detailed description of a possible new method for shipping the tubes.

TWO MARK QUESTIONS AND ANSWERS

1. What is HRM?

HRM refers to a set of programmes, functions and activities designed and carried out in order to maximize both employees as well as organizational effectiveness.

2. Define HRM.

Human Resource Management is the planning, organizing, directing and controlling of the Procurement, Development, Compensation, Integration, Maintenance and Separation of human resources to the end that individual, organizational and social objectives are accomplished.

3. List the objectives of HRM.

To attract and secure appropriate people capable of performing effectively the organizations specific tasks.

To utilize the human resources effectively.

To generate maximum individual development of the people within the organization.

4. Define HRIS.

Human Resource Information System is a systematic way of storing data and information for each individual employee to aid Planning, Decision making and Submitting of returns and reports to the external agencies.

5. List the qualities a HR manager has to possess.

- Fairness & Firmness
- Tactful & Resourceful
- Sympathy & Consideration
- Knowledge of labour related Acts
- Freedom from bias
- Communication Skills

6. What do you mean by Outsourcing in HR?

Outsourcing (Subcontracting) is the process by which employees transfer routine or peripheral work to another organization that specializes in that work and can perform it effectively. Activities outsourced include employee hiring, training & Development, payroll preparation, benefits administration etc.

7. What is Personnel Policy?

It is a statement of intention committing the management to a general course of action. A policy is a plan of action.

8. **What is HRP?**

HRP is the process of forecasting a firm's future demand for and supply of the right type of people in the right number.

9. **What is Managerial Succession Planning**?

Managerial Succession Planning includes training programmes and series of job assignments leading to top position.

10. **What is Job Analysis**?

Job analysis is the process of collecting job related information. such information helps in the preparation of job description and job specification. Job analysis is a systematic exploration of the activities within a job.

Job analysis involves the following steps:

i.   Collecting and recording job information

ii.   Checking the job information for accuracy.

iii. Writing job description based on the information

iv.   Using the information to determine the skills, abilities and knowledge that are required on the job.

v.   Updating the information from time to time.

11. **What is Job description**?

Job Description is an important document, which is basically descriptive in nature and contains a statement of job Analysis.

It provides both organizational information's (like location in structure, authority etc) and functional information (what the work is).

Job Description: A statement containing items such as

- Job title/Job identification/organization position
- Location
- Job summary
- Duties
- Machines, tools and equipment
- Materials and forms used
- Supervision given or received
- Working conditions
- Hazards

12. What is Job Specification?

Job specification is a written statement of qualifications, traits, physical and mental characteristics that an individual must possess to perform the job duties and discharge responsibilities effectively.

13. What is Job design?

Job Design involves conscious efforts to organize tasks, duties and responsibilities into a unit of work to achieve certain objectives.

14. What is Ergonomics?

Ergonomics is concerned with designing and shaping jobs to fit the physical abilities and characteristics of employees.

Nature of job remains same but the location of tools, switches and other facilities is changed to make the jobholder feel comfortable.

15. What do you mean by Job Engineering?

Job Engineering focuses on the tasks to be performed, methods to be used, workflows among employees, layout of the workplace, performance standards and interdependencies among people and machines.

16. What do you mean by Job Enlargement and Job Enrichment?

Job Enlargement refers to the expansion of the number of different tasks performed by an employee in a single job.

Job Enrichment involves adding more motivators to a job to make it more rewarding.

17. What is Telecommuting?

Telecommuting refers to the use of microcomputers, networks and other communication technology such as fax machine s to do work from home, which was traditionally done in the workplace.

18. What do you mean by Recruitment?

Recruitment involves attracting and obtaining as many applications as possible from eligible seekers.

19. What is E- Recruiting?

It involves screening candidates electronically, directing potential hires to a special website for online skill assessment, conducting background checks over the internet, interviewing candidates via videoconferencing and managing the entire process with web-based software.

20. What is meant by Selection?

Selection is the process of picking individuals with requisite qualifications and competence to fill jobs in the organization.

21. What are the external sources of recruitment?

Professional or Trade Associations

Advertisements

Employment Exchange

Campus recruitment

Walk-ins, Write-ins and Talks-in

Consultants

Contractors

22. What is test?

A procedure intended to establish the quality, performance, or reliability of something, especially before it is taken into widespread use.

23. What is Interview?

Interview is a formal, in-depth conversation conducted to evaluate the applicant's acceptability.

24. What do you mean by Halo effect?

Halo effect occurs when an interviewer judges an applicant's entire potential for job performance on the basis of a single trait, such as how the applicant dresses or talks.

25. Mention the skills an interviewer needs.

Plan the interview, establish an easy and informal relationship, maintain control over the time and direction taken for the interview, encourage the candidate to talk, analyze career and interests to reveal strengths, weaknesses, patterns of behavior.

26. What do you mean by Orientation?

Orientation is a systematic and planned introduction of employees to their jobs, their co-workers and the organization. It is also called induction.

27. What is Placement?

Placement is understood as the allocation of people to jobs. It is the assignment or re-assignment of an employee to a new or different job and promotion, transfer, or demotion of present employees.

28. Write the meaning for Training, development & education.

Training refers to the process of imparting specific skills.

Development refers to the learning opportunities designed to help employees grow.

Education is theoretical learning in classrooms.

29. State the need and objectives of training

The purpose of training and development is to maintain and improve effectiveness and efficiency of individuals within the organization. Training is essential for job success. It can lead to higher production, fewer mistakes, greater job satisfaction and lower turnover. These benefits accrue to both the trainee and the organization. The purpose of training is to: 1. To increase productivity and quality, 2. To promote versatility and adaptability to new methods, 3. To reduce the number of accidents, 4.To reduce labour turnover,5. To increase job satisfaction displaying itself in lower labour turn-over and less absenteeism, 6. To increase efficiency.

30. When does the need for training arise?

- The installation of new equipment or techniques
- A change in working methods or products produced
- A realization that performance is inadequate
- Labour shortage, necessitating the upgrading of some employees
- A desire to reduce the amount of scrap and to improve quality
- An increase in the number of accidents
- Promotion or transfer of individual employees.
- Ensures availability of necessary skills and there could be a pool of talent from which to promote from.

31. List the Advantages of training.

1. Leads to improved profitability and/or more positive attitudes toward profits Orientation.
2. Improves the job knowledge and skills at all levels of the organization.
3. Improves the morale of the workforce.
4. Helps people identify with organizational goals.
5. Helps create a better corporate image.

32. What are the off-the job training method?

Vestibule, lecture, special study, conference, role playing, laboratory training, films, case study, simulation etc.

33. What are the on-the job training method?

Apprentice training, coaching, internship training, job rotation, orientation training.

34. Explain vestibule training and Sensitivity training.

A special area or a room is set aside from the main production area and is equipped with furnishings similar to those found in the actual production area. It relieves the employee from the pressure of having to produce while learning. Sensitivity training uses small numbers of trainees, usually fewer than 12 in a group.

35. Define Performance appraisal.

Performance appraisal is an objective assessment of an individual's performance against well-defined benchmark.

36. List the objectives of performance appraisal.

To effect promotions based on competence and performance.

To assess the training and development needs of employees.

To decide upon a pay raise.

To improve communication.

To let the employees know their performance is concerned and to assist them.

37. What is Job Evaluation?

Job Evaluation seeks to determine the relative worth of each job so that salary differentials can be established. It is the process of analyzing and assessing the various jobs systematically to ascertain their relative worth in an organization.

38. What is remuneration?

Remuneration is the compensation an employee receives in return for his or her contribution to the organization.

39. Write a short note on Minimum wage, fair wage & living wage.

Minimum wages are given for sustenance of life plus for preservation of the efficiency of workers.

Fair wage is equal to the rate prevailing in the same trade or equal to the predominant rate for similar work throughout the country.

Living wage is one which is higher than fair wage. Provided for bare essentials plus frugal comforts.

40. Define Incentives.

Incentives are monetary benefits paid to workmen in recognition of their outstanding performance.

41. What is Employee Empowerment?

Empowerment is the process of enhancing feeling of self-efficiency and a sense of owing a job. It is giving employees the means, ability and authority to enable them to do some work.

42. What is Dry promotion?

Rise in status but not pay. A promotion that provides greater status or responsibility but does not involve an increase in pay

43. What do you mean by Cafeteria benefit?

In Cafeteria benefit plan the employees could spend their Benefits, allowances on a choice of benefits options. It is a type of compensation which refers to compensation programmes that allow employees to choose what type and how much of each reward is desired during the coming year. A particular employee benefit selected from a company plan offering a variety of choices that can be balanced to suit individual needs.

44. What is layoff?

The act of suspending or dismissing an employee, as for lack of work or because of corporate reorganization. A period of temporary inactivity or rest.

45. What is Understudy Assignment?

To be engaged in studying a role so as to be able to replace the regular performer when required. A performer who understudies. A person trained to do the work of another.

46. What is self-assessment?

Self-assessment is the process of gathering information about yourself in order to make an informed career decision. It is the first step of the Career Planning Process and is often conducted with the help of a career development professional.

47. What do you mean by Knowledge Management?

Knowledge Management is a process that helps organizations identify, select, organize, disseminate and transfer important information and expertise that are a part of the organizational memory that typically resides within an organization in an unstructured manner

48. What is Compensation?

Compensation is a systematic approach to providing monetary value to employees in exchange for work performed. Compensation may achieve several purposes assisting in recruitment, job performance, and job satisfaction.

49. What are the different types of compensation?

Different types of compensation include:

- Basic Pay
- Commissions
- Overtime Pay
- Bonuses, Profit Sharing, Merit Pay
- Stock Options
- Travel/Meal/Housing Allowance
- Benefits including: dental, insurance, medical, vacation, leaves, retirement, taxes...

50. What is Burnout?

This refers to a condition in which individuals are completely negative about themselves and their lives. This includes feeling worthless, physical and mental fatigue. They feel disregarded, pessimistic about the future and lacking in control of their lives.

51. What is job rotation?

It is a Job design technique in which employees are moved between two or more jobs in a planned manner. The objective is to expose the employees to different experiences and wider variety of skills to enhance job satisfaction and to cross-train them.

52. What do you mean by Transfer, Promotion & Demotion?

Transfer is a lateral movement within the same grade, from one job to another. A transfer may result in changes in duties and responsibilities, supervisory and working conditions, but not necessarily salary.

Promotion is the advancement of an employee from one job level to a higher one, with increase in salary.

Demotion is the opposite of promotion. It is a downward movement from one job level to another, leading to a reduction in rank, status, pay and responsibility.

53. What is VRS?

Voluntary retirement is the golden route to retirement. it is giving an opportunity to employees to retire voluntarily. The most human technique for downsizing the workforce in an organization is the VRS. Voluntary separations cause less pain and agony. It gives people choice and discretion rather than making them the victims of management decisions. The VRS is also commonly referred to as voluntary separation Scheme (VSP) or the Golden Handshake Programme (GHP)

54. Define Performance Appraisal.

It is the systematic evaluation of the individual with respect to his or her performance on the job and his or her potential for development.

55. What is Assessment Canters?

An assessment centers is a central location where managers may come together to have their participation in job related exercises evaluated by trained observers. Mostly used for executive hiring.

56. What is360 degree appraisal?

The 360 degree technique is understood as systematic collection of performance data on an individual or group, derived from a number of stakeholders. In 360 degree appraisal system, an employee's performance is rated by superiors, peers, subordinates and clients.

57. What is Participative Management?

Participative Management refers to the process of involving employees or employee representatives at all levels of decision making. Co-determination is another term for participation.

58. What is Labour Welfare?

Labour Welfare refers to all those efforts of employers, trade unions, voluntary organizations and governmental agencies which help employees feel better and perform better.

59. What are Intra-mural facilities andExtra-mural facilities?

Intra-mural activities consists of facilities provided within the factories and includes medical facilities, compensation for accidents, crèches and canteens, supply of drinking water etc.

Extra-mural facilities are provided outside the factory such as housing accommodation, amusement and sports educational facilities, recreational facilities.

60. What is Arbitration?

Arbitration is a procedure in which a dispute is submitted, by agreement of the parties, to one or more arbitrators who make a binding decision on the dispute. In choosing arbitration, the parties opt for a private dispute resolution procedure instead of going to court.

61. What do you mean by Profile Matching?

Profile Matching is assessments that deliver candidate reports addressing the specific competencies required for success.

62. What is Downsizing?

Downsizing refers to the process of reducing, usually dramatically, the number of people employed by the firm.

63. Explain Socialization?

Socializing is the process of orienting the selected candidates to the organizational culture. It is also the process of adaption that takes place as individuals attempt to learn the values and norms of work roles. It is the process of three stages; pre-arrival, encounter and metamorphosis.

64. What do you mean by reward?

An incentive or reward can be anything that attracts the workers attention and stimulates worker to work.

65. What do you mean by career anchor?

A "Career Anchor" is a combination of perceived areas of competence, motives, and values relating to professional work choices. **Career Anchors** - include talents, motives, values and attitudes which give stability and direction to a person's career – it is the 'motivator' or 'driver' of that person

66. Explain Transfer & Retrenchment.

Transfer involves a change in the job without change in position, pay or responsibilities.

Retrenchment results in the separation of an employee from his/her employer.

67. What is Collective bargaining?

Collective bargaining is the process whereby workers organize together to meet, converse, and compromise upon the work environment with their employers. It is the practice in which union and company representatives meet to negotiate a new labor contract. In various national labor and employment law contexts, collective bargaining takes on a more specific legal meaning. In a broad sense, however, it is the coming together of workers to negotiate their employment.